ELUSIVE GLO

NAVIGO DILIGENTER

Martin Burdick

Neville Pughe

ELUSIVE GLORY

An Autobiography

by

NEVILLE PUGHE

The Memoir Club

© Neville Pughe 2006

First published in 2006 by
The Memoir Club
Stanhope Old Hall
Stanhope
Weardale
County Durham

British Library Cataloguing in
Publication Data.
A catalogue record for this book
is available from the
British Library

ISBN: 1-84104-153-X

Typeset by TW Typesetting, Plymouth, Devon
Printed and bound by CPI Antony Rowe, Eastbourne

Dedication

To my dearest wife

Whose cheerful determination
in the face of adversity
is an inspiration to all
and whose devotion
made much of this story possible

Also to my three sons
David, Richard and Jonathan
who I know will make it all
worthwhile

Contents

Family Welsh origins. Royal Marine background. The Plymouth blitz
1940. Father at Narvik with HMS *Warspite*. Move to Exmouth 1941 via
Lustleigh and Yealmbridge

Life in wartime Exmouth. Starting Prep school 1943. Father in Far East
with HMS *Indomitable*. Sister Diana returns from Switzerland 1945.
Father dies 1951. Mother sails to Malaya to marry our cousin Captain
Leslie Jole MC RM. Scholarship to King's College, Taunton failed

Domestic and social conditions experienced after the war

Difficult start at Exeter School 1949 followed by years of success as a
boarder. Tough regime. Many sporting achievements. Head of School
by 1953. Failed on eyesight to enter Royal Marines

Market gardening. Joined Army. Basic Training at Oswestry 1954.
Sandhurst, sports, 'A' Levels, girlfriends and London Shows.
Under-Officer. Queen's Medal. Commissioned into Royal Artillery

Young Officer Training at Larkhill. Riding and cricket. Arrival in 45th
Field Regiment, Germany. First tests of leadership. 'L/Bdr Wallop'. To
RMCS Shrivenham, 1957. Intermediate Course, Rugby. Summer back
in Germany with '45'. Mechanical Engineering Degree Course, Rugby
balls, cricket and musicals. First car. Parachute Selection Course 'P'
Company. 33rd Parachute Light Regiment RA, Aldershot. Libya. 7th
Parachute Regiment RHA

Broken leg. Failed Degree, resit and failed again. 1962 to Bahrain.
Intelligence Officer to 1st Parachute Battalion. On patrol in the Jebel
Akhdar. Life in Bahrain, Yas Island. Christmas Eve service. Return to
England to marry 1963. Adjutant 27th Army Missile Regiment,

List of Illustrations

Preface

This autobiography originated as a family archive, but it should appeal more generally to all those who have striven hard but never quite made it, whose successes have been few and quite by chance, and who have the good sense to laugh at themselves.

The author's earliest and burning ambition was to join the Royal Marines, but he spent 35 years in the Army instead. He aspired to the highest ranks – Field Marshal at least – but he finished what he describes as less of an illustrious career than a lacklustre one punctuated by innumerable errors, in the one-star rank of Brigadier commanding only half a Brigade. For the next seven years he was a Chief Executive in Local Government, his sense of humour there being wonderfully exercised!

How he reached these less than dizzy heights, and what adventures and misfortunes he experienced on the way, provides a salutary tale for anyone misguided enough to hope for fame and glory without much chance of getting them.

Any profits accruing to the author from the sale of this book will be donated to multiple sclerosis charities, especially the Wessex MS Therapy Centre, Warminster.

The author is indebted to The Random House Group Ltd. for permission to reproduce extracts from *An American Life* by Ronald Reagan, and to HarperCollins Publishers Ltd. for permission to reproduce extracts from *The Downing Street Years* by The Rt Hon The Baroness Margaret Thatcher LG OM PC FR.

The author would like to thank The Memoir Club and Meg Ross, for the help and advice he received in the publication of this book.

Foreword

General Sir Michael Wilkes KCB CBE

Neville Pughe and I have soldiered together for over forty years during which time I have got to know him, his charming wife Linda, and his three boys very well. We were off to a brisk start in the Parachute Brigade during the early sixties, endured the vicissitudes of the so-called 'Cold War' on the North German Plain through the seventies and eighties, and finally on to the sunny uplands of a world not dominated by an omnipresent Soviet threat. Compared with the hectic operational routine of the present day soldier with his Active Service involvements across the world, the background against which we served could be very frustrating. Small wonder then for a man who was in every sense a professional soldier, with a well developed streak of independence, that he might feel that military life should be offering him more.

To set the scene one must imagine a politico-military confrontation across the centre of Europe with two 'alliances' facing each other toe to toe across the inner German border. Deterrence was the watchword and indeed both the tactic and the strategy. Part of the deterrent philosophy involved the threatened use of battlefield nuclear weapons, hence Neville's command of a nuclear delivery battery within his regiment at one stage. This was a huge responsibility and difficult to imagine in our present circumstances. Life was largely static and based on well-established garrison areas. Large-scale exercises punctuated the year in an effort both to convince the 'enemy' that we were formidable opponents and to break the monotony of garrison life. Suffice it to say that, whatever its downside, this confrontation was entirely successful and ultimately resulted in the unification of the two Germanys and the break-up of the Soviet alliance. Neville was to witness this dissolution from a military viewpoint as well as from the rarefied atmosphere of the British embassies in Washington and Bonn as a military diplomat.

The effect of this situation in more personal terms was to polarise one's private life into a round of appointments in either the United Kingdom or Northern Germany. Success in career terms was based on an understanding of the 'Cold War', its tactics, its military politics, and the social manoeuvrings within the NATO garrison scene. It was possible therefore to reach the highest ranks without ever seeing a shot fired in anger. One exception to this was involvement in the Northern Ireland campaign which was being conducted in parallel with the continental deployment.

Neville Pughe's very personal, often intimate, account of his life before, during and after this time makes fascinating reading. It is a bittersweet story of a frustrated Royal Marine who finds release in Army life but, owing entirely to a combination of circumstances, comes to feel that real success eludes him, often at the last moment, despite many achievements modestly understated. That is not to suggest that there is any element of self-pity here, rather the tale is told with a self-deprecating light touch and a wry humour. What shines through is his indomitable spirit and his complete devotion to Linda and the boys.

CHAPTER 1

Early Disasters

I CRANED MY NECK out of the attic window to watch the band, leant further out – and nearly fell to my death. Had I done so, this tale would have been rather shorter. I was only aged three at the time. The splendour of the Royal Marine band, marching and counter-marching on Stonehouse Barracks square, was always compelling watching for me at that age. That was not surprising as the Royal Marines were in my blood, the passion and music of my Welsh forebears in my veins.

I am indebted to my cousin Cynthia Payne (née Jole) for research into the Pughe family history and a detailed account appears elsewhere. It is sufficient for this story of my life to paint the barest outline. The Pughe lineage was traceable back to Hugh Williams who was born in 1773 in the little village of Llanfachreth, near Dolgellau in North Wales. In those days Welsh sons took the name of their father's Christian name, so Hugh's son Meredith, born in Ty Nant, Llanfachreth in 1815, held the surname ap Hugh. Meredith was, like his father, a stonemason; he married Margaret Roberts at Llanuwchllyn church near Bala in 1840. By 1861 they had moved into a picturesque little cottage named Gelli (which in Welsh means a small grove or wood). This stone cottage with its quaint round chimney stands to this day somewhat apart from the village in its own grounds surrounded by breathtaking rhododendrons. Meredith had seven children, among them a son, Owen, born in Llanfachreth in 1841, who rose to be a gamekeeper on the Nannau estate owned by the Vaughan family. As a mark of this superior station, Owen added an 'e' to his surname, henceforth Pughe. Owen in turn had a son named Owen Meredith Pughe, born in 1865. Owen Meredith did well at Llanfachreth school and became a student teacher there. This was short-lived, however, and evidently finding life boring, he was sacked for his indolence. Fearing family disgrace he ran away to Liverpool where he made ends meet by becoming a porter. Then he found his way to Plymouth and joined the Royal Marine Light Infantry.

One of Owen Meredith Pughe's seven children was my father, Morris George Pughe, who, as we shall see, also joined the Royal Marine Light Infantry but at a very early age. He was, like his forbears, of medium

'Gelli', Llanfachreth

height, brown-haired, with large blue eyes beneath astonishingly long eyelashes. He, and all his brothers and sisters, were musical in the Welsh tradition, especially accomplished at singing. But my maternal lineage was Royal Marine and musical too. My great-grandfather William Henry Goss died of TB at the early age of 35 when serving with the Royal Marine Artillery at Chatham. His son was William Thomas Goss, who became the Royal Marines' first commissioned schoolmaster. (The Corps had previously relied on the Education Branch of the Royal Navy to provide learning to the troops.) I only knew him by repute, as he died three years before I was born, but my mother and her five sisters and four brothers had both worshipped and been frightened of him. He was evidently a martinet, but then wouldn't you be with a family that size to bring up on a Captain's pay?

The chief influences of all this background on my life were firstly: I have always thought of myself as of Welsh origin and fanatically support the Welsh Rugby side in every international; secondly: I have been fortunate enough to be musical; and thirdly: I passionately wanted to join the Royal Marines.

For those first few years of my life I lived at my maternal grandmother's house, 85 Durnford Street, Stonehouse, Devonport, a tall edifice of fading Victorian grandeur. It provided a direct view of the grey stone barracks to the front, and a glimpse of Mount Wise beyond and Stonehouse Creek, an inlet off Plymouth Sound, behind. The barrack square to the front, however, with its Royal Marine band, was my favourite view.

PUGHE LINEAGE

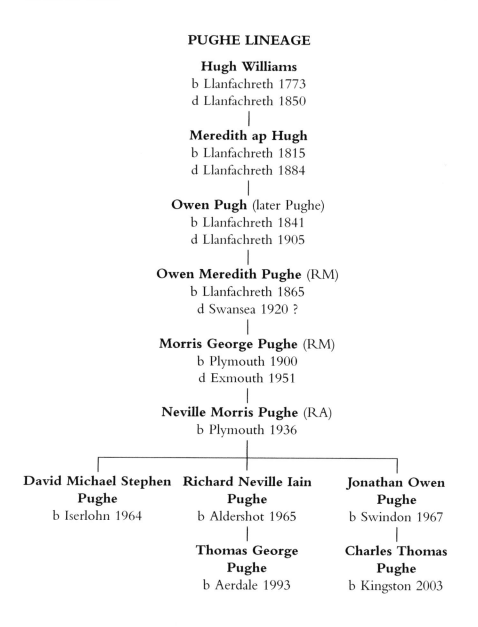

Hugh Williams
b Llanfachreth 1773
d Llanfachreth 1850
|
Meredith ap Hugh
b Llanfachreth 1815
d Llanfachreth 1884
|
Owen Pugh (later Pughe)
b Llanfachreth 1841
d Llanfachreth 1905
|
Owen Meredith Pughe (RM)
b Llanfachreth 1865
d Swansea 1920 ?
|
Morris George Pughe (RM)
b Plymouth 1900
d Exmouth 1951
|
Neville Morris Pughe (RA)
b Plymouth 1936

David Michael Stephen Pughe
b Iserlohn 1964

Richard Neville Iain Pughe
b Aldershot 1965
|
Thomas George Pughe
b Aerdale 1993

Jonathan Owen Pughe
b Swindon 1967
|
Charles Thomas Pughe
b Kingston 2003

In autumn 1939, young though I was, my early memories of those first days of the Second World War remain among my most vivid. That's not actually saying much, for I am generally thought to have an exceptionally under-developed memory, especially for places and people's names. Not, you might say, a sound basis for an autobiography. I can only assure you, dear Reader, that I'll do my best. Certainly those early disasters are etched firmly in the mind's eye.

My grandmother, Grandma Goss, was a little old lady with neat white hair. My sister Margaret Ann, or Maggie for short, and I saw her generally only once a week. That was when we were allowed downstairs from the nursery, presumably on Nanny's day off. After tea on those days – Thursdays I recall – Grandma would play the piano, and I would be required to march up and down the drawing-room to the tune 'We're the Soldiers of the King – me lad!' Then, as in later years, I had a tendency to fall flat on my face when trying to be so upright and military, and more often than not the performance would end in tears. My mother, Dorothy Edith Pughe (née Goss) however was, as ever, proud and encouraging. To help my sister and me learn the intricacies of table etiquette we also joined the grown-ups once a week in the dining room for lunch.

A lot of people lived in 85 Durnford Street, Stonehouse, at that time. In addition to the head of the house, my grandmother, one of her two eldest daughters occupied the attic bedroom – the one from whose window I watched the band. That was Winifred, my maiden aunt 'Pin', so called because she was as thin as one. My mother and father were also there from time to time, the former when she was not visiting my eldest sister Diana who was convalescing from TB in Davos, Switzerland, or following the fleet around Mediterranean ports; the latter, also a Captain RM, less frequently when on shore-leave.

Then there were the servants, some of whom lived in. Mrs Bull occupied the basement, and she did the laundry. The washing was done in an out-house, in a copper boiler, and I can well remember the smell of steam and bags of blue starch. Clothes were wrung out in a mangle, and Maggie and I were for ever squashing each other's fingers in that primitive machine. There was also a cook named Gladys Woodall, and although she did not live in, she was very much one of the loyal family retainers. Finally, Maggie and I had a nanny, or should I say several in succession. The first I remember was the dreaded Nanny Amos who was later sacked, and she was followed by the lovely Nanny Bergham, whom we adored. When Nanny Bergham left to marry a Royal Marine sergeant, her place was taken by a certain Nanny Cook whom we hated. One night at bath-time, we attacked. My sister scratched her face, and I bit her! Nice little people! She promptly left in tears. So we got our beloved Nanny Bergham back. She was a real treasure.

Nanny used to take us for a walk every day. The route seldom varied. We turned right out of the front door of No 85, and after a few yards passed the Royal Marine barracks gate across the road. I always stole a peep at the band, still resplendent in blue uniforms at that stage, and the recruits drilling daily. They were exciting times, expectation in the air, and we could not fail to sense it as we toddled by. Next we would pass on the right Wingfield Nursing Home, where I was born on 10 January 1936. Although I didn't know it then, that was a particularly inauspicious date to be born as old King George V was terminally ill. He died ten days later, 20 January 1936, and confusion reigned over his successor's suitability.

Our perambulation would then take us past a little road called Admiral's Hard, leading down to the creek. There I could see 'my' white ship with its yellow funnel, an elegant cable-laying steam-yacht which always fascinated me. At the bottom of Admiral's Hard was the slipway down to the Cremyll Ferry, the means by which we were often taken over to Cawsand or Mount Edgecumbe for a picnic. Then on down to the end of Durnford Street to Devil's Point, whose rocky pools were a child's delight when the tide went out. There we would watch His Majesty's warships leaving Devonport, and sailing out past Drake's Island, through The Sound and out to sea beyond the Breakwater. There it was that we saw HMS *Hood* sail on her last fateful journey. I remember watching her all the way out to Eddystone Lighthouse, never dreaming that we would never see her, nor Plymouth her men, again.

It was on one of these walks in 1940 that we saw our first German aeroplane. We were tumbling head-over-heels down the grassy slopes of a field called The Long-Room behind the barracks. It was a fine, cloudless morning, and at 11 o'clock precisely the sirens wailed and this single reconnaissance fighter flew unmolested over the City. Not a gun fired – there were none. Plymouth was receiving its first evacuees from London then, and nobody imagined that it could be a target! Later, of course, the barrage balloons went up. One of them was tethered to my white steam-yacht, and whether I dreamt it or actually saw it I do not know to this day, but that balloon exploded one day in a ball of fire. To me that was a disaster paralleled only by the precipitate departure of my ship a few days later. Unbeknown to me, that splendid vessel had answered the call to go to Dunkirk to help rescue the British Expeditionary Force.

The aftermath of Dunkirk, however, did make an impression on me. The sight of bedraggled Belgian soldiers shambling down Durnford Street en route to the Naval Victualling Yard, being offered tea and cakes at every front door as they went, remains with me still. A sense of imminent tragedy hung pregnantly throughout the land, and not only in south-east England. Shortly afterwards the Blitz started in earnest. Night after night we were taken downstairs to sit, wrapped in blankets, on the basement stairs. Maggie and I would suck barley-sugar sticks, while my mother, Grandma and Mrs Bull would take turns at fire-watching above. To me the greatest disaster was when a bomb destroyed my favourite sweet-shop a few hundred yards from the house. But the throb-throb of German bombers approaching, the whine of falling bombs and the crash of explosions overshadowed any ack-ack gunfire there was. Hitler became an ogre to me, and I never forgave him for wrecking my sweet-shop.

My mother, wisely, decided that the time had come to move us to safety, and Maggie and I were despatched to a boarding school, Hill Hayes, at Lustleigh, on the edge of Dartmoor. But dangers lurked there too. Horses ran wild in the front garden one day, and one night we were all awoken by the largest explosion I had ever heard as an ill-directed German land-mine blew up in Lustleigh Cleave. We were hungry, I remember – very. War-time rations didn't go far, and some items of food we ate at that place I detest to this day. In place of vegetables we ate bitter dandelion leaves. Tripe and onions took the place of meat and fish. So desperate was I that I raided the orchard and golloped dozens of little green apples. I shall never forget the ensuing stomachache. It taught me not to steal, though!

We could see the glow of Plymouth burning over the horizon, and the searchlight beams probing the night skies. My mother was there with her friend Maud Milton manning a mobile canteen, bringing succour to the bombed-out, and Aunt Pin was doing voluntary work with the YMCA. We must have been worried, and I do remember vividly the nightmares I had, and the flashing patterns before my eyes. Let's face it, I was scared. Soon the inevitable happened, and 85 Durnford Street disintegrated under a hail of incendiary bombs. My mother had had a premonition of disaster, so Grandma had been dispatched to stay with the Dathans at Tavistock and Aunt Pin to her friends the Smallbones at Ivybridge, so nobody was at home that night, but everything in the house was lost. My parents' household possessions had been in store in Southsea, where they formerly had a flat, but that too was bombed, so my mother shared the distinction with her mother and sister of having nothing left in the world but what they stood up in. All our family treasures were lost: furniture, silver, pictures, family photo albums – the lot.

My father came home from serving with HMS *Warspite* at the Battle of Narvik, totally unaware of what had happened. Imagine his shock on seeing the devastation as he went to Stonehouse Barracks! Having ascertained that we were all alive and where we were, he came out to see Maggie and me. All we were told was that a surprise would be arriving on a train at Lustleigh station. We had almost forgotten what he looked like, but it was a joy to see him, I recall. He was wearing khaki Service Dress uniform, with his three First World War medal ribbons: 'Pip, Squeak and Wilfred'. As a youngster aged 14 on 7 June 1914 he had left school and immediately enlisted as a Bugler Boy in the RMLI. He had faked his age and added back the 'e' to the mis-spelt surname 'Pugh' on his birth certificate. On 27 August he landed at Ostend with the Naval Division in the British Expeditionary Force that Germany's Kaiser dismissed as 'A Contemptible Little Army'. He was in action by 19 September 1914 at Antwerp and the retreat from Mons. His age was then discovered and his exploits as 'The Youngest Old Contemptible' were widely reported in the national press. When we saw him that day at Lustleigh he broke the news to us about the house, but after a short pause, I can remember simply asking what had happened to Sergeant Hopalong, our pet tortoise!

A little while later we had a day's outing to Plymouth, but only ventured as far as Mutley Plain. We had tea in Dingles, which had moved there like many shops after the City Centre was so emphatically destroyed. A string quartet played, just as it had before the war. They played a request for me, 'Wishing', and I sang it, dreaming of joining the Royal Marines and bashing up Hitler! Aunt Muriel Goss joined us; she was our eldest maiden aunt, a full 21 years of age when my mother had been born, and she was engaged in pioneer work in teaching the deaf and dumb just north of Mutley Plain at that time. A typically bossy Goss,

Father – the 'Youngest Old Contemptible'

Muriel was very talented; she played the piano well and her water-colours of Plymouth are exceptionally fine.

But it was time to go. We moved temporarily to Yealmbridge while my father went to sea again – this time on HMS *Malaya*, sister battle-cruiser to *Warspite*. The ship was damaged on a convoy escort run to Malta and he stayed with the crippled ship on its long slow voyage to Norfolk, Virginia for repairs. By the time HMS *Malaya* went to sea again – and blew up in her next, disastrous action, I believe – he was fortunately back again in England.

Yealmbridge was a happy if short sojourn. Quite apart from the relative peace, Sergeant Hopalong was discovered untouched in what remained of the garden in Stonehouse, and he duly arrived there. Sadly, Hopalong found it less agreeable than we did, and he took to his heels and disappeared for good. That was the third catastrophe of the war for me. My mother ran the house as a small hotel, and made the most delicious salty butter, I recall: a real treat in war-time. We also had one short holiday at the Berry Head Hotel, Brixham, from where my mother made wild forays across the Moors to Tavistock and Yelverton on the back of a motor-bike. Skit Poulter was the name of her romantic attachment then, and Edna Dathan her closest friend. The Dathans lived at 'Monyruy', Watts Road, Tavistock, and at one stage towards the end of the War, the whole Dathan family, father, mother and three sons, held commissions in the Royal Navy. The father, Captain Brandon Dathan, was one of my godfathers. The other was the Reverend Leonard Coulshaw, later to become Chaplain to the Fleet, and Honorary Chaplain to Her Majesty The Queen.

But in late 1941 we moved east, my father having been appointed, on 1 July 1941, to what was then known as The Depot, Royal Marines, Exton. Our rented house was a 1920s semi-detached brick building of substantial proportions, and our address was 1 Richmond Road, Littleham Cross, Exmouth, Devon. So began Phase 2 of my early life. For a boy of barely 6, I seemed to have packed in rather a lot so far, especially by way of disasters!

CHAPTER 2

Little Horrors

BUT EVEN IN EXMOUTH we didn't get away from the Germans! No sooner had we got there, and my mother had painstakingly assembled, by virtue of some nefarious dealings with Blackmore's and Crew's Furniture Stores in Rolle Street, a quantity of 'Utility' furniture for the new house far exceeding our ration, than Exmouth was subjected to a series of nuisance raids. The town was bombed and our house was machine-gunned. I witnessed the latter from a sprawled position halfway down the stairs. The most serious damage from that particular event was a smashed chimney pot and some rather dirty underwear! I have never been so terrified as then.

The Germans hit a little seaside town like Exmouth rather hard. During 1941, '42 and '43, 37 high explosive bombs hit the town, causing 54 deaths. I recall the chaos on 26 February 1943 caused by the bombs which struck the Strand shoe shop in the centre of town, distributing footwear far and wide. Otherwise it was the nightly bombing of Exeter that frightened us most. Squatting under the dining-room table, listening to the familiar throb-throb of enemy bombers passing overhead en route to their 'Baedeker Target', was a sound I shall never forget.

Grandma Goss had come to live with us, and Aunt Muriel had also moved away from the Plymouth blitz. She later took up residence in a flat above a chemist's shop halfway down Rolle Street. There she was within spitting distance of Holy Trinity church, which made her feel virtuous and the congregation less so! I remember her giving me kittens one day; she took Maggie and me for a walk to Orcombe Point, and on the day following a machine-gunning raid by enemy fighters the roads en route, Cranford Avenue and Douglas Avenue, were littered with silver anti-radar strips, shell-cases and cartridge clips. They all looked lethal to me, and we had been told never to touch such objects. Muriel, however, kicked every scrap of German metal she saw. I was quite convinced we would have a legless aunt before that walk was over!

Douglas Avenue contained the empty shell of a house which had been hit by an old Lysander aircraft – one of ours. It was Exmouth's first war-time destruction. Cranford Avenue also contained a house named

Trengwainton Lodge in which the Shephards lived – great friends of the family since they and my parents had been Royal Marine comrades and neighbours in Deal in 1933, and again in 1938 in Malta with the Mediterranean Fleet. Colonel Derek Shephard, after being rescued from the Luftwaffe's bombardment of Malta, was now stationed at the Nissen-hutted camp, Dalditch, 5 miles away on Woodbury Common. He took me there one day to ride in a Bren-gun carrier, which was the nearest thing the Royal Marines ever had to a light tank. It shook me up, but thrilled me nevertheless. I was sold on joining the Royal Marines, of course, by then. Cranford Avenue also contained spies – particularly one old man with sunglasses. There were spies everywhere in 1942, we thought. It was a long avenue, and we were always dog-tired by the time we had been to the beach – or what remained accessible of it between grid-iron defences and barbed wire, keeping us well away from the coastal and anti-aircraft gun-emplacements all along the sea-front. Those guns made a great deal of noise and periodically black puffs of smoke in the air as their shells burst around the slow-flying Hurricane tugging its sleeve target. I never saw the target hit.

Walks were, in fact, quite one of the most frequent horrors of my early days. We walked everywhere. Even when my father bought an old maroon Armstrong-Siddeley car, it was always breaking down, so we walked. He usually walked to the Depot at Lympstone, a 5 mile slog down Bradham Lane, through Withycombe village, along the muddy Pound Lane past Pink House Corner to the barracks – and back. He took me walking to Keeper's Cottage and Woodbury Common. To sing in the choir every Sunday at Littleham church, we walked – two miles each way (on Good Friday too and twice on Easter Day). It was no wonder I grew up with legs shorter than my arms; they were well worn down by the time I was 10!

One walk Maggie and I used to enjoy, however, was along Watery Lane, past the curious, rather man-made-looking, hill with the Bofors gun site on its summit and the detachment hut at the bottom, over the stile, across Buttercup Field to 'Paradise'. This was a blissful picnic spot, seldom frequented by a mortal soul save my mother and us. The Morrish's farm was nearby and we made friends with them sufficiently well to obtain fresh cream and illicit butter – untold luxuries in war-time. My mother was a most charming and successful scrounger in that way. To her, rationing was a personal challenge!

Footpaths led from there, across the stream, past ruminant horned cows, one way to Littleham Village, the other way to Orcombe Point.

Given the energy, one could do the round trip, but we seldom managed that. Had we reached Littleham, we might have caught one of the hourly buses, either a Hart's Bus or a Devon General. These plied between Exmouth and Budleigh Salterton, with occasional diversions to Little-ham, East Budleigh and Otterton. Hart's were our favourites; they were decrepit and overloaded, constantly breaking down as a result. This private company had seven drivers, known by us as the Seven Dwarfs, 'Grumpy', 'Happy' and so on. They seldom wore any sort of recognis-able uniform, but they were the sort of people who would stop anywhere to pick you up, and stop anywhere to set a passenger down. Often they just stopped. They always ran late, but they were fun. Devon Generals, on the other hand, were correctly dressed, dull and impersonal. What is more they were often punctual. They were painted grey, and some had a hump at the back of the single deck to house the luggage. Many of them were parked for safety in a lay-by en route to Keeper's Cottage, but I could never for the life of me understand why they could not be spotted by enemy aircraft, lined up as they were out in the open there.

They could have obtained camouflage nets, if they had wanted them, from a local source. Best's garage, barely 300 yards from our house, was converted into a camouflage net factory for the war's duration. I used to pass it on my way to music lessons with Mrs Sargent. That walk was a horror too, as I had to run the gauntlet of the errand boys. 'Brown Guy' and others of his ilk would mock me for the clothes I wore and the class I self-consciously represented, and they threw stones at me.

By 1943 my cousin John had arrived in Exmouth, and he was to be my constant companion throughout my days there. His mother, my Aunt Marjorie, who was two years younger than my mother, had married a Gunner officer called Bill Washington Dyer when he was ADC to the Governor of Sierra Leone. The marriage was short-lived and Marjorie returned to a flat in Grand Parade, Plymouth soon after which they were divorced. Marjorie then undertook to do voluntary work in Malta with Derek Shephard. After surviving the horrors of the siege of Malta, Marjorie was shipped out to Durban, South Africa and she married again, this time a Lieutenant Commander in the Royal Navy called Alex Hambly, who had just survived the torpedoing of the cruiser HMS *Cornwall*. Alex, Marjorie and John, who was her son by Bill Dyer, returned to England towards the end of the war. John's surname was not changed by deed-poll until well after he started at Prep school in Exmouth. They lived a few hundred yards from us at 13 Barnfield

Avenue. My cousin was tougher and rowdier than I, and he never lost the influences of his hard South African upbringing, short as it was. We played together and lived in each other's pockets.

Aunt Pin also escaped from the Plymouth Blitz, and took a job with the Ministry of Agriculture, Fisheries and Food in Newton Abbot, taking a rented house in Totnes. She often came to stay with us in Exmouth at weekends, chancing life and limb by using the Starcross ferry, a rather primitive form of passenger craft which occasionally got stuck on sandbanks in the Exe estuary. Dear Aunt Pin bought John and me bicycles – mine was a rather heavy 'Rudge' – and she taught John and me to ride them. That was a real milestone in our lives: less walking! We would play imaginary games on them, and normally we were the Royal Bicycle Machine-gun Corps, though discretion was the better part of valour when we encountered the dreaded errand-boys.

So came the time to start school. In 1941, on arrival in Exmouth, I had survived mornings only at Littlecot nursery school conveniently near; just past the shops at Littleham Cross. From there after a year Maggie and I went to St John's School at the bottom of Cranford Avenue. I remember little of that, except the uniform was brown, but there I met my first girlfriend. She was a lovely little blonde called Shirley Reeve, and she wore brown knickers. My first stirrings? Hardly, aged 6, but she definitely took my fancy.

Then came the great day in September 1943 when, aged 7½, I went to St Peter's Preparatory School for Boys, Exmouth. I was a 'day-bug', and, joined later by John, I used to walk or cycle to school, down Salterton Road, round Hospital Corner, and down past the Convent Girls' School playing fields, into school. At first I only went in the mornings, because I was thought to be 'delicate'. I had, in fact, had a year of strange high temperatures, akin to glandular fever, for which the sole remedy in those days seemed to be 'M & B' tablets, which old Dr Salter would prescribe liberally to me. I was much relieved after two terms to attend full-time, and boys no longer laughed at me.

The fierce, fine headmaster was Mr Theophilus Rhys-Jones (grandfather of the present Countess of Wessex) who used the cane fairly but with vigour. The two youngest classes were, however, looked after almost exclusively by the formidable Miss Rushton, the only female teacher in the school. Discipline was strict, and we had daily 'drill' – a mild form of PT but in our school uniform. We were obliged to sing 'Jerusalem' lustily at Assembly on Saturday mornings and, because we had a master called Mr Le Soeur who had escaped from the German occupation of France through the Channel Islands, we were also required to sing the 'Marseillaise' and believe implicitly in the valour and invincibility of the Free French Army.

A young, powerfully built, former Welsh Guardsman called Mr Christopher Freer, a talented cricketer who later bowled very fast for Devon, taught me 'Musical Appreciation' after 'Pottery' and 'Carpentry' on Saturday mornings. Those classical music sessions were something I never forgot. Freer's explanation of Beethoven's 'Pastoral' symphony opened my eyes – or rather ears – to serious music. I tried playing a few bars of Beethoven's Moonlight Sonata one day on the piano in the school Assembly Room, when Mr Rhys-Jones came in. He said to me: 'If you can learn to play the whole of the First Movement by the end of the term, I will give you a prize.' That was when I started taking my piano lessons with Mrs Sargent. I learnt it, and I got my prize. It was £5 – a lot of money to me then, and I never looked back, and have enjoyed playing the piano, if with more enthusiasm than skill, ever since.

As I grew older. I came to realise that the 'tone' at St Peter's was not all that it might have been. Mucky little boys hung around the repulsively smelly lavatories more than was healthy. For a time, too, the school was split evenly in a mild form of gang warfare, called 'He' or 'Touch'. One side was called the Roundheads, the other Cavaliers. I had no idea why I was elected to be a Roundhead and was not allowed to change sides. It was years afterwards that someone explained that it depended simply on whether one was circumcised or not!

1944 saw my father return to sea. He went away to join HMS *Indomitable*, one of our Fleet aircraft carriers in the Pacific. Preparations for 'D'-Day abounded in a south coast town like Exmouth. The streets were full of marching Americans dispensing chewing-gum. They looked a sloppy lot to me. Hutted camps sprang up everywhere, in fields as much as in the gardens of all the large houses in the neighbourhood. A half-built, empty shop at Littleham Cross was requisitioned, and the countryside was alive with exercises. There was no mistaking the difference, too, from the Home Guard exercises we had watched a year or two earlier taking place on the railway bridge at Littleham Cross. This time, we and the Yanks meant business, and expectation filled the air. On 5 June 1944 we saw them drive down to the docks to embark. From then on we were glued to the *Daily Telegraph* war maps pinned up in our dining-room. When the Russians started to advance into Germany itself, we even named our Field Spaniel Timoshenko after the Soviet Marshal. Somewhat difficult to credit, a few years afterwards!

I enjoyed school, and soon became quite proud of my efforts at both work and games. My reports were glowing. John thought I was a 'goody-goody', but it was only relative. I am sure it was he who egged me on to throw poor De Gren into a patch of stinging nettles one day when we were walking home from school up Hamilton Lane. We must have been real little horrors. De Gren was 'foreign' – a Polish refugee, in fact – and he stank. He also sang 'O! For the Wings of a Dove' quite superbly – which made him 'a wet'. He earned our respect, however, for never telling on us for that incident, even though he must have been horribly stung, particularly over his bare legs, wearing, as we all did, short grey trousers. John it was, for certain, who induced me to throw a stone in that same lane a few days later too. Misdirected, the stone crashed through a greenhouse. We sheepishly owned up to the owner, and our respective mothers made peace. However, I cannot blame my cousin for my being caught in Mr Brennan's Latin prep one afternoon writing an imaginary love-letter to my long-since forgotten 'girl-friend' Shirley Reeve – just to keep up with the others. That earned me a tanning from the headmaster, and a note to my mother. It was some years before I wrote another love-letter.

I also did all the usual things lads of 7 and 8 do during those years of discovery. I stole my mother's cigarettes, and smoked twenty in about half an hour in the bicycle shed – and was understandably taken to task when it was clear that neither charwoman Mrs Lee, the batman Marine Fox, nor his successors Edgeworth, Rudge, or Mutter who lived-in with their wives, smoked, let alone stole! I also made certain anatomical discoveries with the help of a school chum called Hayter in his mother's garden shed. From both these events, I confess I learnt a lot.

Then, in late 1945, my eldest sister, Diana, came back from being interned in Switzerland. She was still very delicate, with epilepsy now adding to her bronchial troubles. But she was a fighter, and the family seemed complete at last. One relation, however, who had caused me to worry, although I had never met him, was a cousin called Leslie Jole. He had been captured by the Germans during the battle for Crete, and he had suffered all manner of indignities in prison camps in Germany. I once cried at night, just imagining his privations. Another aunt, Nell, appeared from time to time too, and on one memorable day all five Goss sisters were present. Nell attempted to commit suicide off the railway bridge, ostensibly because things were not at all well with her marriage or with the hotel business she was running in Aldershot. Diana, Maggie and I secretly thought that it was simply the noise of all five aunts talking at once that had driven Nell off her rocker.

Diana's continual illness brought the handsome Dr Geidt to the house more than often, and I got to know, in a platonic sort of way, his beautiful daughter Julia. They lived not far down the Salterton Road in a large house called Merton Lodge. Although my mother was very restrictive in how far I could cycle (I always felt frustrated at not being able to cycle to Dartmoor then), I was certainly allowed to go as far as the Geidts' house with many a message or to fetch prescriptions galore. Another friend of my mother who made an impression on me then was Eric Delderfield, a big noise on the Exmouth Town Council. He was the brother of R.F. (Ronnie) Delderfield, the playwright, whose first production *Worm's Eye View* was staged in the Savoy Cinema, Exmouth at about this time, and I well recall seeing and enjoying it.

And so the War ended, and my father returned from the Pacific, now with two rows of medal ribbons, but ill and minus his teeth. He had not been so sick, however, that he had not managed to get himself involved with another woman in Sydney on his way back from the Okinawa Battle. His homecoming was therefore somewhat stormy, as you may imagine, and the next four years were punctured by ever-worsening conflict between my mother and him. For his first year after returning, he was placed in charge of a Polish resettlement camp at Okehampton. Then he went to Eastney Barracks, Portsmouth, where he ran the first of many magnificent Royal Marine Tattoos. But it was not long before the doctors diagnosed angina, and he was invalided out of the Service. From then on he was like a caged lion at home, striking out at everyone. It was a sad demise at the end of a fine career, in which he had risen from being the youngest Old Contemptible, to the Inter-Services Fencing Champion in 1929, and to Major RM. He had been a handsome young officer, who, with clear blue eyes and long eye-lashes, had captivated my mother at a very early age. She married him when she was just 18 years old. He did not come from a very grand family background, his father Owen Meredith Pughe having had a rather chequered career in reaching the rank of sergeant in the Royal Marines, and his grandfather being a gamekeeper at Llanfachreth, near Dolgellau. I often believe that my dear mother, in her feigned snobbier moments, was more horrified about the latter than the former!

The winter of 1947 was particularly nasty. John and I caught chickenpox and were confined to my mother's double bed for what seemed like weeks. It was the coldest winter on record, with deep snow lying on the ground for six weeks. We had no central heating in those days, but each bedroom had an open fireplace. My mother would tramp through the snow to fetch bundles of kindling wood from Otton's, the ironmonger in Exmouth High Street, and coal was delivered by ancient lorry from the railway sidings at Littleham station. The sidings had two spurs; the coal trucks were lined up along one while the other was occupied by two 'holiday coaches' for poor families from the cities to use in the summer.

Leslie Jole now appeared on the scene, and his frequent presence added little to the peace of the household. My father became insanely jealous of him, despite the fact that my cousin was years younger than my mother. There was, however, something to his suspicions, which even we children could not fail to notice. It was all a bit unseemly, and those last two years of my father's life were not our most happy. He died outside the Royal Marine barracks where he had served so long, at Lympstone, in January 1951, seven months after his 50th birthday. I was stricken that he died so young and in such a way. He may have only attained the rank of Major, but after such extraordinary beginnings and being consequently a self-educated man, his action-packed career, spanning two tumultuous wars, was far more commendable, significant and glorious than mine was ever likely to be.

Leslie had been sent with the Commandos to Malaya, where he was fighting the Chinese communist guerrillas with distinction, winning a Military Cross as a Troop Commander. On hearing of my father's death, he immediately telephoned my mother and offered to marry her. She took little persuading that that would be sensible, and that we could continue to be educated privately only if she did so. What a brave man to take on a woman far older than himself, with three children to educate on a Captain's pay! They were married in Penang on 13 November 1951, their best man being Robin (later Sir Stuart) Pringle, a fellow Troop Commander in 42 Commando RM. Eventually my mother had the distinction of having had two silver weddings! But I am getting ahead of myself, for I had left St Peter's Preparatory School in summer 1949.

That was a watershed: indeed the end of Phase 2, one could say. I took a scholarship to King's College, Taunton, and, although I was offered an Exhibition of £30 per term, there was no disguising the fact that I had

Stepfather and Mother, Malaya, November 1951

failed! I consequently sat Common Entrance, and scored 100 per cent in maths and passed with flying colours. There was only one decision my parents could make: I had to go as a day-boy to the best Direct-Grant Public School in the county – Exeter School. John Hambly was already there, as a boarder, and I did not like the sound of it one bit. It had a decidedly rough reputation and I cried my heart out. Nothing would ever be the same again. I had reached the summit at St Peter's; well, nearly: Deputy Head of School and Captain of cricket and hockey. The Head Boy was Michael Southon, a nauseatingly clever boy who was devilish good at soccer too. He won a scholarship to Blundell's and became a successful chartered accountant in time. He got all the glory; my attainments were more elusive even then. But I was taller, bigger and more mature than anyone else there. I was cock of the roost and relatively good at everything. My reports were unbelievably perfect – but I was in for some nasty shocks!

CHAPTER 3

The Way of Life 1947–50

I T HAS OFTEN BEEN regretted by succeeding generations that interesting details of the daily lifestyle of their elders pass into obscurity unrecorded. In the belief that, one day, my sons and grandchildren may be amused by the truth of the lifestyle I experienced in my younger days, I shall try to describe it in this chapter.

The years I shall describe are 1947–50. I was a boy growing up fast in formative post-war years. In 1947 I was aged 11 and still at Preparatory School: a tall, thin and rather serious lad, improving rapidly at sport and showing some aptitude for schoolwork, though not brilliant by any means. My cousin John Hambly and I walked a mile to school and back every day, including Saturday mornings, until we progressed to bicycles. Rain or shine, carrying our school books in a satchel on our backs, we wobbled our way along the relatively empty roads, our green school caps periodically being blown off in the breeze. Our knees were alternately weather-beaten, chafed and sunburned, as we wore short grey flannel or corduroy trousers halfway down to the knees, and grey socks which were supposed to be kept up with elastic garters but were more often than not down round our ankles. Only on becoming a 'monitor' in the 6th Form at St Peter's School, aged 12 or so, did one progress to long trousers, and a very proud day that was.

We lived in a fairly spacious semi-detached house, built in the 1920s: 1 Richmond Road, Littleham Cross, Exmouth. For some unknown reason it was renumbered later to become 2 Richmond Road. My parents rented it, as there were no Service Quarters in the area. It was tastefully but not lavishly furnished as the family had lost absolutely everything in the Portsmouth and Plymouth blitzes. Much of the furniture was of the war-time 'Utility' type, bought or scrounged with coupons. Rationing of any sort was a challenge to my mother, and she managed to charm and wangle her way round most restrictions. The house had no garage, and we, like most families then, had no car. Middle-class families were not too proud to travel on the buses and trains. We often caught a bus down to the town of Exmouth, the noisy, antique Hart's buses running alternately with smarter Devon Generals every 15 minutes both ways for a trifling fare. Bus queues were quite a way of life and an occasion for the exchange of much gossip!

Shopping was mostly completed at the ten or so local shops 200 yards away at Littleham Cross. My mother often telephoned the grocer's, Wilson's Stores, to order her food supplies, which would then be delivered to the house by errand boys on specially designed heavy bicycles with a large basket on the front and an advertisement for the shop slung beneath the cross-bar. As there were no refrigerators or deep-freezes in those days shopping had to be done in small quantities more often. To keep food cool the larder was used with its cold slate shelves, and in summer much use was made of muslin gauzes and standing foodstuffs on saucers of water. Eggs were stored in jars of isinglass. Tea-bags had not been invented then, either, so tea was brewed from tea-leaves in a tea-pot and poured into cups through a metal strainer, or put in a curious double-sided tea-spoon with holes in it to soak in the cup, a metal forerunner of the tea-bag. Fast food, other than fish and chips, was not available. Obesity was not a problem.

We walked a great deal, and were the more healthy for it. A trip to the beach would always be on foot, and two miles each way in the summer heat was quite a slog. We walked the mile to church at Littleham village every Sunday, my sister Diana and I singing in the choir there, sometimes twice a day. We would also be taken by my father or friend of the family Colonel Derek Shephard, for longer walks up to Woodbury Common, normally taking our black field spaniel, Timmy. Timmy, incidentally, like most dogs, was fed on horse meat, discoloured with a green dye to ensure humans were not tempted. Food and clothing rationing was still with us until the 1950s. Deliveries to the door included coal and coke, bread, milk, the mail twice a day, and eggs from the farms. Tinkers called periodically to sharpen one's knives. On our front gate was a forbidding notice 'No Hawkers, No Circulars' but it was a common notice which most disregarded.

1947 was a year of particularly harsh weather. Early, snow lay on the ground for six weeks, and then the summer was long and hot. I recall that winter very well, as for much of the time, it seemed, John and I were ill in bed with chickenpox and measles or something similar. Few houses in those days had central heating, and ours, with its spacious rooms and large sash-windows, was no exception. Double glazing was also unknown. There were open fire grates in every main room, and we were kept warm during those days of illness by a glowing coal fire in the bedroom. Electric fires and even paraffin stoves were used to keep the house warm. Hot water was created by a coke-burning range in the large kitchen, and when my father was away on duty or when he was so ill in those days between his retirement in 1948 and death in January 1951, I used to take turns with my mother in cleaning out and re-lighting that coke stove. The clinker that built up in the stove was considerable and it took quite an effort about once a week to dig it all out.

These years were not happy ones for my father; he had been a heavy smoker, and, although the connection was not understood then, he contracted angina for which there was no known cure in those days, only rudimentary open heart surgery, and few of the drugs available nowadays. He suffered a lot, and was reduced to occupying part of an enforced sedentary life in weaving woollen hearth rugs. Very nice they were too, but what a frustrating come-down! His retirement from the Service also resulted in our having no more living-in batmen in the house, so the heavy chores fell largely to me.

The oven part of the kitchen range was seldom if ever used for cooking. Kindling wood would be dried in it more often than not. There was a gas stove in the scullery for cooking. Next to it was a huge copper basin for boiling linens in. I can remember the smell of steam and blue starch to this day. Washing and drying machines had not been invented, or if they had, their price was well beyond all but the wealthiest families at that time. Washing was otherwise done by hand in the ample sink, using Lux soap flakes, strong detergents not being widely available, followed by squeezing the clothes through a hand-turned mangle. Clothes would be hung out to dry either outside on a rope line in good weather or over the wooden barred contraption that could be lowered from the ceiling over the coke range in the kitchen. Coke was piled in an outhouse just outside the scullery, and delivered regularly by lorry from the Littleham railway sidings.

In 1949 I changed schools, and as my father had retired on a very small pension, it meant I had to go as a day-boy to the nearest Public school, Exeter School. I travelled by train every day, catching the Littleham flier at about 8 o'clock in the morning, and changing at Exmouth, where I was joined by a gang of fellow day-bugs. After half an hour we would alight at Exeter Central. A bus would then take us to Heavitree and we would walk down Manston Terrace just in time for 9 o'clock prayers at Assembly. I never minded the early morning rush, and on occasions when I was late getting up, the Littleham flier, two carriages pulled by a steam-driven tank engine, would wait for me at the level crossing. Returning in the evening, after a hectic day, sport, and loaded down with homework or 'Prep' as we called it, was another matter. I was often dead tired, and dreaded eating my dried-up supper which had been kept warm for too long – micro-wave ovens were not yet invented. I was relieved when eventually I was able to become a boarder.

Society's attitude to corporal punishment in those days was quite different from today. It was regarded as quite a normal, if sometimes an ultimate, sanction against ill-discipline. It was even treated with a degree of levity, there being a cartoon strip in one of the popular children's weekly comics, *Beano* or *Dandy*, in which a schoolboy's pranks regularly resulted in an eccentric headmaster, dressed in black gown and mortar-board, delivering 'thwacks' with a cane on the offending lad's bottom. Public school prefects were permitted to beat younger boys with a slipper for quite minor offences. Boys and adults regarded it as all part of life's rich pattern. At the other end of the crime spectrum, murderers were hanged. The scourge of drugs, however, had not yet hit society.

Littleham Cross was quite a community in those days. Everybody knew each other by sight, at least. The roads were very quiet as few families had cars, lorries were small and cyclists and pedestrians were everywhere. Cars, many of which had no heaters and which were started by a crank handle in front below the radiator, were generally rather unreliable, with frequent breakdowns. It was wise to belong to the AA or RAC, whose patrolmen would ride around on motor-cycle and side-car combinations, never failing to salute you when they saw your metal membership badge on the car. Road surfacing was quite a business, with a noisy old steamroller belching black smoke making the finishing touches. Occasionally a horse and cart were still to be seen, often the property of farms in the neighbourhood. Street lamps, situated on the edge of pavements, had been dismantled during the war, but were now gradually restored to the gas supply. By 1950 most had been converted to electricity and later they were replaced by the taller overhead gantries one sees today.

For entertainment we had no televisions or computers. However, we listened avidly to the radio, or wireless as it was called. This was a large set in a wooden case in the dining room, and it was driven by electrical valves, before transistors were in commercial use. It used to take a long time to 'warm up' and it had an extension loudspeaker wired into the kitchen. We listened to comedy broadcasts such as *ITMA* (It's That Man

Again) with Tommy Handley, or *Much-Binding-in-the-Marsh* with Kenneth Horne and Richard Murdoch. Crime and adventure series too, like the Paul Temple mysteries, and Noel Johnson's *Dick Barton, Special Agent*, were all the rage. Stations were named the BBC Light Programme, the Home Service, the Third Programme and Radio Luxemburg. The 'wireless' stimulated the imagination in a way that visual entertainment never can.

Of course we also often went to the cinema, of which there were three or four in Exmouth, and took part in the local Exmouth Amateur Operatic Society shows at the Pavilion. My sister Margaret was particularly talented in light opera and took leading roles in *The Belle of New York*, *The Arcadians*, *The Geisha Girl* and *The Quaker Girl*. We played the piano, mouthorgan, comb-and-paper (which was easy using the brittle hard lavatory paper of those days), drums (often Mother's saucepans) and ocarinas (the forerunners of panpipes). We played recorded music on a wind-up gramophone, using Bakelite records of a 78 r.p.m. speed. Needles and scratches were always a problem, and woe betide anyone playing these records in the sun. The records would warp and go out of tune. Neither hard nor soft plastic was yet widely in use in the late 40s and early 50s. Plastic wrapping of foodstuffs was unknown, tin cans, cardboard and metal foil being the norm.

I produced a home-made house magazine at 2 Richmond Road. It was entitled *The Richarmstead Magazine*, as we had so many visitors it was as though we were keeping a hotel. I certainly got the bug for such literary and rather corny publications, and later, at Exeter School, produced one for School House. Printing in those days was achieved by typewriter and wax paper. The wax paper, suitably imprinted by the typewriter, would then be put on a flat bed of ink, and paper was then rolled across it. This process was called Roneo-ing, after the make of the flat-bed. It was a very messy and slow business, and a far cry from laser printers, lasers being then also undiscovered. Other magazines around the house included *London Illustrated*, *Picture Post* and the *Boys' Own Paper*.

Such photographic records as we have of those days were limited to sepia brown school group photographs, or snapshots taken with our own small box Brownie. More advanced German Leica cameras did exist, mostly war booty, but films were universally black and white. Colour photography did not become commercially cheap and widely available until the 1960s. A glance at my early albums, however, will show no trace of holiday snaps, for the simple reason that we did not have holidays

of the type which are common today. There were no package holidays
for the masses.

1948 saw the Allied air forces supplying Berlin by air in response to
Soviet encirclement – the famous Berlin Airlift – for months on end,
with propeller-driven transport aircraft. Airlines had no jet liners. We,
like most people, spent holidays in the UK. We stayed on farms in other
parts of Devon, we went on picnics and to the beach, swam, and rode
bicycles and the scruffy ponies brought to the front door by the eccentric
Mr White, played frequent games of cricket with friends, played with
marbles and Dinky toys, cards and board games, learnt ballroom dancing
at the Cranford tennis club teenage tea-dances, and amused ourselves day
in and day out without ever feeling deprived. We never had to be
'entertained' by 'grown-ups' to keep us occupied. In fact, I and many of
my fellows had not been abroad before joining the Army. One of the
reasons young men joined the Forces was 'to see the world'. Nevertheless
our childhood was completely happy without package holidays and
today's school-sponsored sporting and 'educational' trips abroad. Indeed
our knowledge of the world's geography, especially the British Commonwealth and Empire of which we were all so proud and which still
encompassed a quarter of the world, was considerable, mainly through
the medium of our cherished – quite valuable – stamp collections!

Another, somewhat bizarre, collection youngsters made was of
discarded cigarette packets. Smoking was widespread and socially
acceptable indeed cigarettes in packets of 20 or 10 were issued to the
troops with their weekly pay. All manner of work in society was
interrupted for ten minute 'smoke breaks'. No link had then been made
between smoking and heart or lung disease. What litter there was in the
streets comprised mainly used cigarette packets, the cleanest of which
were picked up and pasted into albums. I collected some 50–60 such
specimens, Players' Navy Cut, Craven 'A', Rothman's and Woodbines
featuring among common British makes, and Chesterfields, Camels and
Raleighs among American. Many childhood hobbies, such as train-
spotting, bird-watching, and Dinky-toy, coin and stamp-collecting, were
carried on into adulthood.

Our holidays on farms were memorable: small Fordson or Ferguson
tractors pulled binding machines to take in the harvest, and these
machines with their whirling windmill arms bound the sheaves of corn
which were then manhandled into stooks and left to dry in the fields.
The tractor moved around the field in an ever decreasing circle, so that

the final circuit was accompanied by a panic-stricken rush of rabbits from the centre to the edge of the fields – always a hugely amusing moment. Rabbit pie was a much-appreciated meal. Milking was still by hand on some farms, and I became quite skilled at it. Butter and clotted cream were invariably made on the farms in Devon, and this did much to make up for our slender diet in those days of rationing.

Communications were primitive too in those post-war days; there were no 'mobiles' and our home telephone was a heavy black bakelite instrument with a dial on the front of the base part with finger holes in it to dial the required number. All domestic and commercial lines went through the local exchange, where women connected you to your required number. On picking up the phone one would dial '0' and in answer to the response 'Operator' one would say, 'This is Exmouth 2574. May I have Portsmouth 4762 please.' The request would be repeated with the comment, 'Trying to connect you.' On answering an incoming call one would say, 'Exmouth 2574,' so I can easily recall this number to this day! It was many years before automated exchanges were introduced, and we all felt they spoiled the fun – especially for the operators listening in to the conversations!

One aspect of life in England in those days cannot be overlooked, and cannot be ignored or condemned as somehow 'racist'. There were very few black faces to be seen, and large scale immigration had not become a major political or social issue. In today's 'multi-cultural' UK the days of the 'traditional' British way of life that I was privileged to experience in my youth may be fading into nostalgic memory. In my view there was nothing much wrong with our unique British culture, and it seems a shame that immigrants cannot share it and adopt it rather than try to preserve their own cultural differences, religions and identities.

Having now settled in a part of England where the British way of life is still flourishing and does not seem threatened by the advent of alien cultures, we count ourselves fortunate. Nevertheless, life has taught us that people are more important than places and possessions, and this has become increasingly our maxim and one of our foundations for happiness.

CHAPTER 4

Adolescent Afflictions

I MUST HAVE BEEN repulsive. I was a snooty, middle-class, toffee-nosed, smug, bighead. Everyone else was common. A rough-neck named Carne took exception to me on sight, and one day, he hit me, very hard, on the jaw. I didn't cry, and I didn't hit him back. I suppose I was too astonished. I hated that first term.

I was a day-boy in Crossing House. I travelled every day by train. The first leg was from Littleham Station on a two-coach, tank-engine drawn rattler. Sometimes the train driver would wait for me. Then, changing at Exmouth, I was joined by a few other boys, and we travelled the half-hour or so to Exeter Central. From there we walked or caught a bus to Heavitree and shambled down Manston Terrace to school. We wore black blazers, black ties and blue and red quartered school caps. More often than not there was skylarking on the train and caps were thrown about everywhere, including out of the window. I generally returned home around 6 p.m. every day, exhausted and dirty, or later if I got into a sports team.

Fortunately my reputation as a cricketer had preceded me, and after those first two agonisingly lonely, miserable winter terms, during which I learned the rudiments of rugby football, I found myself put straight into the Colts cricket XI, and life became more bearable. I was kept in the side almost exclusively for my fielding. Hobson, Porter and Sedgewick were my only chums in the 4th Form that year. But I also joined the CCF, and that changed life for the better at once. I was fascinated by Ordnance Survey maps and I even joined the Corps Band, as a stand-in cymballist. When we marched down Exeter High Street on a great occasion, one of the cymbals flew out of my hand and rolled down the street. I broke ranks and gave chase, but by the time I caught up with it, it was halfway down Fore Street hill and badly cracked. It made a noise like a lump of lead for the rest of that unforgettable march.

The school was going through a post-war depression. The masters were old and tired. Several were ragged unmercifully, and from those it was difficult to learn anything but sympathy. Mr Bell, the deputy head, was an exception. His sonorous tones as he brought Shakespeare and

Chaucer to life will be with all whom he taught for ever. Mr Paul, the new Headmaster, too was a breath of fresh air. Young, imbued with the spirit of reform and religion, he pursued excellence and good manners with determination and diligence. Standards inexorably rose. The rowdies were removed and those appointed as prefects were, on the whole, young gentlemen.

In my second year, I threw myself at all sports with renewed vigour. I loathed the work, and during the hockey term failed my mock 'O' Level physics. Getting home late night after night, dog-tired and unable to cope with the maths and physics, who should come to my rescue but cousin Leslie Jole, now my stepfather, back from Malaya. Time and again he would rescue me from my tears, and by dint of logic and working from basic principles, he would show me how to solve those beastly sums. I owed so much to him in those unhappy days.

And so 'O' Levels came and went, and I took and passed about seven. Cricket became my all-absorbing passion, but in the following school year I captained the school hockey and cricket teams, and was vice-captain of Rugby. I was promoted to Sergeant in the CCF and then became Drum-Major. But all this paled into insignificance beside my becoming a boarder and member of School House. The thought of it had appalled me at first, as one had heard dark whispers of the horrors of beatings and homosexuality amongst the boarders. But it was like joining an elite club. We were best at everything, and there was nothing to rival the team spirit of that House.

It was tough, though. It was run under the wholly traditional Public School regime of cold showers, runs, beatings and fagging. Inevitably, the time came when I had to be beaten by a prefect called Fabes, whom I despised. It was a ghastly blow to my self-esteem, but after self-righteously seeking advice from another prefect called Peter Honey-man, whom I had assumed was my friend, I took the punishment for some offence I was convinced I had not committed. It was undoubtedly good for me, it hurt my pride rather than my body, and it contributed too to my subsequent somewhat robust attitude to corporal punishment, for sure.

Life was full of spills and fun, though. My cricket took me to local Devon Club matches. I played for Exmouth 2nd XI. I played for Thorverton Village side, and got horribly drunk on rough cider after one game there. School House won everything, and we always celebrated victories in traditional solemnity with a quaff of cider for every boy.

Meanwhile Leslie was posted to the Royal Marine Small Arms School at Browndown, near Gosport, and we left Exmouth for good. Diana worked on there, first in Haynes estate agents then in Barclays Bank, but Maggie went off to Roehampton for Froebel teacher training. I remember being almost unconscious of such family developments, my whole life seemingly focused on wringing the last drop of experience out of what had by now become a blissfully happy school life.

Then the great day came, in summer 1953, when Mr Paul told me that I was to be Head of School for my last two terms before taking the Civil Service Entrance Examination to the Royal Marines. I was to be simultaneously Head of House, Captain of Rugby, Captain of Hockey, Under-Officer in the CCF, editor of the School House magazine, Head of the Crossing Club – a debating society, senior member of the school choir, a leading light in the Musical Society performing *Trial By Jury* and so on. You name it and I ran it! And was I conceited!

At the start of the winter term in September 1953, as I nervously approached assumption of all these responsibilities, I recall that my priorities must have been roughly as follows:

(a)   Maintaining the sturdy (but unenlightened) Public School traditions
(b)   Nurturing the elitist *esprit de corps* of School House
(c)   Encouraging gentlemanly behaviour and religion (what a prig!)
(d)   Participating in musical activities (having developed into quite a good tenor I became passionately fond of church choral music and Gilbert & Sullivan – my sister Diana and I had been given some vocal training by a Miss Blight in Exmouth in the holidays, the fundamentals of which were to stand me in good stead for the rest of my life)
(e)   Sport
(f)   The House magazine (*Toby II*) which I founded as a successor to that edited by Fred T Jane (of *Jane's Fighting Ships*) many years before, and which I typed myself on an ancient Remington Rand typewriter
(g)   The Combined Cadet Force
(h)   (A very poor last) work

But power went to my head somewhat, and I began what must have seemed a rule of terror in School House. I beat everyone with 'Percy' the slipper; often for the most trivial offences, as I thought it was good for them. I made life hell for the fags, especially my long-suffering yet loyal personal fags, Keith Edmonds, Hughes and later, Peter Short. I justified it all on the grounds of the maintenance of tradition! I felt not the slightest qualms of hypocrisy when I read the lesson in Exeter Cathedral, or piously prayed in chapel (twice every Sunday for School House). I really relished life, and I was tremendously grateful to Leslie and Mother for scraping together an extra term's school fees to allow me to stay on and enjoy my undeserved responsibilities so much – fees which I subsequently paid back, but that's another story. All in all, however, it probably did me no good at all.

Looking back, it is easy to see how much I owed to the tolerance of my Housemaster, Jon Nelson. He and his comely wife Phyl became great friends – parent substitutes to some degree. He supported me when my fairness was questioned by recalcitrant juniors, and he advised me, sustained me and encouraged my better endeavours in every field. I felt I let him down badly on one memorable occasion, however. A small boy reported to him one day that the house tutor had made serious sexual advances to him. I had actually known about this tutor's homosexual propensities a term earlier and had hoped it would solve itself by the tutor's putative departure at the year's end. Needless to say, the tutor left abruptly in a blaze of unfortunate publicity, and I was acutely embarrassed. I told my mother who, as she was so often to do again at critical periods in my life, wrote a letter in the hope I would not know, explaining my woes to Mr Nelson. It was really a question of conflicting loyalties: on the one hand to the School's reputation and on the other to my Housemaster. He understood, and I was duly forgiven. It was a great lesson. Later, after I left Exeter, Phyl had a son, Richard, and I was asked to be a godfather; which I felt was a touching and undeserved compliment.

In March 1954, having taken and passed the Civil Service Exam quite well, I went up to Queen Anne's Mansions in London and took the medical tests for entry to the Royal Marines. There was some doubt about my eyesight, but I was told to go on down to Dartmouth for the Selection Board process anyway. Despite being a novice at knots, I had a lot of fun there attempting the Command Tasks with a co-operative syndicate of candidates, and passed it all with consummate ease. A week later I was told that I had failed the medical. I was thunderstruck, and the bottom fell out of my world.

CHAPTER 5

Sins of Commission

UNDAUNTED, I SETTLED for second-best, the Army. Apart from having had an errant uncle, Bill Dyer, whom I had never met and never wanted to, in the Army, we had no close relations who had deigned to join such people. I knew nothing about the Army and hitherto I had had no wish to know. I had no idea which Regiment to join, and there seemed nobody who could advise me.

Feeling somewhat the black sheep of an otherwise respectable Royal Marine family, I decided to join the Royal Artillery. It seemed to offer the greatest scope for promotion and the most variety. One could serve in units which rode horses, sailed in landing-craft, dropped under parachutes, which fired into the air or over the land. Exciting new developments in technology were apparently at hand, too, like guided missiles, which offered added variations to the artillery theme.

I duly took RCB (Regular Commissions Board) at Westbury and passed with a little effort and a lot of help from my fellow candidates. I actually quite enjoyed the experience, hurling myself and my group of willing victims over imaginary minefields and alligator-infested swamps by means of spars, ropes and barrels. Subsequently at a recruiting office somewhere I signed on, pledged my loyalty to the Queen and received her shilling. At Topsham Barracks, Exeter, I was inspected minutely by a ferocious female doctor. Her methods of checking that I had 'two of everything' struck me as unladylike, and acutely embarrassing!

I filled the weeks of April working at a large market garden in Hampshire, not far from Lee-on-Solent where my parents had moved while my stepfather was at the Royal Marines Small Arms School at Browndown. Mr G. House & Son Ltd were good to me, worked me hard for little pay, got me fit, strengthened my back muscles with long hours of hoeing between countless rows of beetroot, and made me vow never to do such mindless tasks as planting thousands of young cabbages again. Most of all, they made me bring in the silage, and so stank I each evening on return from my labours, that I had to drop all my clothes outside the back door before entering the house. That strong, sweet smell is with me to this day!

With sisters Maggie (left) and Diana, Lee-on-Solent, 1954

On 17 May 1954 I travelled by train to Oswestry in Shropshire, there to begin 10 weeks pre-Sandhurst basic training as an ordinary 'Gunner'. I joined 24 (Irish) Battery, Royal Artillery, part of 17th Training Regiment, and began a wild and unforgettable indoctrination into the life of a soldier in the days of National Service.

We were a mixed squad of pre-Sandhurst POs (Potential Officers), short-service soldiers and recalcitrant conscripts. Some had had cadet experience; others patently hadn't. We were all treated identically, like dirt. God was Lance-Bombardier Urquhart. He was in charge of us and our wooden 'spider' accommodation, and he ruled our lives around the clock. The Troop Sergeant, a more kindly man named Edwards, was less often seen, while our Troop Officer, Captain Gordon-Mclean, a short, moustached officer, who wore brown boots and a battered service cap, appeared but rarely.

The pre-Sandhurst POs with whom I shared every moment of those trying ten weeks remained my friends and rivals for the rest of my military career. James Templer, later an Olympic horseman, was top of my hit list. His father had retired as a Brigadier and they lived in

Woodbury, not far from Exmouth. He was an Old Carthusian and shone at any sport he turned his hand to. Tim Thompson's father was also a retired Brigadier, and he hailed from the same area, Woodbury Salterton in fact. He was a Wellingtonian. He polished his boots so well, one day, that Bombardier Urquhart threw them into a static water tank. Tim was quite unmoved by this form of bullying, and quietly started anew. He was a calm man, and he later won a gallantry MBE in Aden. John Biles, a tall, thin and aristocratic young man, Colin McAllister, who later joined the RASC, and Ted Fellowes, who went into the Green Jackets, were a trio I had less to do with. Tony Weston, Tommy Tucker and Iain Jack, however, were the three with whom I remained close friends ever thereafter, the Scotsman Iain Jack eventually being best man at my wedding.

Iain and I won the Troop 'Initiative Test', which were exercises in cheek in vogue then. We were obliged to set out for a weekend's enterprise, the most imaginative, bold or far-reaching being considered best. I cannot admit to our plan being very daring, but during those 48 hours we did get down a coal mine and dug at the face, we had tea with the Lady Mayor of Shrewsbury and took the fingerprints of the Shropshire Chief of Police. The public were very understanding! I suppose we must have won by the way we told the story, finishing as it did with Iain the Scot declaring triumphantly that we had not spent a single farthing the whole weekend!

Those were a valuable ten weeks, and young men who nowadays go straight to Sandhurst from school or university without experiencing a little of the life of the soldiers they are about to lead, miss something. It's called insight. I learnt to spit and polish, to keep my cool with superiors, to blanco, to garden, to peel spuds in the cookhouse and sweep the roads. I drilled and learnt gun-drill. I did PT and swam naked with the rest. I also got away to play a lot of cricket, so I have to admit to occasionally getting off lightly compared with non-sportsmen. It all came to an end too soon, but our final night at Park Hall Camp ended with some of us locked up in the guardroom! The local pub, the Boot at Whittington, was our undoing, or rather the end of course party there was really to blame. When the Military Police came to clear us out, I'm afraid one of them somehow found his way into the pond. I thought we wouldn't make it to Sandhurst after all, but a kindly CO released us the next morning without condemning us for our high jinks. And so to Sandhurst.

Like all cadets incarcerated in the hallowed grounds of the Royal Military Academy, I can remember little about the first term, except that it was hell. I recall the first day's 'tour of the Academy', which was conducted as a forced march at 180 paces to the minute under a ferocious Guards' Sergeant-Major. Every few minutes we were halted and the name of a building or part of the estate was shouted at us, but we were in such a state of exhaustion, streaming with sweat from the exertions of our 'march', that not one of those names registered with us at all. A quarter of 'Burma Company' junior cadet entry comprised overseas cadets, and they were totally mesmerised. For the British cadets it was a test of sense of humour more than stamina. Much was, in the first term. We did lots of drill, PT, sport and cross-country running. The Juniors' Steeplechase through the Wishstream and over the Obstacle Course was as much a spectacle as a test of strength. But we did become exceptionally lean and fit.

There was never enough food, and I was perpetually ravenous. I resorted, quite often twice a day, to sticky cakes from the cadets' canteen behind Victory College. In between the physical exertions we had academic studies, but the challenge of attempting serious work for 'A' Level maths, physics and chemistry while still sweating from the latest bout of PT or mind-numbing drill parades was too much for many. At one stage our physics instructor, a young civilian with a sarcastic tongue, suggested that I was intellectually idle. I was mortified and mentioned it to my mother in one of my regular weekend letters to her. A week or so later I was performing the not-too-onerous duty of Company Post Orderly when I spotted my mother's unmistakably bold hand on an envelope addressed to this physics instructor. She gave him hell! That was only one illustration of the influence my mother exerted in my life. She was a strong woman, almost domineering at times, but her wisdom and encouragement carried me along in such a way that I shall always be in her debt. However, she could only do so much to protect my intellectual reputation, and considering our perpetual state of exhaustion I still regard it as a small miracle that I passed all three 'A' Levels towards the end of my eighteen months at Sandhurst.

Having been Captain of both rugby and hockey at school, I was in something of a quandary about which winter sport to concentrate on. I found that I had been omitted from the trials for hockey despite having played for Devon Schools, and I wrote a sharp note of protest to the Captain of Academy hockey asking this gross oversight to be reconsidered! I was duly given that chance, but to no avail. The standard of the First XI was very high. I played a few times for the 2nd XI but more often played Company rugger. It was frustrating. Later, in the summer term, I made slightly more progress with cricket, having a regular place in the 2nd XI and occasionally playing for the 1st XI, although, to my huge disappointment, despite long hours spent in the nets, I was 13th man for the Lords match against the MCC. So near, yet so far. Lords was ever thereafter to prove elusive for me.

My main problem at Sandhurst was a lack of money. Very few cadets could survive on the small rate of pay given to a cadet in those days. All relied heavily on subsidies from home to finance their weekend trips to London, which was so enticingly near at hand. On a Royal Marine Captain's pay my new stepfather could not be expected to help me in this way, so I had to save my military pocket money for just an occasional foray. On Sundays I was a lonely figure at Sandhurst, and in desperation I joined the chapel choir, the only cadet to do so from the whole Academy. I loved it. The contrast between the compulsory Sunday morning Mattins services at which 600 cadets gave vent to lusty voices, quite drowning the choir, and the quietude of the Evensong was intense. It was those Sunday evenings I enjoyed most and still remember with affection to this day. Our choir was not at all bad, and the well-trained trebles' voices echoed around the cavernous, half empty chapel every Sunday evening in a most magical way. It was a haven of peace after the freneticism of the week's routine. My Company Sergeant-Major, a Welsh Guardsman named Paton, encouraged me in all this, and he has my eternal gratitude.

I did get up to London to see shows from time to time; *Salad Days*, *The Boy Friend* and *My Fair Lady* were the hits then. I either took my local girlfriend, Judy Shepherd, an accomplished horsewoman whose father ran the Frimley Hall Hotel, or relied on Julia Geidt getting away from Guy's Hospital where she was training to be a nurse. (Her father, you will recall, had been our doctor in Exmouth.) Both were stunningly attractive, and I was much torn between the two. Taking Julia out for an evening in town tended to be more fun, if only because of the subterfuge required to get her back into Guy's Nurses' Hostel after the gates were locked at 11.30 p.m. each night. Many a time in the small hours I had to heave her up over the wall! Judy, however, was a fashionable girl from a wealthy family, whose riding abilities were going to take her to international competitive standard. For the Sandhurst

Summer Ball I chose Judy, much to Julia's disgust! I liked them both. Judy wore a stunning ballgown, and I shall never forget the impression she made on me as she glided down the huge staircase at Frimley Hall before I whisked her away to the Academy. When, many years later, my eldest son, David, held his wedding reception at this hotel, there was a sense of *déjà vu* for me when David insisted, unknowingly, on having his bride Vanessa stand on those self-same stairs for a marvellous photograph.

At the end of my penultimate term at Sandhurst the names of those selected to be Under-Officers in their final term were announced. We were a good year, and Burma Company, which had hitherto taken a perverse pride in regularly coming last in the Inter-Company Competition, had prospered beyond all expectations through our efforts. I was sanguine over my chances of becoming its Senior Under-Officer. I was, however, doomed to disappointment. Philip Arkwright, an Old Etonian and a very good fellow indeed, was chosen, and I was mortified only to be nominated as Second-in-Command, the Company Junior Under-Officer. Iain Jack was also nominated Company Junior Under-Officer of the neighbouring Normandy Company. James Templer, among other fellow Gunners, was to be Senior Under-Officer of Ypres Company. I was shattered, and told my Company Commander, a gallant and charming Gunner major called Tony Matthew, of my sadness. He was sympathetic, but said the competition was severe.

All, however, was not lost! At the beginning of that final term, one crisp September Saturday evening, the Senior Under-Officer of Normandy Company, one Mike Sharpe, was apprehended by the police for riding a motor-cycle without a licence! The following Monday he was demoted to Officer-cadet. Most assumed that my friend Iain Jack would step up one rank into his place. He was, after all, already in Normandy Company and knew everyone there. To my astonishment, however, Tony Matthew called for me and told me that I was to transfer to Normandy to become its SUO at once! Iain must have been equally astonished and disappointed, but he was loyalty itself throughout that term, although Normandy was an unruly Company to lead.

Busy as life was, I found time for the chapel choir, for hockey and for the Revue. One of the huge benefits of Sandhurst lies in the people one meets there. Quite a bond grows up between men in adversity! A fellow hockey player in Burma Company with me was the unassuming Yakabu Gowon, later to become President of Nigeria. Two charming Ceylonese

cadets named Tamatigama and Wanasingha were popular, Tony Weston
and I taking the former on holiday to the Lake District with us in one
of our leave periods. HRH The Duke of Kent was a term senior to me
and not in Burma Company, but he established a record while at
Sandhurst for the shortest motoring time between the Staff College gates
and Marble Arch: 35 minutes. It is a record that still stands, I imagine,
and that was before the days of motorways! Peter Inge was a fellow cadet
in Victory College and he eventually became Chief of the Defence Staff,
the last Field Marshal, The Lord Inge. Chris Bonington, later to become
internationally renowned for his Himalayan exploits, was a fellow cadet
in a neighbouring Company and his potential as a daring climber was
clearly shown when he and Tommy Tucker scaled the central tower of
the Victory College building one night to festoon it with loo rolls!
Normandy Company, however, lacked future stars in my last term. Its
cadets were nevertheless a very nice bunch to be with.

   We had many famous and interesting visitors, too, during my time at
Sandhurst. Lord Louis Mountbatten took one Sovereign's Parade, King
Hussein of Jordan another. I literally bumped into Field Marshal
Viscount Montgomery one El Alamein Day evening, my nose coming
to rest an inch from the largest chest of medal ribbons I had ever
encountered.

   But the last term was more tolerable for one special reason: Senior
cadets were allowed to have cars. My stepfather, Leslie Jole, had gone off
to sea in HMS *Newcastle* and the little old green Austin 7 Cabriolet,
Registration Number CTT 392, which had been sold to my mother for
£50 by her Exmouth friend Molly Palmer, was loaned to me for the
duration. I christened it 'Janet' and it was a car of character. It rattled
along the road to London, or down the A30 to Exmouth where my
mother had returned while Leslie was at sea. Its driver was alternately
deafened by the clattering of main bearings or enveloped in clouds of
noxious oil fumes. It had no heater, of course, and on winter journeys
one had to wrap one's legs in a blanket. I still recognise those lay-bys
along the A30 where I used to stop to restore circulation and clear the
windscreen of accumulated ice.

   End of term was to be 16 December 1955. On that day the 16th
Intake had its Passing Out Parade, the Sovereign's Parade. Major-General
'Poo' Hobbs, a Gunner, was to take the salute in place of one of the
Royal Family. Shortly beforehand I heard that I had passed all three of
my 'A' Levels. That surprised me, but I had worked hard I suppose. I

had no idea what Grades I had achieved; in those days it was not deemed important. I was strongly advised by the academic staff to continue my studies by taking a London University External Honours Degree at the Royal Military College of Science, Shrivenham. It sounded rather boring to me, but I was prepared to accept their advice. I then got on with the Revue, which among other acts involved one under the direction of Tony Weston, who had been brought up in New Zealand, in which we all dressed in grass skirts and performed a Maori Haka. I was in nearly every act in one capacity or another, and revelled in it all. I was, however, dog tired. To cap it all, I was detailed off to be an Ensign Bearer on the Sovereign's Parade, which required a great deal of extra practice under the direction of the Academy Regimental Sergeant-major, RSM Phillips, who had recently taken over from that most famous man, Jackie Lord.

We reached the final stages of preparation for the Great Day, and I had borne the Ensign in high winds and felt the strain acutely. Then two days before the Parade we were having a lecture in the Sandhurst Hall on a subject which has long since escaped my memory, when I received a summons to see the Commandant! The message-bearer whispered, 'You've won the Queen's Medal!' I said, 'Don't be stupid!' and jumped on my military bicycle, not forgetting the correct mounting drill so deeply was it ingrained, and pedalled off up the hill muttering to myself, 'This is absolutely ridiculous! Madness! Who's dropped dead?' I duly reported to the Commandant who offered me his congratulations and said that a cadet called Buchannen had actually come top of the Order of Merit, but as he was ill and anyway had not done as well in the 'Charlie George' (Character Grading) rating as I had, the coveted medal was to go to me. SUO Jack Crutchley, a Rhodesian, was to be given the Sword of Honour. Crutchley, a fine, fit man, had been captain of rugger at the Academy and he was the first Rhodesian ever to win the Sword. I should explain that the Sword of Honour was the more esteemed prize, although it was awarded solely on 'Charlie George' rating. The Queen's Medal, however, was awarded to the cadet who came top in the Order of Merit, a table made up in equal halves from 'Charlie George' and academic results over the whole length of the Course. I believe now – some feel with justification – that the basis of the awards should be exchanged, and perhaps I had done far better than my chum Jack Crutchley. However, one could not be churlish, and indeed, I was numb with shock at my own wholly unexpected and undeserved success.

Receiving the Queen's Medal, Sandhurst, 1955

A frantic 24 hours followed in which I had to learn the drill for receiving the Medal on the Sovereign's Parade, and some poor soul had to learn to carry the Ensign in half the time it had taken me! Parents, friends, relations and schoolmasters had to be mustered to attend the Parade. My stepfather, Leslie Jole, was still at sea in HMS *Newcastle* in the Far East, but everyone else came. It was a great and emotional day. I know my mother cried as we marched onto the damp parade ground that morning to the tune to which I had so often stamped up and down my grandmother's drawing-room in Plymouth so many years before – 'We're the Soldiers of the Queen, my Lads!'

The Queen's medal was accompanied by a small financial award. In response to my mother's suggestion I paid this into Leslie's bank to pay back those ill-afforded fees for my last term at Exeter School. The top Sandhurst award, however, was the Sword of Honour, and this, carrying the real glory, had eluded me!

Fifty years later I came across one of my Sandhurst reports. It stated:

I am most impressed by this cadet. He has poise, competence & ability far beyond his years, & his obvious integrity, high standards & strong character make him a formidable proposition. He is quiet & this deceives some people into thinking him off-hand or sleepy. They couldn't be more wrong.

I hope he will not prove too intolerant of the failings of the many people less competent than himself. Army Council?

High praise indeed, but if this suggested that I was tipped to reach the highest ranks to serve on the Army Council it was unduly optimistic! However, I was to serve eventually on a rather different sort of Council – as we shall see.

CHAPTER 6

Subaltern Slips

THE SIX MONTHS from January to July 1956 must rate among the happiest and most carefree of my life, but they included a regrettable decision that I made which again contributed to opportunities for glory eluding me.

Apart from a small but flattering interlude when I was asked to return to Exeter School to be presented with an engraved shooting stick in front of the whole school, the period was taken up with a Young Officers' Course at Larkhill, on Salisbury Plain. We were twenty irresponsible second lieutenants learning the basics of our profession. The emphasis of the course was naturally on mastering gunnery skills, and much time was spent in learning the technicalities of surveying gun positions and deploying troops of guns. We were taught how to take charge of a 25-pounder gun-position, how to lay the guns for line and elevation, how to give the orders, how to organise the command post, and all the varied and numerous aspects of being a Gun Position Officer were instilled into us by patient and assiduous instructors. No better grounding in the basic tools of one's profession can be imagined.

Our YOs' Wing Commanding Officer was Major Paddy de Burgh, a veteran of Arnhem and a leader of exceptional energy and charm. I grew to hold the greatest respect for this experienced officer, to enjoy his sense of humour, and even began to look upon him and his lovely wife Bridie as personal friends. He was also an officer who maintained and imparted the highest possible standards in every aspect of an officer's life, as much in social etiquette as in technical matters. The YOs were fortunate to be housed in the First World War vintage 'A' Mess in those days, an old corrugated iron building, renowned more for its charming antiquity and comfort than its economy and ease of maintenance. We were looked after by a long-standing group of 'old retainers' of immense character, who, together with Paddy de Burgh, generated an atmosphere of exceptional friendliness, understanding and loyalty. These faithful servants were well known, of course, throughout the Royal Regiment, as succeeding generations of YOs passed through their hands. Seldom did one ever meet an officer in later years who would not speak with great affection for 'Mr Duffy and the others of the old "A" Mess days.' Many can testify to the kindly advice they gave to thousands of inexperienced young officers down through the years.

Separating the youthful, exuberant and irresponsible YOs into 'A' Mess was wise. On many an evening the Mess reverberated to the noise of a particular brand of boisterous games after dinner, games which were taught expertly to us by Paddy and his fellow officers. Paddy was a stickler for ensuring that the life of an officer should be fun as well as professionally rewarding. Occasionally the games went too far, to the detriment of one's clothing, including expensive Mess Kit, but all manner of puerile rough and tumble passed off with surprisingly little damage.

The YOs' Wing adjutant at that time was Captain John Castle, a florid-faced officer whose expertise as a horseman was readily and ably passed on to all those on the course who wished to ride. Most of us did, and beginners were encouraged. Some of us were already accomplished horsemen, like James Templer for example. Many, like myself, had learnt the basics in our youth on hired ponies, and some, like Tony Weston and Iain Jack, took to the saddle more for a dare than with any serious thought of continuing with the sport. Consequently the standard of attire on our twice-weekly early morning rides varied widely, as did the frequency with which certain officers found themselves walking back to barracks, their mount having ditched them unceremoniously in the middle of Salisbury Plain. Fine spring morning rides out across the Plain are to this day some of my most enduringly pleasant memories of the YOs' Course. But to be fair to the less experienced or adaptable officers, much depended on the mount you were given for the day. The rotund piebald Freddie was the one everyone tried to avoid. The poor beast was the butt of everyone's mirth or temper, and on one remarkable evening after dinner, the usual boisterous games were brought to an end by Freddie being ridden up the steps and into the Mess ante-room. It must be said that Freddie behaved on that occasion with rather more decorum than some of the young officers!

As winter turned to summer I found myself playing cricket for the Garrison. I was fortunate enough to be awarded the Tombs Memorial Prize, which included a cheque for £100, for being the top Gunner subaltern out of Sandhurst, and this money was put towards buying a new set of cricket gear: bat, pads, bag and so on. It was a good investment for the future and that all-important first match for the Royal

Artillery Cricket Club in August 1958 against West Kent CC at Chislehurst in Kent. £100 would not buy the very best kit, but I thought it was good enough not to let the side down, and I certainly enjoyed that memorable two-day game with some very talented and hospitable players on both sides. Quite incidentally, in a curious flash-back to the past, I learned that a cricketer well known among the West Kent side was a fine batsman named Brian Harbury who had been acquainted with Mr Freer, the music master and a fine fast bowler, of St Peter's School, Exmouth. Indeed, he had lived opposite the school and had played for Sidmouth CC if I recall correctly.

In late May 1956 we were invited to consider which unit of the Royal Regiment we would like to serve with on completion of the course. Paddy de Burgh let me know that being top of the course (and subsequently recipient of the Earl Roberts Memorial Prize) I would probably be granted my first choice. He was an old Airborne warrior and I was greatly attracted towards joining the Airborne Gunner regiment, 33rd Parachute Light Regiment. I had been on a short parachute course while at Sandhurst – the so-called 'Teddy Bear' course at RAF Abingdon – and proudly wore a parachute on my uniform sleeve, albeit without wings, as I had not yet served in an Airborne unit. But I was faced with a dilemma: I was due to go to the Royal Military College of Science in nine months' time to take an Intermediate pre-degree course, and the Airborne Gunners were apparently leading a rather dull existence in Aldershot. I wanted to go abroad, and I opted for 45th Field Regiment in Dortmund, Germany, instead. What a frustrating mistake! While I learned basic regimental soldiering in the tedium of exercises with the British Army of the Rhine, BAOR, the entire British and French Airborne forces took off for Suez on a real operation! Elusive glory indeed!

However, the die was cast and when the YOs' Course ended in July I departed for Germany as fast as I could. With a tin trunk, a kit-bag and a couple of suitcases I took the train to the military embarkation point, Parkestone Quay at Harwich. Thence by elderly troop ship we sailed to the Hook of Holland. With a certain amount of chaos, soldiers were there distributed to various trains which took them to the principal British military garrison towns in Germany and the Benelux countries. Mine took me to Düsseldorf, deep in the industrial Ruhr Valley, where I changed to a normal German local train with wooden seats to get me to Dortmund.

I was young, had never been abroad before and was full of trepidation. Matters were made worse by there being nobody to meet me at the Dortmund Hauptbahnhof. I contemplated taking a tram, but my luggage would have created a problem. Taxis might be prohibitively expensive and I only had the standard issue British Armed Forces Vouchers (BAFVs) on me, no Deutschmarks. I stood forlorn outside the station. This was not the sort of welcome I was expecting on arriving at my first regiment.

Eventually an Army 15 cwt truck drove up and I asked the driver, who was from a different unit, if he could take me to 45th Field Regiment at West Riding Barracks eastwards on the B1 Ruhrschnell-weg. He obliged and told me that '45' were away at practice camp in Trauen, a remote place north-westwards in the middle of the North German plain. On the way there I noticed how much of the city of Dortmund was still in ruins, eleven years after the end of the war. There were signs, however, that German heavy industry was back on its feet, judging by the belching black smoke from the Bessemer converters and coal mines in all directions. It looked suffocatingly dirty and depressing.

I was looked after on arrival at the barracks by a helpful duty clerk who furnished me with a train ticket for my journey to Trauen the next morning. I was given a room in the officers' overflow accommodation just inside the barrack gate on the left, beyond a concrete bunker which had evidently been a German ack-ack command post during the war. The Mess itself was outside the barracks across the road, but in those days of National Service, there was such a large number of unmarried subalterns in the Regiment that all the rooms had been taken up. The Mess was closed, anyway, on this occasion, and I had to eat cold sausages and mash in the soldiers' cookhouse.

The next day I was taken in good time to the station, and more by luck than good judgement, as I spoke no German, I selected the correct train to take me on a long and slow journey to Trauen. I arrived by early evening and was kitted out by the Quartermaster with the necessary clothing. A member of the Mess staff showed me my room upstairs in the old hunting lodge which served as a Mess in an otherwise primitive hutted camp, He advised me to be promptly down for breakfast at 7.00 a.m. I ate a hurried meal by myself and went to bed feeling rather sick.

The next morning I felt no better, but strove to make myself presentable before going downstairs punctually to meet my brother officers at breakfast. As I stole down the creaking staircase I could hear nothing but a faint rustle of newspapers. Nobody was talking. I peered nervously over the banister and saw to my horror that about thirty officers were present, including the CO. They were all sitting at the table reading newspapers, with nothing in front of them but a bottle of gin. There was one place vacant and in response to my murmured, 'Good morning, Sir,' the CO nodded to my place. I sat down in front of my gin bottle. I looked up and down the table and at my neighbours. In deathly silence each of the officers took occasional swigs from their gin bottles. One or two cast a supercilious and expectant look in my direction. I quickly plucked up courage and took a swig. It was Gordon's neat gin, and I spluttered. No reaction. Nothing. I took another larger swig and this time summoned up the courage to turn to the Mess waiter behind me and ask for a newspaper as boldly as I dared. At this the Commanding Officer said in a loud voice, 'Well done, Neville. Welcome to the Regiment!' and everyone burst out laughing. My neighbours then explained that *their* bottles were filled with water! We all then had a proper fried breakfast and I had been duly initiated into the Regiment.

I found the Regiment in fine fettle. They had not long been back from Hong Kong where they had been stationed after distinguishing themselves hugely in the Korean war. The Regiment contained a good number of seasoned and experienced officers. It was still equipped with World War Two vintage 25-pounder guns, quads and limbers, and some very unreliable 15 cwt trucks. Officers in the field dressed bizarrely in khaki No 2 dress caps, battledress, gaiters and boots, and, in the absence of any form of waterproof clothing, white trench-coat style mackintoshes by which officers could easily be identified at considerable distance, day and night, by friend and foe alike. I was appointed a Troop Leader in 70th Field Battery RA. The Battery Commander was Major Sam Lucas, a real gentleman and experienced soldier. Under his understanding leadership I learned much in this, my first Practice Camp. My task was chiefly one of map-reading around the training area and leading my four guns in a timely and tactically orderly fashion from one gun position to another. People were kind and I was even forgiven for losing the guns completely on one occasion. This was possibly due to the fact that the guns actually arrived at their destination before I did on that occasion, the Gun Sergeants' knowledge of the terrain being far superior to mine.

An early test of my leadership was, however, presented in a surprising way. The guns were lagered up in a German village one night, and on departing in the early hours to occupy a gun position by dawn, I was pleased to note how expertly the guns all deployed. I was therefore somewhat taken aback on doing my rounds of the gun pits later to find the old Bombardier in command of 'A' sub-section reeking of alcohol and asleep at his post! It transpired that he had taken the opportunity of the lager to visit the village Gasthaus where he got himself exceedingly drunk. Being a seasoned professional, however, he still managed to get his gun into action before falling asleep under the influence of plentiful German beer. The loyal members of his gun detachment put me to the test by insisting that all was well, but I decided this was not exactly the way to behave in preparing for war and the said Bombardier was duly despatched to the Guardroom and subsequently disciplined by the CO.

All in all, although I learnt much, I was not overly impressed with the Regiment's tactics in the field. Back at barracks, however, it was a different story, and I treasure to this day the comradely spirit and fun we experienced, even though for me, it was all too short a stay. I sailed Star Class and Sharpies at the Möhnesee almost every weekend, I played hockey and cricket, I sang the nights away with the Officers' Mess skiffle group, I played the great grand piano in the Mess dining room. I went shopping at the YMCA 'Stonk Club' nearby and in Dortmund city. I took in everything I could about the regiment, its history and customs, and made good friends among the subalterns. Its hockey side was particularly strong recording much success in both the Regimental and the Army Inter Unit Cup competitions, the team including such stalwarts as Captains Peter Farmer-Wright and the ebullient Sidney de Cruz, Lieutenant Peter Hole and the unrelated Major R.S. Hole (who must have cursed his parent's sense of humour in giving him those initials!)

Professionally I took my first steps as a regimental officer and the learning curve was steep. Take for instance my very first spell of duty as the Regimental Orderly Officer. The routine duties of inspecting the cookhouse, visiting the guardroom and mounting the guard and so on were straightforward and relatively small hurdles to surmount on my first day, but that night, at 2.00 a.m. I was called out by the local military police to accompany them to a nearby married quarter, the neighbours adjacent to which had complained of noise of violence. Mustering all my courage, I, the green bachelor second lieutenant, strode purposefully into the small house. I stood stock still on the threshold when I saw the mayhem inside. There was blood all over the walls, the furniture was in disarray, and the wife of a very drunken bombardier was slouched in a corner with her clothing torn, her face bruised and bleeding.

'Right!' I said quietly, 'Bombardier, the neighbours have complained about the noise. You have clearly assaulted your wife, and appear to me to be the worse for drink, and I am taking you to the guardroom immediately. Corporal,' I said turning to the military policeman, 'call for medical help for Mrs X and take the bombardier away!' I quite surprised myself at the firm calmness of my voice. Imagine, then, my amazement when the wife sprang up and cried, 'Please don't take him to the guardroom. It was not his fault. I asked for it! You see, sir, I like it!' To say that this innocent young second lieutenant was somewhat taken aback is an understatement, and it was an early lesson in the darker side of life and an experience never forgotten.

The Assistant Adjutant was a man called John Soar, and, when he was posted, I inherited from him the Regimental mascot, a dog of dubious parentage who resembled a white terrier with one black ear, and who went by the name of '121 Lance Bombardier Wallop AIPO'. 'AIPO' stood for 'As In Pint Of', and 'Wallop' was a fully fledged member of the Regiment, with a Company record card, conduct sheet, pay book and identity discs. He was in many ways a typical soldier. He could be immaculately behaved one day, and unruly the next. Obedience tended to be a matter of whim or mood, rather than of training and tradition, however. After a couple of months of unusually good behaviour, 'Wallop' had been promoted to Lance Bombardier, and the promotion was duly announced in Regimental Routine Orders of the Day. A week or two after I took him on, unfortunately, he had to be demoted again for cocking his leg in the Mess corridor. He was an affectionate dog, and his one and only vice was directed at the regimental cooks, whose white uniforms clearly and regularly gave him the insuperable urge to snap at their legs. Despite that, he received generous quantities of bones from them.

Wallop was my constant companion, even going to the camp cinema with me on occasions. Sadly, one day in the autumn, when he was walking with me along Route 1, we passed a cornfield opposite the cemetery there, and he must have spotted or scented a rabbit, as he was off like a shot, bobbing up and down in the tall wheat. To my dismay and horror I saw a farmer raise his shotgun, and when Wallop bobbed up the next time, the farmer shot him dead. In Germany the law is on the side of such farmers and 'stray' dogs are not welcome on their land. The Regiment was heartbroken, but none more than I. His name was recorded in Regimental Orders for the last time and he was given a fitting and dignified funeral.

I made many good friends in the Regiment during this short period of six months up to January 1957, among them many talented National Service officers. Richard Francis was one of the most talented thespians and musicians among them, having been a colleague of Julian Slade of *Salad Days* fame at Oxford. He, Brian Rowbotham and Toby Woolrych formed the skiffle and cabaret group, giving many an impromptu but highly professional performance in the Mess Keller Bar. Such events served to fill the long evenings impecunious subalterns were forced to spend in the Mess. Few boasted the luxury of car ownership. Chris Morris's old Austin Ten was always breaking down, although, surprisingly, Austin spares could still be obtained from a pre-war stockist in Duisberg. To go skiing in the nearby Sauerland or at Winterberg in the Harz Mountains, one went in military transport on the pretence of teaching one's soldiers winter warfare. It was fun and fit-making. That December there was a good covering of snow in Germany and I learnt to ski quite well, finding it exhilarating. Back in barracks, in contrast, I ventured to volunteer myself as a bridge player one evening. My mother was a fanatically good bridge player and she had taught me some of the rudiments. I partnered Rory O'Callaghan, the senior subaltern, of whom we were all a little in awe. Half way through the third rubber he was clearly exasperated with me, and, piercing me with a pitying stare, he said cuttingly, 'Don't you know what two clubs means, boy?' I never played again.

Such lessons, and the lighter side of regimental life too, were all too soon over for me, as the academic grind of the Royal Military College of Science beckoned in January of the year 1957. RMCS Shrivenham had pretensions to being the Army's own University. The Army Board, quite rightly, was striving to increase the number of University Graduate officers in the Army in the belief that the future technical challenges of warfare demanded better qualified and more intellectual officers, especially in the Support Arms, such as the Sappers (Royal Engineers), Gunners (Royal Artillery), REME (Royal Electrical and Mechanical Engineers) and Royal Signals. Apart from a dozen or so places at Oxford and Cambridge, no places were reserved for Army-sponsored students at any other British University in those days. I suppose Universities in general were filled to capacity coping with the post-war influx of men and women whose degree courses had been delayed until hostilities ceased. Thus it was that around a hundred young officers per year were encouraged to try the three-year London University External Honours

Degree courses in General Science, or Mechanical, Electrical or Civil Engineering arranged for them at Shrivenham. Indeed, so keen was the Army to get officers to sit for these degrees that they were prepared to bring suitable candidates up to the minimum starting requirements of London University in a short 5-month 'Intermediate' course at Shrivenham. One of the London University degree starting requirements was an 'O/A' Pass in Chemistry, and since the three 'A' Levels I had passed at Sandhurst were Maths, Advanced Maths and Physics, I was one of the unfortunates persuaded to spend 3 months concentrating solely on obtaining the extra exam pass in Chemistry. I regarded it as a total waste of time, but nevertheless was persuaded that I should do everything necessary to get a degree as it would all be worthwhile in the long run, both for my career and for the general good of the Army and, if I left the Army, it would be a useful qualification to have up my sleeve.

Shrivenham was a marvellous setting in which to study and generally enjoy life. The college buildings had been erected under the Hore-Belisha Reforms in 1938 with a view to housing a complete air defence Artillery Brigade. They were modern, spacious and tastefully arranged in the grounds of the eighteenth-century mansion, Beckett Hall, on the eastern outskirts of Shrivenham village. After being converted to the Royal Military College of Science, one block comprised two halls of residence, Roberts and Kitchener Halls, while the other main block, half a mile away, was converted into lecture rooms and laboratories. Beckett Hall accommodated further students and a substantial library. Within the grounds there was also a cinema, a theatre, stables, a golf course, swimming pool, tennis courts and numerous rugby, hockey and cricket fields. Across the main road on the outskirts of Watchfield village and RAF airfield there was a NAAFI shop as well as quarters for the numerous Other Ranks stationed at the College. Their task was to support the large student body which comprised not only degree students but middle rank officers on Technical Staff Courses, Guided Weapon Courses and so on. In fact the presence of a few Other Ranks among so many officers underlined the rather quasi-University status of the place. Officers were obliged to wear uniform and attend lectures or practical work all day. Quite what an unfortunate lance-corporal was supposed to do by way of saluting when passing 150 officers walking to their lessons was never officially resolved. The College was neither properly military nor properly a University. It was neither fish nor fowl. Among degree students it was generally felt that the civilian academic staff were not all that good either, and compulsory attendance at lectures did not always fit the academic need of degree students who in 'real' universities would probably have had private tutorials and attended few time-consuming lectures.

But I am glad to say that the boring academic regime of RMCS Shrivenham was made tolerable by the almost limitless opportunities for sport. The social life of the Intermediate Course was particularly energetic, although making the shorthand title of the course 'The Intercourse' in no way reflected a low moral standard. Female company was principally notable by its absence, except for a College Ball once per term, when girlfriends were put up in local hotels. Women, of course, secretaries, wives and others from the neighbourhood also appeared in the College operatic society, which I promptly joined and in whose performance of Gilbert and Sullivan's *Yeomen of the Guard* in March I took a place in the chorus. Otherwise I seem to have occupied much of my free time playing rugby for the College 3rd XV or recovering from the post-match binges in the local pubs of Faringdon. I had been a No 8 forward in my schooldays, and had been selected for Devon Schools in that position. Now, however, I was up against hefty men in the altogether rougher game that was English club rugby, and I took to playing centre three-quarter. Tommy Tucker and Tony Weston joined me in the 3rd XV, a splendidly 'social' side. John Living, a Sapper subaltern, was captain, and in an age when few subalterns possessed cars, his enormous Lancia (or was it a Lanchester?) conveyed almost the whole side to and from the Faringdon pubs. One night the inevitable happened and he drove off the road at the spot where the road 'unexpectedly wiggled' between Faringdon and the College on the A 420. As the front axle struck a concrete post, the fine wooden superstructure of that elegant limousine parted company with the chassis. The fifteen or so bodies inside were propelled into the ditch where, drunk and limp, they lay on top of each other roaring with laughter. Only one officer, Bill Abbott of the REME, was injured. I believe he dislocated a shoulder, but it was a miraculous escape. It was not to be the last time I came off the road during my time at Shrivenham; once I accompanied Tony Weston's Morris Minor into a hedge and on another occasion Nick Whatley's Riley into a field, both of these incidents occurring at night on muddy corners in the lane between the College and the White Horse Inn, Uffington! I have held a healthy respect for driving in muddy lanes ever since.

In spite of all the frivolity and wilder times, we did do some work, boring though it was, and, after a short holiday in Devon with Tony Weston, when we visited my aged Aunt Pin in her twelve-bedroom Rectory, Brookdale, in North Huish (later a hotel) we all duly sat the exam in June, which I regarded a gross interference with the cricket season. We left the place confident we had passed and July 1957 saw me back in Germany with 45th Field Regiment RA again, much to my relief.

Practice Camp that summer was at the desolate Rheinsehlen Camp, and I thought that huge improvements had been made in the tactical professionalism of the Regiment in the field. Indeed, the 45th Field Regiment's reputation as a regiment that excelled at gunnery and sport seemed fully restored, and I was proud to be part of it. I also took time to dig out of the Battery Office safe the day-by-day diary written by a certain Lieutenant George D.S. Truell, the Gun Position Officer of 70th Battery RA at the Battle of the River Imjin. I typed up the relevant entries and placed the script in my copy of Captain (later General Sir) Anthony Farrar-Hockley's (also an Old Exonian) wonderful account of that battle in his book *The Edge of the Sword*. I felt quite strongly after this research that 70th Battery deserved the battle honour 'Imjin' in its title just as much as 170th Light Battery which was granted that distinction together with the American Presidential Citation, the ribbon of which is worn to this day by members of that Battery. Fate was to pay me the compliment later of commanding 170th (Imjin) Battery RA, and loyal and proud as I was of the distinction conferred on this Battery, I, knowing what I did of the historical detail, still held a sneaking regard for '70 Battery' and felt the honours should have been shared.

After another enjoyable but all too short sojourn with '45' I returned heavy-hearted to Shrivenham in September. Gunners were only given a choice between taking a General Science degree or Mechanical Engineering. Tommy Tucker and Tony Weston chose the former, I the latter, although I had severe misgivings as to whether such things as Hydraulics and Mechanics were my particular bent. I felt therefore much in need of distraction from the boredom of academic subjects while so many of my age group in the Army were engaged in exciting soldiering in Borneo, Kenya, Cyprus and other far-flung outposts of what was still a considerable, though rapidly diminishing, British Empire. As before, rugby football came to the rescue, and this time I was promoted to the 1st XV under the fine captaincy of Lieutenant Phil Winchcombe

REME. I thrived on being a centre-threequarter. Our fly-half was Lieutenant Bill Eggleston RE with whom I had been at prep-school in Exmouth years before, and my fellow centre was also a Sapper, Lieutenant Nick Whatley, with whom I became very friendly, but who used to tease me in a childish way almost to distraction. Unfortunately I suffered a slight injury to my neck and throat in one match and had to forego the March operatic society show. I was also in the chapel choir, so fortunately the problem was fairly short-lived.

Being familiar with school and club rugby in Devon led me to volunteer to organise an Easter rugby club tour of the West Country. We stayed at the Seven Stars Hotel in Totnes, and played against Torquay, Paignton, Newton Abbot, Kingsbridge and Thorverton. For some of these games we were even given some gate money, which certainly helped with our expenses. It was a great success and a memorable pleasure. My friend Nick Whatley decided to combine the tour with his honeymoon, his poor new wife having to suffer their wedding night directly above the rowdy singing from us below at the bar!

In the summer of 1958 I first went on a canoeing trip with Tony Weston down the Thames, an experience remembered chiefly from its discomfort when our attempts to sleep in a tent beside the river were so often disturbed by water rats. Then officers on the Engineering Courses had to do three weeks of what was called 'Workshop Practice'. This comprised a fairly loosely supervised period of instruction in practical engineering in the College's old tank hangars, now converted to industrial laboratories and workshops. In fact, I found this experience quite satisfying for two reasons: first, many of the industrial processes like welding, casting and hydraulic pumping I found quite absorbing; and second, I could make illicit use of the workshop metalwork facilities to repair my newly acquired 1931-vintage MG J2 motor car, registration number TJ 502. At first I nicknamed it 'Montgomery', but later 'Gonewrongery'!

This car was my pride and joy. Its pipe-work was copper, its large radiator the finest of chrome. Its black bodywork gleamed, and I painted the engine block with aluminium paint. True, it did possess certain disadvantages, not least the volume of spray its driver and passenger were subjected to whenever it rained. Not only would the canvas hood not fit properly, and the passenger door had an annoying habit of flying off in one's hand, but the front wheel wings were like simple bicycle mudguards, so that on turning any appreciable corner in the rain, spray was thrown up between the wheels and the bonnet, onto the windscreen and into the cockpit. This design was not guaranteed to win favour with a young lady being taken to a ball in her best evening dress! Nevertheless it was fun, and a very good car on which to learn mechanics. It did about 150 miles to the big-end, and to get it from Shrivenham to Devon or Portsmouth and back, where my parents were now living, was a no mean feat of engineering. During this particular summer break I was indebted to Nick Whatley who, with my help, stripped the whole engine down in his garage in Swindon, repaired the big ends and put it all together again, leaving a multitude of bolts and screws over, which was temporarily rather worrying.

That summer too, I played a lot of cricket, and, thanks to my cricket mentor at the College, Major Ian Biggs RA, included some memorable two-day matches for the Gunners at Woolwich, a pleasure that lasted right the way through to September. The side was blessed with some cricket stars doing their National Service, such as Brian Luckhurst, who went on to play for England. Then it was back to the grindstone. Although I had passed the first year's exams quite easily, the second year promised to be harder graft and even greater boredom. The rugby club, as ever, came to the rescue, and this time it was even more demanding of my time as I was elected Vice-Captain to a charming Captain called Hugh Roland-Price. These elections were really by default as our star players were unlikely to be regularly available to play for the College. Greg Read and Alan Parker played for the Harlequins and Dicky Moyle played for Richmond. These, and my talented fellow centre Mike Handfield-Jones (later killed in Aden), were also often away playing for the Army or Combined Services, but when they were able to turn out for us it gave me the greatest thrill to be playing alongside such gifted rugby players. We gave illustrious sides like Oxford University Greyhounds and Cambridge University LX Club good runs for their money.

The College Operatic Society performed that March and I took the lead tenor role. The orchestra, drawn from all over the county, was good under William Pountney, but the show itself was a trifle lightweight. Just before Easter we organised the Rugby Club Ball, which was always a very elaborate affair. For the previous year's Club Ball I had asked Julia Geidt to come up from Guy's Hospital, and she had stayed at the Crown Hotel in Faringdon. We had had much fun and I was really fond of this lovely blonde girl. She was doubtless patient with me, suffering from riding in the old open MG, and having to climb up on the porch and through a window of the hotel to get her back to bed in the early hours. During the intervening year, however, Julia had found a young doctor at Guy's to her liking and then married him. I went down to Winchester to see her wedding presents and bid her a fond and tearful farewell. I did not see her again for 45 years! For the 1959 Club Ball I therefore had to find someone new, and this proved easy. Tony Weston's girlfriend, Caroline Barnes, lived in Newbury, just over the Marlborough Downs, and among her riding chums was a farmer's daughter, Diana Dodd. Caroline recommended her, I took her to the Ball, and a very charming girl I found her to be. Later I took her one weekend to meet my parents at their Royal Marine quarter in 'Tea-Pot Row' in Eastney Barracks, Portsmouth. Although, to my considerable embarrassment, my mother gave Diana a large photograph of me, the visit left me in no doubt that Diana was not going to be the right girl for me to marry, and I saw progressively less of her thereafter.

After another wonderful summer of cricket at the College when the Cricket Club was captained by me under the guidance of Lieutenant

Self (left) in The Jolly Roger, *Shrivenham, 1959*

Colonel Geoffrey Burch RA, Tommy Tucker and I decided that, rather than return for another short spell with a regiment in Germany, we would volunteer to go to Aldershot and take the Airborne Selection Course, otherwise known as 'P' Company. This was a severe physical test by any standards, and we were not really sure that our undoubted rugby fitness would be sufficient for this rather more gruelling fortnight's course. Most thought we were mad to try, but in a spirit of bravado we did. To the uninitiated it is difficult to describe precisely or politely the torture of this famous 'P' Company course, as many would think one is shooting a line. Officers get a particularly raw deal on it, as they not only have to complete all the obstacles and exercises themselves, but they are expected to encourage and lead the others (the others being Other Ranks). Periodically, just for the devil of it, the Army Physical Training Corps staff sergeant instructors would invite a squad to 'assault' their section officer in some playful way like robbing them of their PT shorts during a strenuous exercise in the gymnasium. This too tended to take more out of us poor souls than one might expect.

During the weekend in the middle of the course, Tommy and I went to a pub and set about T-bone steaks and beer in a half-crazed manner. Thus reinvigorated we struggled through the final week and were called to see the Parachute Regiment Depot Commander to hear the result. To our dismay we were told bluntly that we had failed. Tommy and I looked at each other in amazement and disbelief. More than that, we were furious.

Tommy blurted out. 'But Sir! Do you know that we have given up our leave to volunteer to come on this course?'

I added, 'Indeed, Sir! We needn't have come on it, but we've given it our best shot, without the preparation the others on the course will have had. Why have we failed?'

The Commander peered somewhat sheepishly over his desk. 'Would you like to come back and have another shot?' he enquired kindly.

We answered without a second's hesitation, 'Certainly NOT, Sir. We think we should have been passed this time, and once should be good enough!'

The Commander paused in thought and chewed his pencil. 'OK,' he said. 'You have actually passed. I was only waiting to see your reaction!'

We were delighted, and I felt that I was now well on the way to redressing that terrible error on the YOs' Course, and one day soon I could join the coveted Airborne Gunners.

And so in September I embarked on the last stretch of my boring three-year degree course. Having cruised through Parts I and II now, I harboured few doubts that I would achieve the BSc(Eng) qualification I sought, even though the failure rate among students at that time was averaging nearly 30 per cent. I worked assiduously, but continued my energetic life of sport, singing and drinking. I have to admit, however, that my drinking habits came to an abrupt end one day. After a particularly strenuous rugger match the team was indulging in its usual evening of beer and vulgar songs, and a large Sapper second-row forward by the name of 'Jungly' Drake, who was renowned for doing hare-brained things, bet me a fiver that I could not drink a pint of port in one gulp. Foolishly I took him on, and, since I had already consumed about eight pints of beer, I felt somewhat the worse for wear afterwards. I staggered off to the Mess and recall very little more until waking up in the morning feeling not only very sick and depressed but also *compressed*. My dear friends had encased me unconscious in a roll of coconut matting carpet, and I had to be rescued from this by the batman. I suffered from alcohol poisoning for three days, and touched neither beer nor port for many months afterwards.

The rugby club became more serious in this, my last season. Under the guidance of Lieutenant Colonel Don Isles, with Tommy Tucker as Vice-Captain, we trained hard and played well. My fellow centre-three-quarter was Lieutenant Mike Handfield-Jones, who played for the Army and Combined Services, and my own game continued to improve as a result. Released from the duty of helping run the club, I was able to give more time to the operatic society and I cannot recall a more enjoyable show than our production of Gilbert and Sullivan's *Princess Ida* that spring. I took the lead tenor role of Hilarion, and my other two 'sisters' were Lieutenant (later Major General) Niel Carlier and Mike Parsons, and what fun we had.

My crowning achievement in this year of 1960, however, seems to have been leading a very talented and successful cricket team. Lieutenant (later Major General) Richard Peck, who also played for the Army and Combined Services, Ian Dobbie, Pat Sampson. David Corsellis, Ian Runciman, Nick Whatley, Ian Weller and Bob Bell, under the chairmanship of Lieutenant Colonel Kevin Taggart, formed a great side, and I couldn't have felt more happy. The only problem was the small matter of my degree Finals. I found the last year's syllabus very demanding, and when I tried 'spotting' questions – almost impossible to do in an externally set exam – I feared I had failed in one of the five

Captain (seated 3rd from right) of RMCS Cricket XI, 1960

main subjects. I subsequently learnt that I had indeed failed in one Mechanics paper, and so failed the entire exam and the whole degree eluded me. Nothing to show for 3½ years' hard work and frustration.

Nevertheless relief came quickly in the shape of the realisation of my ambition to be an Airborne Gunner. I was posted in July to 33rd Parachute Light Regiment in Lille Barracks, Aldershot. There, after doing my obligatory 8-jump parachute course at Abingdon, I made myself at home and gained friends among my fellow officers with whom I have never lost touch. The spirit of cameraderie in that regiment surpassed all others. I joined 41 Parachute Light Battery and who should be my Battery Commander but Paddy de Burgh! I was appointed Battery Gun Position Officer (GPO), and my two section commanders were 2nd Lieutenants Mike Wilkes, later to become General Sir Michael Wilkes, Lieutenant-Governor of Jersey, and Tony Harnett, both of whom were to serve later with distinction with the SAS. Captains Peter Steer and Derrick Frost were the OP officers and Troop Commanders, and the two Battery Sergeant Majors were Danny Cummins and Ken Johnson, to whom I shall always be grateful for all the advice and help they gave me.

We were a tight knit Battery, even though 25 per cent of the soldiers were National Servicemen and only with us for eighteen months or so. We were a tough lot too, but very skilled in gunnery, being equipped both with 4.2 inch mortars and the new 105 mm Pack Howitzer. We had to be prepared to operate either of these different weapons at short notice, depending usually on how many aircraft and platforms were available from which to heavy drop parachute them. I became absorbed in the technical aspects of deploying these weapons, and Danny Cummins and I developed between us variations in the standard drills most appropriate to our Airborne role. I got to know my soldiers extremely well, defended them against undue bullying by the Regimental Sergeant Major, and supported them in their efforts to rival and beat the other two Batteries in the Regiment, 29 and 97. I took them out on all sorts of minor tactical manoeuvres in the Aldershot area, irritating them to death on occasions, but none the less having enormous fun. The Battery performed well, too, in the highly competitive weekly Gun Drill held under the expert supervision of Major Harry Rice, the Regiment's Second-in-Command.

Within a few months we went on a major exercise to Libya, the UK's principal desert training area in those days when a friendly King ruled the country. Exercise SOLINUS involved the whole of the regular 16th Parachute Brigade, the 10th Territorial Parachute Battalion and, as enemy, units of the Royal Marines Commando Brigade. We flew from RAF Lyneham first to Malta, from where, after 24 hours refuelling, the Airborne assault was mounted. One of my soldiers was left behind there as he had failed to surface in time after spending the night in the red light area of Valetta, but he did catch up with us on the second wave, looking spruced up and pleased with himself! We dropped the mortars without mishap and deployed far into the desert at night. The post-drop adrenalin was still flowing in Mike Wilkes' veins on our first gun position, and when I saw him giggling and generally larking about, I had cause to speak to him rather severely and publicly. I then sent him off in the darkness of a wintry desert night in radio silence to find the Battery Commander on some important tactical mission, which is not easy in an environment completely lacking in reference points. Navigation even by day was not easy, as in the days before GPS or satellite aids it was achieved by the use of dead-reckoning and sun-compasses, the latter being useless at night and midday, of course. Mike fulfilled the mission I gave him with remarkable aplomb. He said that he never forgot my ticking him off that day, and he never failed over the succeeding years of his exceptionally fine career to assure me that every subsequent promotion or award was due to that sharp lesson he learnt! I am sure he was only flattering, but if I did in some small way help that fine and popular officer's spectacular climb to stardom, then I can rest satisfied that I achieved something.

The exceptional comradeship we enjoyed in this regiment, part of the Airborne Brotherhood, elitism, male bonding, call it what you like, extended beyond my Battery to surmount the natural rivalry between Batteries. Among the subalterns Chris Bateman, who was the GPO of 95 Battery, Bill Cornock, Andrew Norton, and Bob Redford from other Batteries remain among my firmest friends to this day. But we were no angels. '33rd' had a reputation for toughness and spirited behaviour, especially when in barracks. Evenings in the Mess were memorable, and there was a series of raids and counter-attacks between us and the young officers of the neighbouring 9th Parachute Squadron, Royal Engineers. Damage was generally superficial and invariably paid for and repaired quickly. And we could be cruel to anyone within our own ranks who declined to take part.

One night my friends and I decided that the newly joined regimental education officer was 'wet' as he had gone to bed rather than join the party. Thunderflashes, which were produced as if by magic, and a dustbin were taken to this poor man's bedroom. The thunderflashes were ignited, placed swiftly into the dustbin, the lid was placed on firmly and the 'bomb' was thrust into the middle of the bedroom of the still slumbering officer. The door was slammed shut and from inside there followed the expected explosion. The door was immediately re-opened and the dustbin lid had made a neat hole in the ceiling. The room was full of white dust and the picture of the education officer sitting up in bed, blinking dazedly through his thick spectacles in a fog of ceiling dust, is with me to this day. There were no hard feelings and the hole was repaired the next day by us semi-skilled plasterers.

We were lucky in having an understanding President of the Mess Committee in the shape of a bachelor major called Jimmy Lothian. Under his direction we redecorated the whole mess when we moved to Oudenarde Barracks some months later, making a rather sleazy-looking 'night-club' out of what had been a billiard room in Victorian days.

Imagine, therefore, with all this traditional and characteristic roughness in the Regiment, what a shock it was when the news was released that we were to be converted to a Royal Horse Artillery Regiment! We were at once the butt of derision from the rest of the Brigade. 'RHA?' they jeered. 'What does that mean? Rocking Horse Artillery? Rather Hairy Arsed?' We too wondered what effect it would have, what changes would have to be made and what sort of officers and men would be posted in to the regiment now. One thing was certain: all new entrants would have to get through 'P' Company, whether they were elite RHA or not. They must meet the criteria of the Brigade and Airborne Forces generally.

One of the first new RHA faces to appear in the regiment was the officer who was to take over from our much admired Lieutenant Colonel Toby Caulfield as commanding officer when we became 7th Parachute Regiment RHA. To put it politely, this officer failed to allay our fears that the nature of the regiment would change quite radically. Indeed he said somewhat tactlessly that he was certainly going to make it change. That was an unfortunate blunder, as most of the regiment would be remaining, and most of the Brigade thought of us as a spirited, proud unit and rather good at our job. Fate however was our salvation, as this officer, after making a token appearance at 'P' Company, went away to Abingdon for his parachute course and injured himself sufficiently badly to have any Airborne assignment ruled out.

Our initially rather 'bolshey' attitude to the new title, dress and customs of the RHA designation extended to an important social event soon after the change. Lieutenant Chris Bateman was to get married, and he and his guests, including a sword guard of honour outside the church, were to be dressed in No 1 Blues Uniform complete with the new RHA accoutrements. Chris asked me to be in charge of the guard of honour, and there was a lot of nervous giggling about how to put on the golden cord RHA busby lines, which we disrespectfully called 'yellow rigging lines'. I glanced at a regimental magazine and to me it appeared that these cords were slung under the right shoulder, and so the groom and all the officers of the guard were dressed accordingly. The wedding proceeded according to plan on the Saturday and among the photographers was one from the *Tatler* society magazine.

On the Monday following the wedding, I was summoned to the Adjutant's office. He was apoplectic with rage and anxiety. It had been noticed that all our officers were incorrectly dressed, the busby lines on the wrong shoulder, and I was to cancel all press photographs immediately, especially the *Tatler* ones, lest the regiment be disgraced and publicly derided! I could scarcely contain my mirth, and felt that it should have been Chris Bateman's decision anyway, but he was on his honeymoon by then, and I had no option but to carry out the Adjutant's instructions. Needless to say, as time went by, we managed to get ourselves properly dressed as RHA officers, and still retain our Airborne spirit, this no doubt helped by the fact that very few officers indeed were replaced by what we feared might be 'prissy' horsemen. As time went by, the regiment became, of course, just as proud of the enhanced status of being both Airborne and RHA, combining both of the best traditions of the Royal Regiment.

The most significant event for me during this period, however, was meeting Linda Chetwood. She lived at Larkwood, Upper Chobham Road, Camberley and had been taken to Chris Bateman's engagement party by Lieutenant Tony Harnett who, I thought, rather fancied her. Somehow during that party Linda and I got talking, and I was, among other things about her, very taken with her open sense of humour. After a couple of hours I decided that this was definitely the girl for me. A few months later I took her to the lake at the Royal Military College, Sandhurst, and asked her to marry me. To my chagrin she said she would have to think about it, which was a severe blow to my self-esteem. After all, I had no doubt at all that *I* would marry *her*! She kept me waiting for a response for 24 nail-biting hours. She agreed and I went to see her barrister father to ask, in a most formal and traditional way, for her hand in marriage. It was the best thing I ever did.

CHAPTER 7

Captain's Calamities

I WAS ACTUALLY PROMOTED to Captain on 16 December 1961, but the celebrations were rather subdued. This was because I was still in hospital at Aldershot having my badly broken leg seen to. Some brave soldier in 216 Parachute Signals Squadron had fallen on the ball almost immediately after we had kicked it off at the start of a rugger match against them. He fell on my right foot as well as the ball, and I was travelling at sufficient speed for both fibia and tibia to break with a noise that reverberated all the way down Queen's Avenue! I was encased in plaster right up to the top of my groin, and even such basic procedures as sitting on the loo became very awkward. To bath I had to encase the whole leg in a plastic bag. It then floated on the surface, which meant that if the bathwater was at all deep, my head tended to get submerged! It was upsetting, I was miserable, and the damned thing didn't come out of plaster for nine months! I even sold my MG, as there was no way I could drive.

As I was pretty fit, the surgeons thought it was unnecessary to send me to the Services' rehabilitation centre at Headley Court. They thought the bones would heal more quickly if I romped around on Salisbury Plain on crutches, and that is what I proceeded to do. Slipping over on the ice and snow, tripping over heather and bogs, and falling in and out of military vehicles as an awkward passenger became all part of life's rich pattern for me. It was extremely tiring. The plaster cast was broken and replaced a dozen times. My bones persistently failed to knit. After one such visit to the Aldershot military hospital I was so frustrated and disappointed that I would have to endure yet another six weeks in plaster that I asked my stepfather to come and fetch me in his car and, after I clambered up the long flight of steep stairs to my room at his quarter at Eastney, I fell onto my bed and wept. This, I thought afterwards, was not a creditable thing for an Airborne soldier to do!

But life did contain some consolation. One evening I was leaning on my crutches in the Oudenarde Barracks Mess, where we had temporarily moved while Lille Barracks was being rebuilt, a week or two after Chris Bateman's engagement party, when I saw Linda again. I always said I couldn't escape her! She was very good to me over those months of torment in my plaster cast, but it was frustrating. Eventually Paddy de Burgh decided that, as I had failed that one subject at Finals in that awful Mechanical Engineering Degree, it would be better for me to return to Shrivenham, sit down and have another shot. I was grateful to him for that at the time. Although I couldn't bear to be away from regimental life for too long, it would give me a chance to put my leg up and let it heal.

And it did heal, and after a few spells of physiotherapy the badly wasted muscles quickly returned. I bought a new car – hardly 'new' as it was a vast 10 year-old Wolseley 20 h.p., which did 25 miles to the gallon of petrol and about 30 miles to the gallon of oil! My love-affair with such a luxury motor was cut short by the arrival of a red-hued bank statement. I sold it to a rugby friend, Mike Lord, and bought a decrepit Hillman instead. I then retook the whole of the BSc (Eng) Part III exam – and failed in one subject again – a different one – so I consider I obtained a moral degree over the four years. But I didn't care. I was out! I burnt my crutches and three months later I was back on the rugger field again in Aldershot playing the same opponents. I caught sight of the man who had put me in hospital last time and, as soon as he got the ball, I tackled him so hard that – I cracked my collar bone! No plaster this time, though, only a sling for four weeks. Somebody told me that I might be injury-prone, but I wasn't inclined to take any notice of such a suggestion. Anyway, we were about to go to the Middle East, and I didn't want to miss the rugger out there!

In August 1962 'G' Battery flew out as part of 1st Parachute Battalion Group to Bahrain. We should have been there a year earlier. But when Kuwait had felt threatened by Iraq and called for British help, Paddy de Burgh had been on holiday in Greece and couldn't be reached. Major Bob Lyon was told to take 'F' (Sphinx) Battery RHA to Kuwait to support 2nd Parachute Battalion instead of us. By the time we went out in support of 1st Battalion, we had moved the British base to the cramped naval base at Jufair, Manama, Bahrain. On arrival I called into Jufair to see the F Battery GPO, Robin Duchesne. He was lying on his bed with suppurating sores all over his legs and thighs – not a pretty sight. But it showed his fanatical dedication to rugby football, as these wounds had been received on the hard, sandy pitch at Jufair, and he refused to take any notice of the fact that the humid climate prevented grazes from healing properly. However, a new camp was being started as we arrived, and much of our time was to be spent toiling in the heat of the relentless sun, laying concrete foundations and erecting Twynham huts out on the barren ridge at Hamala. Officers did this too, much to the surprise of a visiting group of Labour MPs bent on uncovering class distinction in the desert!

I was then lucky enough to be appointed Battalion Group Intelligence Officer. It meant that I was fully detached to the Infantry and accompanied the Battalion Group CO, Lieutenant-Colonel Pat Thursby, up and down the Persian Gulf visiting our potential operational areas in Kuwait, and also the Trucial Oman States in their almost feudal state before oil wealth totally changed their landscapes. It was the most immense fun; I adored the heat and deserts. I have never been fitter and browner than I was then. I played hockey and cricket almost every day when not out on reconnaissance, visits or patrols. I played a couple of games of rugby on the sandy pitch at Jufair, where successive Batteries of 7 RHA laid the foundations for years of supremacy at the game back in the UK. I swam in the warm pool there, where on one occasion Paddy de Burgh struck his head on the bottom trying to demonstrate a new style of diving from the top board.

Having always been a keen gardener I decided to try to grow roses in front of my hut. I thought that if Cockers could grow them in Aberdeen, then they could probably grow anywhere. I duly signalled: 'Urgent. Please send 12 tough roses.' Some months later I reported back: 'Roses thriving in the sand, liberally dosed with water and camel dung.' Cockers immediately replied: 'Excellent! Send 12 tough camels!' But those roses did attract every fly in the Arab world! As Intelligence Officer I also had to supervise the civil labour working at Hamala camp. That meant pay parades, hiring and firing. To help me I had two Intelligence Sergeants. One had learnt Arabic at Durham University, the other spoke little Arabic but plenty of Swahili and Urdu. I need hardly recount which of these was understood by the natives best!

On one occasion I took the four-man Intelligence Section on a brief expedition to the southernmost tip of Bahrain island. There we traversed the desolate, uninhabited salt marshes, abandoning our Land Rover on its deflated sand tyres and metal sand channels before continuing warily on foot. We camped and swam naked in the shimmering shallow sea, dried ourselves in seconds in the searing sun, and withdrew cautiously, counting ourselves lucky that our vehicle had not sunk while we were away.

After a few months I was relieved by Geoffrey Brierly, an infantry officer, and I returned as a Troop Commander to the Battery. One of my first tasks was to take a group of three NCOs with me on a patrol in the Jebel Akhdar region in north Oman. It was probably the best period of active service I ever had.

Ostensibly those patrols were designed to 'show the flag' in conjunction with the Sultan's Armed Forces. They were named 'OMEX' (Oman Exercise) patrols, but every now and then, some residual activity by the Imam's rebels, so resoundingly defeated by the SAS a year or two earlier, bubbled to the surface again. My patrol was warned that we might encounter just such a resurgence, and that promised to be exciting.

We flew to Sharjah in a RAF Beverley transport aircraft and thence in a Twin Pioneer propeller aircraft to make a bumpy landing on the primitive airstrip at Fort Saiq up in the Jebel. With a diminutive white fort dominating the local landscape, the scene was straight out of a P.C. Wren novel. We found the ration cache left by previous patrols contained exclusively the Compo menu nobody liked: mutton, Scotch style. We set out the next morning on a local acclimatisation patrol to Bani Habib, a nearby village much battered by RAF bombing during the height of the campaign. Despite lingering distrust of foreigners, we were met very civilly by the Wali and the elders of the village. They confirmed that there was much talk in the Jebel of the impending return of one of the leading rebels who had been receiving training in Saudi Arabia.

The following day, guided by the local Loan Service Officer, Spike Powell, and accompanied by a section of ferocious-looking Baluchi tribesmen seconded to the Sultan's Armed Forces from Pakistan's North West Frontier Force, we set out eastwards through the arid mountains. We stopped at Hayl Yaman, a settlement perched high on the saddle of the barren Wadi Duwaykhilah, and there our guide interrogated some very nervous inhabitants about the rumours we had heard. They confirmed that an important rebel was expected in the area of this village quite soon and that he would possibly be coming in with the next caravan from the east. Among the usual goods for trade on the backs of the mules, we might, they revealed, also anticipate some weapons.

Leaving our heavy baggage to follow on the backs of our own pack-ponies, we set off fast for a good ambush site on the 'main road' (no more than a tortuous, rocky mountain path) in from the east. As there were no maps, we had to rely entirely on Spike's knowledge of the terrain. This was, however, going to be my first glimpse of action and

Arrival at Fort Saiq (self 3rd from left) 1962

my moment of glory, so we followed hard. I discussed tactics with my heroic band as we breathlessly climbed towards a sharp bend in the track, hoping to get there by nightfall.

The sun was beginning to set as we reached the appointed spot. Time was running out and the rebel caravan would arrive any minute. Just as I was directing my team into fire positions, Bombardier Horton to the right, Lance Bombardier Hoskins to the left and Gunner Pickering in depth, the bearded face of an Arab rounded the bend! He was followed by two more, together with two or three skinny pack-mules. We at once stopped laying our clever ambush and ran past the caravan and beyond the bend to determine whether there were any more newcomers around the corner!

If there had been, they weren't there by now! Feeling distinctly foolish, cheated really, we returned to help the Baluchis, now chattering excitedly, to guard the prisoners and search the baggage train. Spike decided that he would take his time interrogating the three Arabs, especially the one proudly wearing a United States Air Force sergeant's uniform jacket!

It was, however, soon clear that the rebel leader we had hoped to encounter had not been caught in our brilliant trap. True, we had captured an assortment of weapons, chiefly American in origin and rather ancient. But as night fell, we had little choice but to move the caravan back to Hayl Yaman, escorted by the Baluchi soldiers and our long-suffering Loan Service Guide. We four 'paras', however, would remain holed-up in the ambush site on the off-chance that our wanted rebel would follow on during the night.

He didn't. Spike appeared as the first rays of the morning sun topped the precipitous, inhospitable mountains, and we set off eastwards across the ridges, leaving the Baluchi soldiers to follow. We climbed for what was probably no more than a couple of hours, at a speed which at the altitude we were now at, left us gasping and sweating profusely. At 7,000 feet in hot sunshine, Bombardier Horton, our only smoker, was in particular distress. Then a shot rang out! It was a long way off, and as far as we could judge, it came from a cave high up on the mountain face, across the other side of the vast and sheer Wadi Halfayn, whose depths were lost in pitch-black shadow.

Spike said he thought it wasn't worth the effort to go chasing this thousand-yard sniper. It was, after all, only a single rifle shot, at very long range, and it would take hours to get down into the wadi floor and climb the other side. I decided otherwise, and he was very tolerant. I cursed myself for being armed only with a short-range Sterling sub-machine gun, which would have been ideal for clearing a cave, but with the prospect of the rebel escaping from his lair, whoever went across that wadi had to have a rifle. Bombardier Horton was the man to go, I thought. He had the most sense, he was second-in-command, and we would give him covering fire. I cannot recall today what else influenced that decision, but I suspect a little malice of forethought not wholly unconnected with teaching a smoker a lesson.

To cut a longish story short, Bombardier Horton, accompanied by two Baluchis, did clamber down into the wadi bottom, across the floor of that cavernous ravine, and climb very swiftly up the other side, while we covered him and sprayed the mouth of the cave sporadically with fire. When he got there the rebel had either flown, or he'd not been there in the first place; we shall never know. It is infernally difficult to locate the exact point of origin of a single shot, as much in wide open and featureless terrain as in built-up areas. At all events, poor Bombardier

Horton was so shattered when he returned that I had to leave him at the ambush site for a full day to recover.

After a day patrolling on the south-east edge of the Jebel, during which I gazed in wonder at some of the most spectacular scenery I had ever imagined, we gathered Bombardier Horton and made off northwards to the highest point on the Jebel. We moved as fast as we could, in the hope that, if the wanted rebel were still in the area, he might well be making back the way he came, and we might cut him off. We camped in a shallow wadi that night, and sat around huge thorn-scrub fires which the Baluchi had lit. I thought it most unwise to sit silhouetted by these fires, but Spike and the Baluchis laughed at the very idea that anyone would take them on. They cooked our mutton, Scotch style, dosed it liberally with curry powder and wrapped it lovingly in chapatis. They thought it delicious; it still tasted like compo mutton, Scotch style, to me.

The next morning we reached Sograh, a village cut into the steep sides of a narrow wadi. The inhabitants lived as troglodytes and many had never been outside their wadi. We were the source of much curiosity and we lingered there half a day. The trail had gone cold by the next morning, and we surrendered all hope of catching our rebel. Instead we amused ourselves shooting a gazelle which was, strictly speaking, a protected species. It was no mean shot by Lance Bombardier Hoskins and I finished off the poor beast with a dozen shots to the head with my useless Sterling. We roasted it that afternoon over an open spit. It tasted like the most tender of veal, and as we lay in the shelter of a west-facing wadi that evening, the majestic peaks and rocks of the Jebel Akhdar all around us, I wallowed in a sense of great contentment. The view, however, reminded me of pictures I had seen of the North-West Frontier of India, and a wave of frustration enveloped me as I contemplated our missed opportunity to come to grips with the enemy.

The following two days were spent in reaching down into the Bani Kharus to overlook the town of Awabi on the edge of the coastal plain to the north, and a headlong rush back to Saiq along the tracks to its north and west. We were bounding with energy and vigour, and I have seldom felt so fit. We climbed to 8,000 feet before we plunged southwards towards the fort. Bombardier Horton had given up smoking – for ever, he vowed – and the other two were in marvellous form. We outran our sure-footed Baluchi friends across those burning mountains like nobody before or since. When we reached Saiq we at once challenged them to a shooting match on the range, and won that convincingly too! A day's relaxation in the hills around Saiq, enjoying particularly our makeshift shower, and we came to the end of our short but exciting sojourn. We were sad to return to Bahrain. Once there, life continued in a fairly humdrum way, with plenty of sport, air-conditioning eventually being installed, and occasional evenings 'nimbling', as party-making had it in our 'para' vernacular, at the Awali Oil Company club, and endless hilarious evenings of 'Scat' in the Mess with my chum the padré, Freddy Preston, for whom I occasionally played an antique harmonium at his makeshift church services. Nevertheless, I found the wholly male environment a particular strain and it was tough to be away from Linda now that we were engaged.

We exercised in the Trucial States, parachuting into the desert on the Abu Dhabi coast, observed by the aged ruler, Sheikh Shakbhut. He was reputed to keep the wealth of his small nation under his bed, and to have remarked after our impressive parachute assault that he would prefer to see a few more fast camels! RAF Beverley transport aircraft landed the guns on an improvised airstrip at Jebel Ali in Dubai, and we tugged and pushed the vehicles and guns through miles of soft sand track through sweltering Sharjah towards the foothills in the east, on what is nowadays a main road, I suspect. An especially unforgettable parachute exercise on the remote island of Yas in the Gulf nearly ended in disaster for some of the many soldiers who suffered serious dehydration there, and more nearly ended in death for Paddy de Burgh and 'SNOPG' (Senior Naval Officer Persian Gulf) who was visiting our artillery live-firing exercise when a miscalculation at the Battery Command Post caused a round to land immediately in front of the OP where they were standing. It was, in fact, one of the most dangerous peace-time exercises I ever went on. The heat was intense, and I well remember on the low-level flight there, the remarkable sight of the combined sweat from twenty heavily laden paratroopers literally running along the floor of the Beverley aircraft as it approached the DZ. In such circumstances it was not surprising that heat exhaustion was widespread amongst the bare rock and sand of Yas Island and at least three men had to be taken to an RN frigate lying off-shore and be packed in ice.

Christmas 1962 saw us back in Bahrain, with Hamala Camp nearly finished. My roses were flourishing, and we started regularly riding the Sheik's horses, which redressed any deficiencies in camel manure. Paddy de Burgh told me that I had been put on the short list for becoming an ADC to General Bill Stirling, the GOC Middle East in Aden, but I did not relish that and made the excuse that I was about to get married and ADCs should be single. Yes, I was dreaming of home and Linda and that had priority for me now. The padré arranged a midnight carol service for Christmas Eve. Fortunately the battalion band had arrived and I did not have to play the wheezing old harmonium pedal-organ with which I normally accompanied his services, with its one defunct pedal which puffed sand when I pressed it. The night sky was clear and a myriad of stars shimmered down on empty rows of chairs in the desert. The officers arrived and the band struck up the first carol. Gradually, one by one, the soldiers slunk in, filling up the rows from the back, hoping their mates didn't see them. By the end of the third carol, there was standing room only, and the whole Battalion group was there to a man, singing their heads off. In the quieter moments between the music, men's thoughts no doubt were, like mine, far away at home. It was a most moving occasion.

And so to England and my wedding. After a memorable 'stag night' at a pub near Farnham, at which Linda's young brother, Denis, then aged 18, became sensationally the worse for wear, I, feeling a bit white around the gills myself, got to the wedding on time at St Peter's Church Frimley, on 19 January 1963, in a snow-storm. Iain Jack escorted me up the aisle to marry Linda Chetwood. Reception at the Camberley Heath Golf Clubhouse was followed by a nightmarish trip to London airport to catch a midnight flight to Gibraltar. It was raining heavily when we arrived at the Rock, and the bus journey along the coast to Torremolinos left us ill-kempt, ill-tempered and much the worse for wear. We shuffled into the only hotel that Torremolinos boasted in those days, dragged ourselves into the lift, and two and a half floors up it stopped! We nearly spent our whole honeymoon there in that lift, which I suppose mightn't have been too bad, but the lift attendant was with us! Eventually we were rescued, and while our sexual inexperience did not contribute to a wholly fantastic honeymoon, we succeeded in doing all that we wanted, learning fast(!), and had a blissful holiday in what was then a relatively unknown and peaceful spot.

And so, on return, Linda and I started on a journey which would see us moving house 22 times in 28 years. We started in a modern flat in Tenby, South Wales, while I did a short course at the Air Defence School, Manorbier. From there we went to Amesbury, Wiltshire, and lived, or rather survived, the joys of married life in Flat 2B, the Abbey. The lofty ceilings of the old Abbey were no protection against a particularly cold winter. With electric and paraffin heaters going full

The best thing I ever did

blast, one could get warm only by being wrapped in a blanket and standing on the furniture. The loo was really a throne room, the pedestal perched regally on a dais at the far end of a bare room of palatial proportions. Electricity came intermittently by means of a shilling in the meter. By the end of my Captain's Course at Larkhill, in April, we had had enough of that accommodation.

But far worse was to come! I was posted to 27th Army Missile Regiment, Napier Barracks, Dortmund. The regiment was equipped with the American 'Corporal' nuclear guided weapon invented by Professor Braun, who provided the V1 and V2 for Germany in World War 2. After the light scales of equipment and high speed of life in the Parachute Brigade, the slow reaction and lumbering convoys of enormous vehicles in a Corporal regiment could not have presented a more unwelcome contrast. Heaven knows why I allowed myself to be sent there, but I was easily persuaded that guided weapons represented the art of the future, and everyone should get involved.

Poor Linda! We were given a sub-standard flat under the Hoesch Steelworks: 16 Magdeburger Strasse, not far from the red light district of

Dortmund. Soot poured out of the sky, so much so that it crunched underfoot in the courtyard and up the steps to the front door. Linda's family were not military, but any lingering ideas she might have harboured about the glamour of army life were rudely shattered by those slum conditions. It was three months since our honeymoon, and morning sickness told its own story. We endured that flat all through Linda's first pregnancy, far from kindred spirits and other Britons. The only saving grace was the presence of Tony Weston and his wife, Caroline, in the neighbouring regiment, and Linda and Caroline became immediate and lasting good friends. One foggy day in January 1964 I drove Linda to Iserlohn to see Caroline, who had just been admitted to the maternity ward. As she stood at Caroline's bedside, her own labour pains began. 'Wow!' she said, 'it's contagious! Quick, darling, drive back to the flat as fast as you can and fetch my things!' I drove like a devil possessed through the fog, there and back, and that night, in the early hours of 9 January, I had the good fortune to help David Michael Stephen Pughe into the world. I found the experience of seeing that complete and perfect little creature emerging into the world a most moving and religiously significant event.

We stuck it out in the down-town flat for long enough for David to get bronchitis and for the diesel-oil stove to explode, spraying the whole flat with oily soot, before at last being allocated a brand new quarter just outside the Napier Barracks gates. Leimkuhle, the street was called, and we moved in before curtains were even provided. With neighbours close enough clearly to see into the bedroom, we crawled between bedroom and bathroom on hands and knees for the first few weeks. We had a sensational house-warming party, with plants mulched into the lawn with whisky, and fine artistry, particularly of a vast nude, provided by our guests on paper hung on the walls. I became Adjutant and life began to look up.

I played a lot of cricket, and was at one time the only white man in our regimental team. Our gunners of West Indian extraction were not, however, the best of soldiers. But, as Adjutant, I was in a strong position to see that they were safely locked up in the Guardroom all week and let out only for cricket matches. Morale was not exactly low in that slow-moving, slow-thinking, heavy regiment (it took eight hours to bring a Corporal missile into action) but it had an exceptionally high court-martial rate. As Adjutant I was kept very busy in Dortmund, and we had every crime in the book. But I had my reward at regimental

firing camp. This took place annually at Benbecula, in the Outer
Hebrides. I had no operational duties on the range, where we fired these
vast fireworks out to sea, or wherever else they were apt to land, and so
I took to walking in a big way. Shortly before we left those islands in
1964, I led seventeen soldiers on a 55 mile speed march from Loch
Maddy to Loch Boisdale. Only three of us completed it: Lance
Bombardier Surgenor, a fit young PT instructor; Gunner Riseman, a
veteran soldier who had fought in Korea; and myself. I got there in 10 ½
hours non-stop marching, a speed record which stands to this day.

On return to Dortmund my tour was now half completed. Despite the
joys of off-duty life with Linda and our first-born son, sailing at the
Möhnesee, visiting Arnhem and the Osterbeek Airborne cemetery for
the first time and making other excursions, I was looking for a rest and
a change from the pain of being Adjutant in such a regiment. But first I
had to do something for the better soldiers in it. I encouraged as many
as possible to volunteer for Airborne forces. To give them a taste for the
physical entrance standards required, I ran my own version of 'P'
Company. The course included weekend exercises in the gymnasium
and an assault course which ran over buildings and up the chimney-stack
of the garrison incinerator. After a number of people had jumped off the
roof of a low brick building halfway round the course, and onto some
planks below, Gunner MacKenzie jumped and, with a yell and a rending
of wood, he disappeared out of sight below. He had fallen into a sewer!
We tore the remaining planks up, and attempted to reach him, but he
was a long way down, wallowing around in sewage, spluttering and
shouting that he couldn't swim. Furthermore he was bleeding profusely
from huge gashes across his chest. As I formed a human chain to reach
him I could see my own court-martial pending. Mackenzie, however,
was very game, and he completed the course, only stopping to get
injections against septicaemia and every other known water-borne
disease once a doctor had been summoned. Sadly, only a handful of those
Airborne hopefuls made the grade. One, however, was my Assistant
Chief Clerk, Bombardier Stenning . He came to me one day, shortly
before I left, and said that his wife was six weeks pregnant and he had to
make a quick decision as to whether to leave now for the Parachute
Brigade or wait until after their child was born. I advised him to take
Fate by the forelock and go at once. He did, and never lived to regret
it. After a distinguished career with 7th RHA, he was commissioned into
the Army Air Corps. I'm glad I did somebody some good in that funny

unit. Linda returned to the UK ahead of me as No 2 son was on the way. She stayed with her parents in Camberley and Richard Neville Iain Pughe was duly born at the Louise Margaret Maternity Hospital in Aldershot on 31 July 1965.

Then in August 1965, Linda, the two young children, and I moved to Oxford. I was appointed to be Adjutant and Training 'Major' of the University Officer Training Corps at Manor Road. We lived at The Slade, Headington, and I used to walk to work each day, glad to be alive in the fresh air of a wonderful English spring. We thrived there, immersed in the world of students and dons, but academic stuffiness balanced to perfection by the friendly and informal club atmosphere of the OTC. It was amateur soldiering, but great fun. I was repeatedly surprised by the cadets, because military matters were done either so well or so badly. There seemed nothing between these two extremes. The combined Arms exercise I wrote and ran at Sennybridge, in South Wales, that summer, gave me enormous professional satisfaction.

Oxford was also the ideal environment in which to study for the Staff and Promotion exam, and I would have had no excuse for not passing it as well as I did, despite surviving a car crash on the way to Aldershot to take it! The otherwise relaxed workload allowed me more Gunner and Stragglers of Asia cricket than at any time before or since. I 'managed' several games, that is raised the side and captained it on the field, and played on many different grounds, including the impeccable HAC ground at Armoury House in the City of London, and at Sandhurst and Shrivenham, but most matches were played at the home of the Royal Regiment at Woolwich. This was quite a distance from Oxford and often I went by train. Linda, with two small children and starting a third pregnancy, was a veritable 'cricket widow' that summer, left behind at Oxford without very many friends in the neighbourhood and normally without the car. If she was lonely she never said so, and was a real Trojan. I went all out to make my mark on the Gunner cricket arena that year. I bought a pair of rimless glasses to improve my all round vision (some years later to be replaced with the new-fangled hard – and uncomfortable – contact lenses which I needed for parachuting and exercises as well as for sport) but the ultimate accolade of a place in the Gunner side to play the Sappers at Lords eluded me. I was an opening batsman and my highest score on the superb batting strip at Woolwich that season was 84, but it came too late to stand up to the competition from David Phipps, Peter Salisbury, Denis Williams and other really top-class batsmen around at that time. There were also occasions that year, and in subsequent years, when drizzle, a duck and a dropped catch were all I had to show for a weekend's 'pleasure' at cricket. At one time I called myself 'the most consistent low-scoring batsman in the Gunners' but nothing ever deterred me from extracting the maximum pleasure from this quintessentially English game.

By the end of that fine summer we had made a lot of friends at Oxford, mainly at the OTC and University. The young regular officers now able to take all sorts of different degrees at Oxford were a particularly cheerful group to be with. We basked in such events as the Chancellor's Garden Party in the immaculate grounds of Trinity College, and we loved the city and its incomparable atmosphere. When September came around I had to move on, and we were loath to leave it after less than fourteen months.

I was off to the first leg of the Army Staff Course. It was planned that I joined Division II for fifteen months at Shrivenham before going to the Army Staff College, Camberley. The main problem for Division II was quartering for the first three months. Our second son, Richard, had been born in Aldershot in July, and, as we evidently still hadn't found out what was causing it, Linda was pregnant again. We were offered a sub-standard, semi-detached, tiny, Other Ranks' quarter in Watchfield. It hadn't been occupied for years. Grass, elephant-high, barred our way to the front door. The flaking entrance opened into the kitchen. The loo, replete with wild-life, lay through the kitchen at the back. We were lucky to be given an extra upstairs bedroom from the neighbouring less densely occupied house. Not surprisingly, by Christmas in those cramped conditions, with Linda hugely pregnant, our nerves were becoming sorely tried. For the first and last time in our married life, Linda lost her temper with me and actually chased me, only half in jest, round that grisly kitchen one day with a carving knife!

It was ironic that after Christmas it was decided that as I had, to all intents and purposes, a degree behind me, I should have been placed on Division I with the Graduate officers. I therefore started afresh in January on this course, and those humour-testing horrors of life in the aptly named Folly Crescent had all been unnecessary. We soon moved into a new Quarter on the edge of the Military College estate, in Bower Green, overlooking farmland. Linda's trials and tribulations were not quite over yet, though. The happy event of the birth of Jonathan Owen Pughe on 7 February 1967 at the RAF hospital, Wroughton, was followed shortly afterwards by our car, a large blue Simca which we had brought back from Germany with us, breaking down and requiring spares only obtainable, apparently, in France. It was six weeks before that car was roadworthy again, during which time Linda would be faced with a walk to the NAAFI shop, pushing a heavy coachwork pram with two offspring in it and a third toddling beside it. Not surprisingly she often looked tired, but I never recall her complaining. She had the patience of a saint and the stamina of a real trouper.

Life at Shrivenham during that year of 1967 assumed much the same pattern of my previous years there. I returned to run the cricket side again, and rejoined the Choral Society. That spring, however, I vowed that Offenbach's *Orpheus in the Underworld* would be my last appearance as a solo tenor. Prancing around the stage like a prune in a purple skirt was something I didn't consider I could readily face again! We had a wonderful family triple christening at Shrivenham that summer, both my sisters, Diana and Maggie, having given birth to children at much the same time as our Jonathan had arrived. The academic content of the Course was substantial but unremarkable. Had it not been for some pretty indifferent instruction, about which we loudly complained to the Commandant, it might have all been more worth while. The most valuable study modules were undoubtedly those on modern management techniques, such as critical path analysis and computer programming. Yet broadly speaking, we couldn't wait to get away.

But our plans for moving with our friends to Camberley at the end of the year were dashed when I was chosen, instead, to go to the RAF Staff College at Bracknell. It wasn't exactly my choice and mid-morning sherry parties were not entirely to Linda's liking. But it had its moments, and we and the Royal Navy students got on well together. Professionally it was an absorbing time to be with the RAF as they were having to depart from their long obsession with bomber raids on Moscow to determine how to deploy the jump-jet Harriers forward with the troops in close-support. I had to press the Army's case both for the closest possible support from these new aircraft and for the introduction of armed helicopters in the Army Air Corps. Both were emotive issues at that time. I learnt a lot and grew to understand the RAF, but I must admit to being glad that the alternative society of Camberley was not far away. We were well housed in Hawk Lane, however, right on the sports field, and again I played hockey and cricket to my heart's content. That summer of 1968 was enjoyable for the family too. We paddled at West

Wittering, visited old Aunt Pin at Brookdale and had a hilarious stay on a farm at Upottery. My stepfather Leslie had by now left the Royal Marines and entered the oil industry. His first assignment after a period at Shellmex House in the Strand, was to Huddersfield, which my mother tended to call 'Shuddersfield'. The only blot on our landscape that year was a short spell of misunderstanding between Linda and my mother, of the sort that often happens between a mother and daughter-in-law, but which, I am happy to say, was more than amicably resolved as the months and years went by.

Then came news of our posting. I was so dismayed with mine that I resolved to resign my commission. Linda and I even discussed emigrating to Australia!

Chapter 8

Major Mischances

W E THOUGHT BETTER of both those courses of action. Instead I wrote a letter to the Military Secretary respectfully pointing out that I was suited by neither inclination nor experience to the particularly awful staff appointment I had been given in the Ministry of Defence, London. He kindly invited me to visit his Stanmore offices and speak with one of his Deputies. I did so and mustered quite some passion in pointing out that an Airborne Gunner, recently educated in a Joint-Service environment, knew nothing of the Army's requirement for jeeps, lorries and hovercraft with which the branch I was about to join seemed exclusively and most unglamorously to deal. The good Brigadier listened with more patience than I deserved. He explained that it was quite normal that postings for those attending other Staff Colleges were considered after Camberley students had taken the pick of the plum jobs. That only increased my misery. He then he told me an eternal truth: a job is what you make it. 'Go and do it,' he commanded, 'and I assure you it will be better than you think!'

He was right, and it taught me a very good lesson. I was, of course, exceptionally lucky to find that my boss in London was none other than that wise and intelligent Brigadier Dick Simpkin, who had been my Colonel General Staff at Shrivenham. He set me two tasks: to determine what wheeled vehicles the Army would require in the 1980s, and to define 'mobility'. He also told me that I would have just eighteen months to do it in – a shortened tour.

I was now a Major, a Staff Officer Grade Two, filling what was later to become a Lieutenant Colonel's appointment. To help me I found I had two Retired Officers in my dingy office in the Old War Office Building in Whitehall. Henry Lancefield-Staples had retired from active service some years before as a full Colonel. He lived in Eastbourne and commuted daily, arriving around 10 o'clock and leaving at 4 o'clock, breaking the day's tedium with an ample lunch at his club. After lunch he would plug in an earphone and listen to the racing from Newmarket, snoozing fitfully. He signed his one letter a day in the morning, with a flourish fit for a king. The length and majesty of his signature brought an air of authority to the most trivial directive.

My other assistant was Peter de Mey, a retired Major, late of the SAS, a member of the Special Forces Club and a likeable rogue if ever there was one. He kept quite respectable hours, but slipped out of the office every now and then to attend to his 'other business' – the provision and maintenance of fruit-machines! He lived in a delightful thatched cottage in Toot Baldon, a village near Oxford, and the two of these gentlemen were real characters, most civilised, and a guinea a minute. They were also decent enough to take over all the routine and mundane work of the branch, leaving me to get on with the two tasks Dick Simpkin had given me.

The saving grace of the Ministry of Defence is that much depends on the initiative and application of junior staff officers. Unlike many other nations, British Forces tend to work top-down only as far as broad directives go, and for day-to-day business, very largely bottom-up. I was therefore left to get on with drafting my paper on vehicles and finding out all about mobility without interference from above. Both proved fascinating studies, which took me on several trips abroad. I worked rather hard, and found the commuting from Fleet, where we had a MoD hiring, very tiring. On occasions I would fall asleep on the late train returning from London, to find myself well down the line towards Basingstoke, and having to catch a train going back the other way. Eventually, Henry found the increase in pace too much, and he resigned, shortly afterwards succumbing to a very nasty heart attack. He was eventually replaced, but not before Peter de Mey and I had become snowed under with excessive paperwork.

The rewards were few, but it was nice to be asked to brief senior members of the Army Board and Ministers direct, without having senior staff officers acting as intermediaries. The choice of vehicles for the Army assumed a high political profile, and I was inevitably drawn into procurement decisions as well as stating the general requirement. Tony Wedgwood Benn was Minister of Technology at the time, and Denis Healey our Secretary of State for Defence. Whether my view that Volvos fulfilled the Army's needs better than Land Rovers prevailed over the political and industrial arguments presented by Mr Benn was a source of much interest during this hectic period. I do not consider the fact that I lost that particular argument was in the end a source of great satisfaction to the British Army. However, life was busy and fun. I enjoyed my travels to Norway to see the new oversnow vehicles we had just introduced for the UK contingent in the Allied Mobile Force (Land), and

I got some excellent skiing there at Voss. Later I went to Washington DC to support General Jackson, the Master General of the Ordnance, to lecture to the Allied Quadripartite Forum on Mobility, and while there took a trip north to see the Niagara Falls.

It was stimulating to find how much further down the road than our American, Canadian and Australian allies we seemed to be towards defining mobility in absolute terms rather than relative. My system was based on a Swedish idea, but it involved matching indices of soil trafficability and ground pressure, among several parameters, in an endeavour to specify to manufacturers more precisely the exact degree of mobility required in a military vehicle. Its aim was laudable but it was an intellectual exercise beyond the grasp of many, and the whole idea was eventually dropped. My paper on vehicles, however, was taken by the Army Board shortly after I left London, and my successor was awarded the MBE. Dick Simpkin, however, had been generous enough to give me two successive 'Outstanding' Annual Reports, which set me on the path to swift promotion and rather higher profile appointments.

During my tour in London we had bought an old Ford Anglia estate car and we were accommodated in an MoD hiring at 13 Longmead, Fleet. David had started at the local primary school but there they initially expected this left-hander write with his right hand, and teaching standards seemed to us anyway abysmal, so we were pleased when eventually the time came to move. In September 1969 we had a memorable late holiday in a leaking tent at Llyngwryl on the north-west coast of Wales, the only other occupants of the field being some miserable-looking sheep. I regretted the experience did nothing to deter the family from camping again, possibly as were rescued from the worst Atlantic gales by James and Rosemary Gordon. Lieutenant (later Major General) James Gordon, who at that time was with the Air Defence Regiment along the coast at Towyn, had been my Assistant Adjutant in 27th Missile Regiment and he and his family became close and enduring friends of ours.

Shortly before we were due to leave Fleet we resolved to look for a house to buy, and after a while we found something that was not too awful, not far away in Crowthorne. I then did my sums and reckoned that we might just be able to squeeze the mortgage repayments out of what was left of our meagre pay after school fees were met, but in no way would we be able to find the money to buy carpets, curtains and furniture, of which, of course, we had virtually none of our own. First priority was to pay all the insurances I had taken out for the boys' future education fees. I had put them down for that fine west-country school, Blundell's in Tiverton, with second choice Exeter, but the family centre of gravity was clearly moving away from Devon now and it was important to be nearer grandparents for fetching at half terms and delivering to airports at ends of term when we were abroad. So, rather late in the day we switched to Wellington, and we faced the prospect of heavier fees and associated expenses, as the Army boarding school allowance was likely only to cover half. So we failed to close the deal. It was one of the worst decisions of our life and a decision that, in the light of the subsequent boom in house-prices, we were always to regret.

In July 1970 we spent a wonderful family holiday in the Lake District, staying at a house overlooking Lake Windermere, owned by Jon Nelson, my old Housemaster. Sadly our scrambles around the Langdale Pikes were to prove to be the last time that Linda managed to climb any considerable mountain. August 1970 was time to return to regimental duty. We had bought a new car – our first brand new one – a Ford Escort Estate, and loaded to its axles we set out for Germany again. The tour was, in the family tradition of the Royal Regiment of Artillery, to be with 45th Field Regiment RA once more, and I was to command 170 (Imjin) Battery. The only snag was we had to suffer Dortmund again! Housing was still an unresolved problem there, and I had been asked to leave Linda in the UK until a suitable quarter became available. Neither she nor I were at all keen on that idea. If I was to be an effective Battery Commander, with all the social responsibilities that entailed, I needed her with me. So, brave girl, she came. And where did we live? She could scarcely believe it, but in a cramped flat back in the same grotty area of down-town Dortmund as we had survived with difficulty six years before!

After a couple of months of torture I resolved to make a fuss, and we were then offered another cramped flat, this time in the attic of an old German house on the busy, noisy Ruhrschnellweg. But it was not far from West Riding Barracks where the Regiment was. Our first night there was hilarious. After the move, we clambered exhausted into a rickety bed a second or two before midnight. As we did so, there was a roar as a coal train rumbled past the house, the church clock right outside the window struck twelve with a resounding crash that shook the flat, and the bed collapsed! We tried hard to entertain people from the Battery there, but it was like eating in a railway carriage, complete with noises off!

After Christmas we at last moved into a decent quarter, in Max-Eyth Strasse, in an area of Dortmund known as the Gartenstadt – the Garden City. It was opposite the barracks, and suited us very well indeed. I then had an enjoyable six months commanding the best Battery in the British Army and running the Regimental Officers' Mess. I was told that I managed to do both competently and with flair. We certainly showed off a lot. With marvellous support from the Battery Captain, Bill Winchester, and my new Battery Sergeant-Major, Mike Mitchell, who had been to Public School in Devon, we set up a Battery History Room, made up flags and scrolls, won the inter-Battery hockey cup, and did a thousand good things in the field with the utmost panache. They were good days, made even better by the presence of our old chums Tony and Caroline Weston as friendly rivals in another Battery of the same Regiment.

We were then given the exciting news that we were to deploy to Northern Ireland. Major Nick Jones, who had been with me in the Parachute Brigade, was Second-in-Command of the Regiment and he and I went off to see a unit that had just returned from a tour in the increasingly troubled Province. Our job was to find out how things were tackled over there, and then to write Standing Operational Procedures for the Regiment, as no official tactical doctrine had yet been established for the British Army's first Internal Security Operations on the streets of part of the United Kingdom. We then accompanied the Commanding Officer, Lieutenant Colonel Patrick Ellwood, on a reconnaissance of our forthcoming tasks in the 8th Brigade Area of Ulster, which included Londonderry and all the western Border country southwards as far as, and including, County Fermanagh.

As we were being briefed by the Brigade Headquarters Staff that June day in 1971, the first serious casualty occurred among British soldiers trying to quell riots on the streets. Our reconnaissance took on an extra degree of earnestness. What were euphemistically called by the Press 'disturbances on the streets of Belfast and Londonderry' were nightly becoming more vicious. Our anti-riot drill was firmly based on the doctrine of 'forming square' developed by the British Army over the years for its colonial troubles. The squares were manned predominantly by men armed with batons, and they used dustbin-lids as shields. Little enough protection against bombardments of stones, concrete slabs, nail-bombs and bottles filled with flaming petrol. But it all looked grimly exciting, and I was looking forward to the action.

But my hopes for this sort of action were dashed at the end of the reconnaissance when Patrick Ellwood told me that 'Imjin' Battery was to be detached to County Fermanagh. He thought that I would enjoy the fairly independent role down there. I returned to Dortmund downhearted. We carried out the same training as the rest of the Regiment during the following weeks, but I gave my men instructions to be prepared to take all that they could in the way of sports gear and Adventure Training equipment to Northern Ireland, for this was going to be a very quiet and boring tour. With the number of lochs in south-west Ulster, I anticipated a lot of canoeing and fishing, but absolutely no action in that quiet neck of the woods.

The last few weeks of preparation were frenetic, but I was not at all happy that we were training in the most appropriate way for any tasks I could foresee in the rural areas of Ulster. There was too much emphasis on static guarding and riot 'drills' and I was determined to introduce as much mobility, fitness and flexibility into my Battery's training as possible. In the final days of the training, each Battery was to go through a 24 hour test exercise in which the CO and Nick Jones would throw everything they could think of at the Battery to expose any loopholes in their drills and procedures. The exercise included a severe test of anti-riot formation tactics, the 'rioters' being provided by a large number of exceedingly enthusiastic 'mobsters' from other sections of the Regiment, who showed no mercy to their colleagues trying unsuccessfully to shelter behind phalanxes of dust-bin lids.

Now, the approved tactic for a platoon engaged in riot control was to conceal three or four men inside the 'Square' who were to be the 'Snatch Squad'. When the mob got close enough to the 'Square', the Platoon Commander would give the Signal for the 'Snatch Squad' to break out from behind the phalanx of shields and run forward to arrest indicated ring-leaders. In my view, this tactic was at best foolhardy, and at worst useless. I could see this small group of 'snatchers' themselves being 'snatched' by the mob, and anyway, whether heavily equipped soldiers could run fast enough to catch the young stone-throwers was highly problematical. I therefore resolved to reduce my 'Squares' by at least a full Section of 10 men, who would be held fully concealed down a side-street to a flank. As a mob then closed to within throwing range of the thinly manned 'Square' our soldiers in it could more easily move back or to the sides to avoid the worst of the bricks and bottles. More importantly, however, at a given signal the concealed Section would move in from the rear or flank of the mob, which, if surprise were sufficient, would enable them to come to grips with the ring-leaders immediately and in sufficient strength safely to make arrests.

Needless to say, I told nobody of such ideas but told Lieutenant Tony Rice, son of Harry Rice of 33rd days, my most enterprising subaltern, to use these tactics on our test exercise. The surprise achieved was considerable, the success total and the consternation of the CO and Nick Jones undisguised. Indeed, I was taken to task in no uncertain way at the post-exercise conference for adopting such unconventional tactics, but eventually their success had to be conceded. This had a very significant bearing on subsequent events in my part of Ulster, as this story will show.

It was on 5 August 1971 that I arrived, together with leading elements of my Battery, at Lisgoole School, Enniskillen, County Fermanagh. It was a beautiful, sunny day and the surrounding countryside looked lush green, inviting and tranquil. I sighed deeply as Major Tony Wilson (later Brigadier commanding 5 Brigade in the Falklands) of the Light Infantry Company completing their four month emergency tour there described the situation. His men had, in his view, done an exceptionally good job, maintaining a high level of patrolling in Land Rovers around the Border lanes and villages. As in any rural community, rumours had prospered of all sorts of deadly deeds by countless villains, but most of the 'suspicious activity' he told me about was, I surmised, a figment of well-developed imaginations. This was clearly going to be an uneventful tour, and I thought that I would go to Omagh the next day and see John Turner, the charming CO of the 17/21st Lancers, to whom my Battery was now formally attached, and at least see what the chances were of my getting some horse riding from time to time there.

Over the next three days my Battery arrived in stages, relieving the Light Infantry Company man by man in the overcrowded accommodation of that old school building. I paid courtesy visits on the police and the Mayor of Enniskillen, and there were few grounds for believing that anything would disturb the peace of the countryside. Then, on 8 August, Inspector Harry Curry, the RUC Divisional Military Liaison Officer, arrived at Lisgoole School unannounced. He said that there was to be a major swoop the next day to 'lift' all known terrorists in the Division! I could scarcely believe it. He went on to tell me about the numbers involved and the breadth of territory which we would have to cover within a very short period in the early hours of the morning. I would need every man I had to escort the police to each of the suspects' homes.

My last men were still arriving from the aircraft at Aldergrove, and as they touched down they were driven with all speed to Lisgoole, there to be hastily equipped and briefed. Every single man, cooks and REME vehicle mechanics included, were to go out on the operation. Only a small Battery HQ team was to remain at base. I repeatedly sought from the police that day meaningful grid references of the target houses. It was wholly in vain, as few, if any, of the policemen who arrived that evening knew how to read maps.

More by luck than skill we rounded up some 23 of the 30 or so names on the RUC's list in my operational area that night. It was plain to me that not all of those arrested could in any way be considered threats to security. Several were middle-aged or elderly men who claimed that they had had nothing to do with the IRA since the 1920s, let alone the 1955/56 Border Campaign. A few rusty old weapons were found, but very little incriminating. I assumed, however, that the RUC and Intelligence knew what they were doing. For our part, it had made an exciting start to the tour, although in later years, that Internment Operation was deemed to have been a trifle counter-productive. Certainly it livened up the Province, and brought Catholics out onto the streets of every town and village in Ulster within a few days.

Inspector Curry then told me that, on Saturday, a huge protest meeting was being planned by local Republicans for the crossroads area in Enniskillen town centre. When I did my reconnaissance on the Friday, shop windows were being boarded-up in anticipation of rioting. I spent some time at the Police Barracks making a thorough plan. I was given extra Ferret Scout Cars by CO 17/21st Lancers, and these I deployed in pairs to the Border crossings, to report in good time to me and to the police, when there was any significant increase of traffic from the Republic of Ireland towards the town.

By 08.30 on the Saturday morning their reports were positive. Very large crowds of Catholics were converging on Enniskillen town centre, and they continued to arrive all morning, leaving cars parked on the outskirts of town and walking in the last two or three miles. There was no real shortage of car parks in Enniskillen then, so they were obviously mindful for the safety of their vehicles and the most favourable position from which to make a getaway. Things looked ominous. The crowd of several thousand gathered quietly enough, and the few RUC men present looked on from a distance. I stayed in the Police Operations Room in radio contact with Inspector Curry who was observing events at the crossroads. Leaving one platoon carrying out Border patrols, and guards at base, I had two platoons with me concealed in the Police Barracks. My aim was not to raise the temperature by revealing our presence too soon.

At noon the first speaker started to address the throng from the temporary platform erected on the street corner . A series of rabble-rousing speeches was then delivered by incensed Republican spokesmen well known to the police. Then cars driven by enraged Protestants drove into the town centre in an attempt to assert their right to free passage. The crowd swiftly turned into a furious mob. I at once deployed Captain Freddie Clements' platoon to the scene. They moved swiftly and precisely into position, forming Square in the approved manner in full view of the chanting mob. There was a momentary lull. The mob glanced uneasily at the troops standing calmly, batons and shields at the ready. It looked for a moment as if the situation might be saved, but renewed appeals by one of the leading speakers to 'set the town alight' created frenzy. They turned to attack the platoon and the shops. Inspector Curry's despairing cry over the radio is with me to this day. 'Oh by Jesu, Neville, its gone up! Its all yours!'

I immediately gave three orders to my men. Tony Rice's platoon was to move at the double from their concealed position up the nearest side-street to intercept the mob as it rampaged down the Enniskillen main shopping street. Freddie Clements' platoon was to disperse the crowd using CS gas grenades. The Scout Cars of the 17/21st Lancers were to close in rapidly towards the town, stopping and arresting any rioters making for their parked cars. I myself then sped towards the scene.

As I entered the town centre my Land Rover clattered over tons of debris in the street. A tyre burst, sounding like a rifle shot. We drove on in the wake of Freddie's platoon which was pursuing the mob at running pace down the main street. Tony's platoon rushed in from the flank, increasing the speed of the mob's headlong rush down the street. Windows were smashed as the frenzied mass ran down the hill. As two men stopped to light a torch to throw into a shop, Tony Rice's men pounced and arrested them. The two platoons chased that mob all the way out of town. By the time they saw they were pincered by the incoming scout cars, the mobsters slowed to walking pace and attempted to look like respectable citizens out for a Saturday stroll! My Land Rover bucked and leapt over the metal rods, bricks, pieces of wooden platform and shop windows, as it crashed its way down the street, sounding for all the world like an ancient chariot. It was all over in half an hour, and we were exhilarated.

The good citizens of Enniskillen were shocked beyond words by these unprecedented events. I was visited that evening by a staff officer from Brigade Headquarters who had been sent to ask me 'what had gone wrong'. I was stunned. I was convinced, and remain so to this day, that we saved Enniskillen from being burnt to the ground. We did it by a combination of sound planning and effective, speedy reaction to events. Above all, my tactics of mobility, flexibility and flank snatch squads had been completely vindicated. Only the RUC appreciated, however, how well we had contained an ugly situation and averted more serious damage.

The following weeks saw a continued and steady rise in tension. All the Customs Houses at the main Border Crossing points were blown up or set alight by IRA gangs in the dead of night, crossing from and returning instantly to the safety of the Republic. Even with the help of a Battalion of the newly formed Ulster Defence Regiment, I did not have enough troops to set up ambushes every night on all these Customs Huts. Intelligence was at best sketchy, and normally non-existent. Most of our operations were speculative, and consequently very expensive in manpower and time. Customs Houses were, in any case, unoccupied at night, and my principal task, I believed, was to protect life rather than buildings. The RUC were increasingly nervous, and often declined to accompany our patrols into the remoter areas of the Division.

Then we were fired upon from across the Border. Nobody, fortunately, was hit, but at that stage of the campaign we were forbidden to shoot back into Eire. Such instances became more and more frequent. A road running parallel to the Border for five miles or so in the south-west of County Fermanagh became known successively as 'Ambush Alley' and 'Hellfire Pass'. I put in a strong plea to Brigade HQ to permit us to return fire, for life was going to be lost before long, and we could not simply stop using the roads in the Border areas, as that would be regarded as surrendering territory to the terrorists.

I was visited by the GOC Northern Ireland himself. I briefed him on all the recent incidents shown on the map in my operations room, and he paid close attention. When he came to leave by helicopter from the hilltop field behind the school he said, 'When you are next shot at from across the Border, you have my permission to return fire, and if you hit a gunman you can nip across and drag back the body!' This was a huge fillip to morale. 'But,' he added darkly, 'on no account must you tell anyone I said so!'

The next day we were visited by reporter Robert Fisk of *The Times*. He probed and probed about the rumour he had heard that we were about to be given political clearance to fire across the Border into the Republic. We kept him guessing, but took him for a comprehensive tour of our whole operational area by helicopter, which thrilled him enormously. He was kind enough the next day to write in glowing terms a front page article for *The Times* on my Battery's recent exploits.

As the days and nights passed, we became embroiled in more and more hectic activity. Every patrol could expect trouble. The terrorists started to carry out raids further into the north. A policeman was shot dead outside Kinawley RUC station at 8 o'clock in the morning, and the gunmen were back across the Border within minutes. There were too many routes and unauthorised crossing places to patrol every one. For our own security, too, our patrol programme had to be random, to set no regular patterns. This was especially so as Lisgoole School could only be approached along a single lane to the north and one to the south. I determined to rely more and more on helicopters, and the field behind Lisgoole School reverberated night and day to the sound of RAF Wessex helicopters flying in and out, often in atrocious weather.

One day I was called out to the RUC station at Belleek, on the westernmost tip of the Province. This small town, where the famous pottery is manufactured, lies on the eastern shore of an inlet in the River Erne estuary. The police station, which backs onto the shore, is overlooked by a hill in Republic of Ireland territory. That hill provided a gunman with the ideal fire position from which to engage the police station with impunity. The local RUC sergeant told me that he had heard a very strong rumour that the IRA were planning two attacks: one on the police station and the other an explosive attack on one of our vehicle patrols as it crossed the Rosscor Viaduct three miles to the south-east en route to Enniskillen. He looked extremely nervous and I was inclined to believe him when he said that he thought the attack on the patrol would take place that very night. It was only rumour, rural gossip, but we had so little to go on.

I had long ago permanently stationed a Section at this RUC outpost, and I briefed Sergeant Binns, its leader at the time, about the need to approach that bridge with care and on foot when he crossed it that night. I could not spare any further troops to set an ambush on the off-chance this information might this time be true. If, however, he got any more 'rumour' from the RUC or anyone to whom he spoke, he was to let me know, and I would call for more reinforcements from Omagh. On the way back, I stopped short of the bridge. I walked forward slowly, accompanied by my escort, leaving the driver, Lance Bombardier Salmon, and radio operator in the Land Rover. The stone bridge was under repair. There was scaffolding around and underneath the near arch. I glanced around and saw two or three men chatting earnestly with an elderly couple at the front of their nearby house. I didn't think much about that at the time, except that I felt it wise not to be seen too closely inspecting the bridge. I said to my escort, under my breath, 'If I were a terrorist, that is where I'd place the explosive. Right there on the scaffolding under the arch!' We turned on our heel and left for base. I turned over and over in my mind on the way back, how I could raise an ambush party from my overstretched resources, and whether Sergeant Binns would do the right thing that night.

I hardly slept a wink that night, but at 04.00 a.m. the telephone rang beside my bed. It was Sergeant Binns, and before he spoke, my heart

A Bailey bridge spans the blown-up Rosscor viaduct

sank in anticipation of what he was about to say. However, although his patrol was safe, the Rosscor bridge was 'blown to smithereens', he said. The explosive had been laid on the scaffolding under the nearside arch, exactly as I predicted. Fortunately, there were no casualties. Sergeant Binns had patrolled very warily that night, taking twice as long as usual by going on foot. The terrorists evidently got fed up waiting, and decided in the end simply to blow up the bridge, giving themselves time to get away across the Border some mile or two away. So the rumour had been real intelligence this time, and I had missed an all-too-rare opportunity to ambush the IRA! No failure has ever irked with me so deeply and so long as that one. There is no doubt in my mind, that tired and short of troops or not, I should have taken four men and laid that ambush myself. If only . . . if only . . . if only.

The Beleek RUC station was shot at a few nights later, a 0.5 inch calibre anti-tank bullet passing clean through the upper story from rear to front, narrowly missing our machine-gunner looking out of the front window! The IRA even dragged up a World War 2 Boys' Anti-Tank rifle for that attack, and unleashed a hundred rounds or more of all types at the startled troops and police inside. There was no hesitation over the volume of fire we returned on that occasion! However, emboldened by such 'success', the IRA returned in broad daylight two days later and opened fire on our patrol as it moved tactically down the main village street en route to the RUC station. An RUC constable was accompanying the patrol, and as bullets ricocheted around the street, he ran forward to get a local villager out of the firing line and into cover. He slipped as he did so, falling heavily onto the road in full view of the gunmen on the hill across the inlet. The Bombardier leading the patrol, on seeing the danger to both the villager and the policeman, yelled to the other soldiers to give him covering fire, and he rushed forward without thought for his own safety and brought both of these shocked and frightened people in turn into the cover of nearby buildings. In risking his life in this way, he thoroughly deserved the gallantry award I later recommended he should receive.

Belleek continued to exercise my attention throughout the remainder of our tour in County Fermanagh, not least because of the difficulty we now had of getting there. Helicopters tended to be shot at if they landed troops too close to the Border, so I took to sending men up there surreptitiously at night by canoe! Those who had done a bit of Adventure Training in the past felt somewhat more at ease in this tactic than others. My operational masterstroke was not universally admired by the less daring. Whether it fooled the IRA or not I have no idea.

And so to Operation Ashburton. This was the code-name for the blowing-up of all the roads crossing the Border. As a gesture to placate public opinion in Great Britain it may have served some purpose, but as a practical anti-terrorist measure it was doomed to failure from the start. As fast as roads and bridges were blown, farmers, many of whose land was bisected by the irregular Border, either filled in the holes or found a way round the obstructions we so diligently laid. As fast as we carried out our tasks, generally at night, the locals countered. Then republicans north and south of the Border rallied around chosen sites, initially simply to demonstrate vocally their opposition, but later accompanied by IRA gunmen. Hidden in the background, the gunmen would open fire on our troops as they closed in on the spot just short of the Border where our explosive was to be laid. To me this seemed a wholly advantageous development, because at last we could engage the IRA in a gunfight, bringing our superior firepower to bear. If we were crafty, too, inserting troops covertly in advance, we could bring them to action and fight them on our terms.

Thus it was that one morning in late October, four or five IRA gunmen chose to fire on what they thought was a very small guard force for the Royal Engineer party preparing demolitions on a rather remote road crossing the Border near Rosslea. That was the signal for four Ferret Scout Cars and a reinforced platoon of men, which included several General Purpose machine-guns, to emerge from cover and engage the enemy with everything they'd got. Over *two thousand* rounds of 7.62 mm and 0.5 inch were fired at the gunmen within the next 30 minutes or so. Freddie Clements, in charge of the operation, could not claim afterwards that any gunmen were hit, as they were cunningly concealed behind stone walls. Be that as it may, the IRA did not try a similar tactic again for a very long time to come. For my part, not least of the enjoyment I derived from the incident was seeing the look on the Military Police Incident Investigator's face when he heard just how many shots had been fired that day!

Captain Brian Porter was my other Troop Commander. He was a most phlegmatic character, and one ideally suited to the sort of tense situation he found himself in one day during Operation Ashburton. A certain bridge was to be blown up, but this time, a peaceful crowd of republicans moved forward and stood defiantly on the bridge. After a while, a platoon of the Irish Army arrived to the south of the bridge. The crowd withdrew and what the Press described as 'the first confrontation' between the two armies took place. Brian Porter kept his head. He played for time. After a while, he told me over the radio that the Irish Platoon Commander and he were sitting down together underneath the bridge, smoking, and discussing what to do next. Although it was certainly an unprecedented development, I was at no time seriously concerned, and thought that those on the spot were best placed to resolve the problem amicably, and disengage. Imagine, therefore, my surprise to receive a call from Brigade HQ to say that the Prime Minister, Mr Heath, was, I was led to believe, in direct contact with the Brigade Commander, wanting to know what was happening. It transpired that this was being viewed in Whitehall as a major international incident! I told the Brigadier that he could assure Mr Heath that I had given Captain Porter instructions to quietly withdraw by mid afternoon, and then return later under cover of darkness and blow the bridge. I don't believe that I was ever reassured that this plan of action met with Cabinet approval, but in the end that is what we did, and that was that.

170 (Imjin) Battery's four month emergency tour in Northern Ireland was therefore very eventful, and I suppose it might be possible to write a complete book about it. It had its quieter moments when, for example, I was able to snatch a few hours fishing in a local loch. Lieutenant Colonel Hank Bowen, of the Royal Engineers, commanded the local territorial battalion of the Ulster Defence Regiment, 4 UDR, and we were to become long-standing chums over the subsequent years. His Territorial adjutant was a local bank manager who held the fishing rights on a remote loch to the south of Enniskillen. At Hank's request he took me dry fly trout fishing there on a couple of occasions, and I was quite taken with the sport. I think the Irish trout were particularly stupid, for they rose magnificently to the flies my host placed so expertly before their noses. Mike Mitchell, my BSM, did some impressive coarse fishing almost daily in the river behind Lisgoole School too, and my breakfasts benefited hugely from freshly caught perch. He drew a most amusing cartoon for me, which I framed, depicting himself in full combat dress fishing, while an IRA terrorist leered at him from behind a bush and all manner of explosions erupted around on the horizon.

Life was generally hectic and exciting. Space does not permit me to complete the tale here, but my adventures included a nocturnal and illicit

My Battery's Northern Ireland tour!

foray with Inspector Harry Curry over the Border to recce IRA haunts, and the arrest of a Westminster MP – Frank McManus – on suspicion of being a member of the Provisional IRA! Missing, too, from this narrative, must regrettably be any mention of all the kind people who made our life worth living; those with whom we could relax, as with Lord Harry Erne in the comfort of Crom Castle. In many respects, however, our tour of duty was no more sensational than many subsequent sub-units' tours in that demanding part of the Province in those dark times of the early 1970s. However, the level of activity we encountered was certainly unexpected and very exciting. I am only sad that, in the last days of our operations, the inevitable happened and the IRA ambushed a patrol returning along the only road from the south to Lisgoole School. A massive culvert bomb blew the top off a Ferret Scout car of the newly arrived 16/5th Lancers, killing the Corporal whose head was out of the top. The Scout Car was accompanied by a Section under the least reliable of my Junior NCOs who was so shocked by the bloodshed that he completely failed to take the follow-up clearance action in the area immediately surrounding the ambush. (Colonel Grivas described a similar incident in his Memoirs of the EOKA campaign that he led against the British in Cyprus in 1955–59. The thought that we again might have let a much-wanted terrorist escape again, fifteen years later, gave me little rest for some time afterwards.) However, this was, miraculously, the only casualty we suffered during that tour, and I considered that we were extremely lucky.

We returned to the more humdrum life of BAOR well satisfied that we had performed creditably, and that we had made a lot of lasting friends among the local people and the RUC. The IRA had, alas, proved as elusive to our best efforts to entrap them as glory was to me. Nonetheless, I'd won my first little medal ribbon!

The remainder of my tour as Commander of a wonderful Battery paled into insignificance after such a stimulating tour in Ulster. Nevertheless I tried hard to make the humdrum life of BAOR interesting and productive. My superb Battery Sergeant Major, Mike Mitchell, and I set up a Battery History Room which warranted a visit even from the Master Gunner, Field Marshal Sir Geoffrey Baker. My first and only oil painting was hung there, depicting – from painful memory – an unsuccessful ambush at Mullan customs house! We played much sport, and the Battery hockey team was especially successful. In the field and on parades we unashamedly showed off, flying the Imjin pennant everywhere, and deployed the silver for visitors, among whom was the Divisional Commander Royal Artillery, Brigadier Richard Ohlen-schlager, whom I believe we must have impressed for it was his backing which secured my next surprise posting. In between times we had some wonderful family holidays in Cavalino, Venice, and the Moselle Valley. On one notable occasion when camping beside Lake Constance we were erecting the tent, and in tugging at the wet canopy my hand slipped. It shot back and I hit my rimless spectacles hard, making the edge of the glass dig into my right eye. Although we stayed where we were that night, I could not sleep for the pain and in the morning it was evident that the eye was damaged. I certainly could not drive, so Linda, poor girl, drove us all the way non-stop back to Dortmund to see the Army doctor. I wore a dashing patch over one eye for a few days, after which, amazingly quickly, the eye healed with no after effects at all. The boys were growing apace by now and family life was ever more fun. In my next job it might have to take second place.

CHAPTER 9

Staff Laughs

LIEUTENANT COLONEL PATRICK ELLWOOD gave me quite a shock when he called me to his office one day in spring 1972. He said that I had been selected to be Brigade Major of 16th Parachute Brigade! This was an extremely rare honour for a Gunner officer, and I could not believe my luck. I must confess to having a few misgivings, however, as I imagined a major part of a BM's duties would be writing military exercises and operation orders. Unfortunately, as I had learnt my staff duties at an RAF Staff College, I had never actually written an Army operation order before. I realised that I would have to learn rather fast on the job.

I handed over 170th (Imjin) Battery RA in June and for the first time, I was able to spend time with the family, motoring home to England via a short camping holiday in the Moselle Valley (the boys in a tent and Linda and I in the *Gasthaus* over the road!). We moved into a vast Victorian quarter in North Camp, Farnborough. It was called Albert House and it's now a car park. In the halcyon days when it was built, I suppose the whole house would have been occupied by a major and his family, with his horses kept in the stables at the end of the long garden. Now, the house was divided between two majors and the stables were leased to a family of gypsies. Our minute dining room was the one-time servants' parlour next to a palatial kitchen.

We arranged for our two eldest sons, David, now 8½ and Richard, just 7, to start boarding school in the September term at St Andrew's School, Horsell, Woking, a school which had been recommended to us by Mark and Anna Coe. Mark was a contemporary of mine at Sandhurst. Although he had joined the Royal Engineers, we had always kept in touch and they had been good family friends of ours, particularly since the Division 1 Staff Course at Shrivenham. It was therefore of special sadness to us later when Mark was shot and killed by the IRA outside his quarter at Bielefeld, in Germany. We were always grateful to him for recommending such a good school for our boys. But now our youngest son, Jonathan, was still only 5½ and he was placed at a local primary school, much to his disgust. I had time to take all three boys to London for a visit to HMS *Belfast*, and to go to see my parents who had now moved south from Yorkshire to Cheam. I confided in Leslie my apprehensions over the appointment ahead of me, and he was, as ever, splendidly encouraging.

In August I duly reported to the Brigade Headquarters in Aldershot and took over from Major Mike Tarleton, a Greenjacket, within a week. (Poor Mike subsequently died of a heart-attack, which for someone so young and fit was a terrible shock for his family.) The following Monday, as I arrived at the office, the Brigade Commander, Brigadier Tony Ward-Booth, called for me and the DAA & QMG, Major Peter Kingston MC. He told us that we were to report immediately to the planning staff of the UK Commanders-in-Chief Committee at Wilton, and commence work in the greatest secrecy on an Airborne invasion of Uganda in order to rescue British citizens there threatened by the reign of terror being conducted by President Idi Amin. As we sped off in the Brigadier's staff car, I remarked wryly to Peter that I had hardly expected my inexperience in writing operation orders to be exposed quite so soon and in such critical circumstances!

To my surprise, my difficulties were compounded by the complete absence of any basic planning staff tables for the Brigade. For the sort of peacetime exercises which the Brigade had conducted for so long the airlift was negotiated on the basis of the troops required for a given exercise framework. For the Uganda Operation the critical path was the limited capacity of the staging airfield in the Seychelle Islands to take more than twenty-two C130 Hercules aircraft. I asked Peter what the basic viable force level was for each element of the Brigade; was it a Troop or a Section of Engineers in the Airborne assault role, and so on. I needed, I said, to know what the basic building 'bricks' were to construct a balanced force. Unknown to me at the time, the term 'brick' was then swiftly adopted by every unit on operations in Northern Ireland, following the Parachute Regiment battalions' example, and to this day the basic patrol unit of force is known as the '4-man brick'.

We played with figures endlessly, altering our plan as intelligence and air-photographs of the golf-course DZ in Kampala and the airfield at Entebbe came in. The RAF, it must be said, were none too keen on the risks involved in the planned operation, particularly as Entebbe airfield was bristling with Libyan air-defence guns of various sorts and undoubted lethality. But given the chance of deploying a few Phantom ground-attack fighters, they were prepared to have a go. The Brigade and the requisite numbers of aircraft were prepared, platforms rigged and

troops given final refresher training, all in the greatest secrecy. At Mr
Heath's behest, we maintained that state of readiness for six weeks,
before, much to our disappointment, but perhaps to the considerable
relief of the British inhabitants of Uganda, the need for the operation
receded. My operation order, incidentally, was, I thought, a masterpiece,
but for obvious reasons, only a very few people ever saw it!

Autumn 1972 was busy for Parachute Brigade units as the Northern
Ireland troubles were at their height. Even so, we managed to conduct
a major Airborne exercise in Denmark. The DZ was pitted with deep
holes filled with water, into which the two bulkiest officers in the
Brigade fell ignominiously. The Heavy Drop loads narrowly missed
various farmhouses wide of the DZ which nearly caused international
difficulties, but by and large it was a fairly uneventful excursion. I learnt
an important lesson from Brigadier Tony, however, and that was to
decide when to sleep. At one stage of the exercise I was making no sense
at all of his instructions to the Brigade and he rightly deduced that I was
dog-tired through lack of sleep. I felt foolish being ordered to bed in the
middle of an important exercise, but one man cannot do everything, nor
is one man indispensable! He did pay tribute to my 'calmness' under
pressure however: something I remember my mother calling 'slow in the
uptake' in my father! Exercise DEEP FURROW, as it was named, was
however notable for one thing, and that was its place as the first major
overseas exercise of the newly formed UK JATFOR (United Kingdom
Joint Airborne Task Force), and I became an ardent supporter of the
concept of this quick-reaction brigade.

Back at Aldershot I found myself one day standing in for the Brigade
Commander at the annual inspection of 3rd Battalion, The Parachute
Regiment, a fine unit just back from a United Nations tour in Cyprus.
I was with the unit throughout the day, and found the Commanding
Officer reacted rather strangely to the instructions I gave him on behalf
of the Brigadier. I later mentioned this to the Brigadier but nothing more
was said. A month later the battalion deployed to Northern Ireland
where, at the second or third Brigade Commander's Orders Group, this
same Commanding Officer had a nervous breakdown. This did not
surprise me, and it was later admitted, it should not have surprised
anyone. That officer was reputed to be brilliant, but all his reports over
the years had indicated a tendency to 'flap' under pressure. Not for the
first time, real operations had caught out an officer who should not have
been placed in command.

HQ 16 Parachute Brigade 1973

Self (front row 3rd from left) as Brigade Major

By spring 1973, the Brigade Gunner Regiment, 7th RHA were back from Ulster, but virtually the whole of the remainder of the Brigade units were deployed in the Province. It seemed to me pointless for Brigade HQ to remain in Aldershot in these circumstances, there being no possibility, for political presentational reasons, for the Parachute Brigade HQ to move to Northern Ireland too. I therefore suggested to the Brigadier that we moved, lock, stock and barrel, to Cyprus for six weeks, leaving a Post Orderly behind to forward the mail! He could see no good reason for objecting to this proposal, so in May I duly took the whole HQ staff with me to Alexandria Barracks, Dekhelia, joining 7th RHA's exercise there. It was immense fun, and while there, we teamed up with the Commando Brigade who swept ashore in majestic style on one of their amphibious exercises. The Brigade Major of the Commando Brigade – in a sense my opposite number – was Major Julian Thompson, and he and I started a long and firm friendship at that time.

Cyprus was, for me, almost as much heaven as Bahrain had been. I have relished hot sun, deserts and blue sea ever since my first exercise in Libya in 1960. Unfortunately, one day I took part in a small parachute

Ladies Mile DZ, Cyprus, 1973

exercise and landed with a vicious thump on my backside. The DZ was just outside Akrotiri, a salt flat beside Ladies Mile beach. It looked like soft sand from the air, but it was rock hard on impact, and I had twists in my rigging lines and came in hard backwards. It was not until a month or so later, however, when I was back in Aldershot and out for a jog, that something twanged in my back, and I was crippled with what was diagnosed as a crushed disc.

I went into the Cambridge Military Hospital, Aldershot for a month's bed-rest and treatment, notable mainly for the hilarious fun I and fellow Airborne sufferers, Dare Farrar-Hockley and Roger Southerst, had at the expense of the nurses. I also tried painting 'The Laughing Cavalier' by numbers, but being on my back the paint kept running and it turned out to be 'The Crying Cavalier'. At the end of this spell I felt as weak as a kitten and in no sense cured. What was so galling was the thought that I might not be fit enough to participate in the next UK JATFOR overseas exercise, in Turkish Thrace. This was to be the largest Airborne drop on Europe since 1944, and I was to lead the British team to select the DZ and write the exercise play. I got out to Istanbul in July and met the American and Turkish recce teams. Skilful diplomacy was called for. The American 82nd Airborne Division was chary of dropping onto anything rougher than what I considered to be a billiard table, while the Turkish Airborne Battalion would have dropped on the peak of Mount Everest if they had been told to! A typical British compromise was agreed eventually, but I confessed to being secretly worried about the course of a dried-up river bed running across one corner of the chosen ground.

After the initial recce of Thrace I donned a blazer and flannels and visited Istanbul, that fascinating city where west meets east. I bartered for onyx lampstands in the Souk, ventured into the Blue Mosque, and, while admiring the rough map of the old Ottoman Empire inside the outer gate of the Topkapi Palace encountered an elderly Turk who said: 'It may not have been as big as the British Empire, but we got more out of it!' The array of magnificent treasures inside confirmed he was doubly right!

When the exercise took place that autumn, I struggled down the aircraft with my weapons-container being half lifted for me by the officer behind me. I landed with everything crossed, especially my fingers, and felt not a thing! Surprisingly, very few paratroopers, out of the 1800 who dropped, fell into the dried-up river bed. Those who did broke ankles and legs of course. Sadly, one first-rate young corporal of the 2nd Parachute Battalion failed to get out of very complicated twists in his rigging lines, and plummeted to his death in front of hundreds of spectators from NATO countries.

Despite this, overall it was a most successful exercise, although it started a little inauspiciously when Brigade HQ personnel were so widely scattered that control was being exercised at one stage by the Brigade Commander, Major Tony Harnett, and I sitting under a thorn-bush. Others were dealing with the casualties. Tony was supposed to be an umpire, but he ripped off his armband and badges of rank just in time to impress the American Divisional Commander, Major-General 'Dutch' Kroesen, that he, the 'radio operator' was in touch with everyone – which by some miracle, he was! It was also an instructive exercise, but it came as no surprise to us a year later when the Turkish Parachute Battalion which had exercised in Thrace with us failed to make much progress after it dropped south of Kyrenia, in the Cyprus invasion. No Turkish officer above Captain had jumped; it was considered too dangerous for more senior officers! As a much battered major myself, I felt that perhaps they had a point!

I nearly lost my name, however, when I sent the Guards Independent Company into an heliborne *coup-de-main* operation onto a bridge deep in the enemy's rear during that exercise. I thought it was a master-stroke of tactical improvisation, well suited to the élan and drive of the Guardsmen. However, I had forgotten to tell the umpires! The bridge, as it happened, was very near the Turkish border with Communist Bulgaria, and it was guarded night and day by Turkish soldiers armed with live ammunition. As our gallant heliborne troops roared in nap-of-the-earth, it took those simple Turks a little by surprise, and weapons were cocked. Fortunately, Colonel John Bagnall, formerly our Commanding Officer of 7th RHA when it took on that title, was in the area and saved the day. It could have been rather a nasty international incident and I was obliged to express my thanks to him with a case of the very best champagne when we returned to the UK. Many may have thought that I was let off pretty lightly!

The injury to my back really demanded an end to my sporting career. However, I continued to play some reasonable cricket, for which I suffered, but I also took up dry fly trout fishing again. I joined the Officers' Fishing Syndicate at Bourley Lake in Aldershot and obtained a half rod on the Officers' stretch on the River Dever near Barton Stacey, Hampshire. I thrashed the water with my usual lack of patience, and was not really surprised at my lack of success. On one occasion on the Dever, the boys offered to throw stones at the fish which they could see lying in the clear chalk stream 'laughing at me' as they said. The only consolation I got from my hopeless efforts was the peace and quiet offered by the surroundings to those stretches of water.

I also took up flying, embarking on a PPL course in a primitive light aircraft at Blackbush airport. But I had logged only a few hours when the 1973 Middle East crisis sent the cost of aviation fuel sky-high, and I felt I could no longer afford to continue. It may have been just as well, as my instructor, Mike John, later crash-landed his aircraft in fog and killed himself.

I was very sad to leave 16th Parachute Brigade at the end of the year. The spirit of Airborne troops the world over is incomparable, and I had made some great friends among them. As a Gunner in that appointment I had been treated very kindly by everyone, especially the Parachute Regiment Battalion COs. I had become a fervent advocate of Airborne operations of the type practised by UK JATFOR. I was convinced that the very low level approach to a target area by a stream of Hercules transport aircraft flying in close formation under radar cover, popping up at the last minute to drop their loads, was a perfectly reasonable and viable operation of war. Such tactics were not without their critics, however, especially among those who had not served in Airborne Forces, and who denigrated the whole idea as an expensive pastime reminiscent of World War II. There was a good deal of professional jealousy about in the Army, and many were envious of Airborne Forces' elitism. It was possibly not altogether pure chance that I, a Gunner, with ostensibly no axes to grind, was put in to the key job of Brigade Major at such a time. I was able to look at matters as objectively as anyone, and I became more enthused as time went by. I must admit that I was exceedingly proud of holding this prestigious appointment of Brigade Major of 16th Parachute Brigade, and remain so to this day. My regard for Airborne Forces as a whole remains as strong as it is for the Gunners. The glamour of Airborne Forces never blinded me to their possible shortcomings, and I myself, largely because of the time I spent injured, only completed around 35 or 40 jumps, which was really a very small total compared with those who spent many years with Airborne troops. I felt I did a good job in this Brigade, nothing glorious, but it had been an exciting and satisfying appointment.

But the time had come to move on, as I was to be promoted to Lieutenant Colonel at the first opportunity, indeed ten days before my 37th birthday. I handed over to Major (later General Sir) Michael Rose, whose tour must have been far less fun than mine, as the UK JATFOR role as well as the break-up of 16th Parachute Brigade took place during his tenure in one of those cyclical losses of popularity for Airborne Forces which occur in the wake of all too frequent Defence Reviews

As a family our time in Farnborough had not been without its sadder moments, and in particular when, in January 1973, Linda's father Denis died suddenly of a stroke at the age of 67. He had had a distinguished legal career, being a Senior Bencher in Chancery, but he never spoke of his war-time exploits as a Wing Commander in the intelligence staff of the RAF and SHAEF. He had not long retired from being a Master of the Bench of the Middle Temple and a glowing obituary appeared in the *Daily Telegraph*. A memorial service was held at the Temple Church in London on 27 February 1973. Linda and her four brothers spent some time during the following year helping their mother, Yvonne, to move into a new and smaller house in Camberley.

We ourselves moved house on New Year's Day 1974. It was one of the shortest distances we had ever moved, Farnborough to Camberley, and it was undoubtedly one of the most chaotic moves as a result. My Ford Escort estate car EM484B arrived at No 4 Duke of Cornwall Avenue, Camberley, more festooned with mops and kettles than usual, and certainly more so than was dignified for a member of the Directing Staff at the Army Staff College!

We then had 2½ years of fun and interest. Linda took a part-time job working for a blind solicitor in Camberley – an altogether fascinating experience. All three boys were happily engaged at St Andrew's School, Woking, and I relished teaching young Majors and Captains enormously. It was hardly teaching; it was more like guiding syndicate discussions and play-acting for Presentations on the Alanbrooke Hall stage. I was a member of the Basic Tactics Team – not an onerous task although my learning curve was steep not having been to Camberley as a student myself. But it was all very stimulating. I also got some excellent cricket, playing for the College First XI for the first two summers, and I was Chairman of 'The Owls' social team for the third year. Most enjoyable of all my duties, however, was to lead the Airborne Team on the Battlefield Tour in Normandy in June of each year. Only those who have organised those unforgettable events can understand how rewarding they were.

My valued ally in matters Airborne at Staff College was my old chum Julian Thompson who joined the Staff at Camberley shortly after me. One day we learnt that changes in the syllabus were being considered to ease the pressure on the programme. The Deputy Commandant had suggested that the time devoted to studying what were called 'Out of Area Operations', that is Operations outside NATO, was to be severely pruned. The précis for which I was responsible on Airborne Forces would in future only be issued to students without any programme time for discussion. Julian and I were incensed, firmly believing that if there is only one thing which is certain in politics and war it is that the unexpected will happen. Very grudgingly, Brigadier Tim Morony acceded to our arguments, something which he was not renowned for doing very often, but we had staked our commissions on the outcome of our discussion with him, we were so upset. So some instruction remained. Thank God it did! Eight years later, when Julian was sailing into the South Atlantic prior to recapturing the Falkland Islands, I sent him a signal saying 'How right we were!' I suspect it was little comfort to him, at the time, though!

While supposedly examining the future of the 6th Airborne Division part of the Battlefield Tour and the availability of guest speakers – a

simple task bearing in mind the youthfulness of most of the participants
in that Division in 1944 – I had a term 'swinging', as it was quaintly
called. My task swiftly completed, I spent the rest of the term buying and
furnishing our first house. It was a brand new semi-detached house on
the edge of an estate. It had four bedrooms and a lovely view over the
park in Warminster. It cost £10,500 and we scrounged all sorts of odd
bits of furniture, mostly from a second-hand furniture shop in Warminster called Welch & Arnoldi, a Wilton off-cut fitted carpet, and curtains
which Linda made; all this for the princely sum of £600! We chose
Warminster simply because prices were cheap there and the proximity
of the Army's School of Infantry might mean plentiful, well supervised
letting opportunities. It was just habitable, and we let it through a local
estate agent as soon as we decently could. It was a sound investment, and
our friendly insurance agent was quite right when he predicted that it
would prove a better way of achieving our forthcoming school-fees
targets than the insurances we had taken out for that purpose years before
and which were rapidly being made worthless by inflation.

The reader will recall that the boys had been registered for three good
West Country schools at birth; Exeter School, Blundell's and Allhallows.
We paid a visit to Exeter while we were at Camberley and found the
future of the boarding element in some doubt, so, as with the future
assistance of grandparents ever in mind, we needed to have the boys
located in the south-east of England, we switched our allegiance to
Wellington College. To the relief of my bank manager, all three boys
gained scholarships to that famous school in due course.

These years between 1974 and 1976 were particularly happy ones for
the family, and I look back at snaps of the boys in our family photograph
album of those years with the greatest of pleasure and satisfaction. The
boys looked a delight, generally dressed alike or similarly. My mother had
knitted identical woollen polo-necked sweaters for them, first brown
ones and then heather mixture, and in summer they would often be
wearing those useful and hard-wearing German leather shorts which we
called *Lederhosen* but which were not the traditional Bavarian type of
coarse long shorts with decorated bracers, but soft dark green leather,
tight at the waist, very short, which showed off their sturdy legs. I'm not
sure if the boys entirely liked them as they were 'different', but they were
practical, hard-wearing and easily washed when dirty. Whatever they
were wearing, they looked fit, healthy and happy. They were a great
credit to their mother's caring upbringing, and were our pride and joy.

(Left to right) Jonathan, Richard and David, Farnborough

After enduring two terms at the local primary school, Lorraines on the edge of the Old Dean council estate, Jonathan at last joined his brothers at St Andrews. We have a splendid photograph of the three of them at this time dressed smartly in their school uniform of green caps, blazers and grey shorts. I tend to agree with those who regard it a pity that fashions change and boys of this age nowadays wear long trousers, often scruffy jeans and trainers. Then, in 1975 and 1976, our three lads were all thriving at school, doing well at sports and work. More we could not have wished for them. I recall what fun I had during frequent walks with the three of them on Barossa Common which lay immediately beside our Quarter. We named various landmarks along the paths there in accordance with items in the *Winnie the Pooh* books. A certain track junction would be known as Pooh Corner, a prominent tree, Eyeore's Tree and so on. Imagine how beneficial this 'code' was later when they were doing CCF exercises on the Common from Wellington. They knew the terrain like the back of their hands, sufficiently to come in first in any competition.

During the summer of 1974 my mother, still living at Cheam, celebrated her 70th birthday. It was a fine day that 3 July, and there was a grand gathering of the clans, with numerous photographs taken of her surrounded by her children and grandchildren in the garden. It must have been a very happy day for her. My elder sister Diana was there with her husband, schoolmaster Christopher Everest, and their three children, Lucinda, Simon and Jenny-Louise. My second sister, Margaret, known as Maggie, had joined us from Zambia, together with her second husband, John Bather. The Bather family line was extensively listed in Burke's *Landed Gentry* 1969, and John's ancestors were also Welsh ('ab Atha'). Their two sons, Matthew and Sebastian, born in Africa, were also present. The latter served later with the Gurkhas, secured a degree in Japanese at Cambridge before retiring as a Major and joining Cap Gemini, the worldwide management consultancy firm.

Later that summer we took a short holiday in Devon, staying with dear old Aunt Winifred, 'Pin', at her seventeenth-century Rectory known as Brookdale in North Huish. She had been a life-long spinster until she married Sammy Foster Deacon who owned Brookdale, a wonderful country house with twelve bedrooms, set in a lovely valley garden with a babbling brook running through it. Sadly he died of cancer within a few years of their marriage, and Pin lived alone in this rambling house, accompanied only by her black Alsatian. She spent much time and energy rushing from room to room with buckets, trying to catch the water which leaked through the deteriorating roof with ever increasing frequency. But we had fun there that August with the boys, going to the seaside at Bantham and Thurlestone, tramping over Dartmoor's Three Bridges, Hay Tor, Brent Tor and Dartmeet. We then took Pin with us to Brixham, but while trudging up a steep and cobbled road, Linda said she was having some difficulty walking. Her left leg seemed to be weak. We returned to Brookdale, and just before dinner I heard a yell from upstairs and, dashing up the broad staircase, I came across Linda lying on the floor, having slipped on the mat covering the linoleum surface of the landing. Brave as ever, she said it was nothing, and later went to bed pretending the ever-increasing swelling around her ankle didn't exist. It was August Bank Holiday weekend, and not a good day for going to hospital, but since she was unable to sleep all night and there was a distinct possibility that the ankle was broken, we went to Torquay General Hospital the next day. After interminable waiting, she was duly X-rayed and encased in plaster. She hobbled around on plaster and stick for several weeks thereafter, and in retrospect, this leg was probably showing the first signs of the weakness that later beset her, of which more anon.

During our 2½ years at Camberley, we made, as ever, a number of good friends among our DS colleagues. James Templer, with whom I had joined the Army, lived next to us in Duke of Cornwall Avenue, and cavalryman Tony Mullens (later Lieutenant General Sir Anthony) lived opposite. It is an endearing feature of Service life that one is constantly meeting up again with old friends. It was during our time in Camberley too, that our first acquaintances were made with German officers, both at the College and in the Embassy in London, which was to pay dividends later. Among the students were Majors Schmoldt and Spiering, on the staff was Oberstleutnant Berthold Schenk Graf von Stauffenberg, and at the Embassy Major Christoph von Plato.

Shortly before the end of my last term on the Directing Staff I was obliged to attend a short Commanding Officers' Course at Larkhill. We were reminded of everything one needed to command a multi-million pound regiment, from how to spot poor accounting to how to plan a nuclear attack. The latter involved use of 'damage radii templates' and 'tables of desired effects' such as how far one wanted to have 'tree-blow-down' while minimising radiation problems to one's own troops. I have to admit the whole process left me cold. I simply could not believe that using weapons somewhat larger than those that had obliterated Hiroshima and Nagasaki was ever a practical possibility on a battlefield in Europe. I suppose that we had to go through the process, however, as part of a meaningful nuclear deterrent, known at that time as 'Mutually Assured Destruction', aptly known as 'MAD'. A lighter and yet valuable session on the Course was provided by a Quartermaster who disclosed to the embryonic COs many of the secrets of their nefarious trade! These amusements aside, the company was also good, as seven of us on the Course had been together in 24 The Irish Battery as Gunners in 1954: James Templer, John Biles, Tommy Tucker, Tony Weston, Tim Thompson, Iain Jack and me. We had our photo taken at Woolwich, the caption to which was exaggeratingly 'The Magnificent Seven'!

Returning to Camberley for the end of term I elected to go on my third Battlefield Tour as Directing Staff. Linda and the boys joined me in Normandy for a few days' holiday after the Tour was over and we then went straight on, in our newly-acquired, second-hand, brown Vauxhall Victor which was to be registered by British Forces Germany as MQ653B, to join the regiment to which I was posted as CO – 26th Field Regiment – once more in Dortmund! En route, the car developed a strange asthmatic wheeze when under pressure, as if sensing the turgid air of the Ruhr Valley, if not the trials and tribulations which lay ahead.

CHAPTER 10

Commanding Catastrophes

THE 26TH FIELD REGIMENT RA was known as a 'good' regiment, not brilliant and dashing, but professionally sound. I visited the officers' posting branch in Stanmore to find out what the 'officer plot' was, that is, which officers were due to leave and who was to take their places in the near future. The three Battery Commanders were Major Nick Bird in charge of 16 (Sandham's Company) Field Battery RA, Alan Gordon (elder brother of James) at the helm of 17 (Corunna) Field Battery RA and Paul d'Apice leading 159 (Colenso) Field Battery RA. They had all done well under my predecessor, David Goodman, and, although they all admired him and were loyal to his memory, to give these officers their due, they were to transfer their allegiance to me equally impressively. However, Alan and Paul were due to leave for pastures new quite soon and I looked down the list of possible contenders for these coveted positions. I chose Majors David Gay, who had been in 16th Parachute Brigade, and Andrew Cattaway who was a highly talented all-round officer whom I had known at Oxford University when he was taking a languages degree there. The postings officer told me that it was somewhat 'irregular' for a CO to 'choose' his Battery Commanders in this way. If it didn't go well then it could be bad both for the CO and for the officers concerned. I am glad to say that it worked perfectly, from both points of view.

The Director, Royal Artillery, Major General Tim Morony, saw me in his Woolwich office prior to my departure for the Continent. He said: '26th Field Regiment is a good regiment, a happy family and it is on the crest of a wave.' He had very little else to say and I was not at all encouraged. I wondered whether he meant that the wave was a breaker or one a long way from the shore gaining momentum. I was determined, if not inspired, to make it the latter.

David Goodman, my predecessor, had indeed had a successful tour in command. The regiment had had a good tour in Northern Ireland by all accounts, and he had moved the regiment with its three Batteries of somewhat archaic 105 mm 'Abbot' self-propelled guns from Larkhill to Dortmund. Once there, he had concentrated on enhancing the Regiment's already fine reputation for technical expertise in gunnery, and on forging close links with the Guards' Armoured Brigade for whom the regiment provided direct artillery support. He left for a staff job in Hong Kong in euphoric mood.

Within a few days of my arrival this euphoria rebounded on me in a most uncomfortable way. The Gunner Brigadier at Divisional HQ called me to say that my predecessor had, in his view, overgraded all the Warrant Officers in their annual confidential reports. He required me to rewrite them, downgrading them all one notch. I could not imagine how any staff officer could have given the Brigadier such extraordinary advice, but it was a course of action wholly at variance with the Military Secretary's guidelines and one which put me in an impossible position. If I told my Warrant Officers of the Brigadier's wishes they would at once lose faith in my ability to stand up for them. If, however, the Brigadier was right in saying they were all too highly graded, then, when it came to my writing their annual reports, I would have no option but to down-grade them myself, again failing to win universal acclaim! Either way I was the loser! I therefore invited the Brigadier to come down and speak to the Warrant Officers himself.

He was very cross, but down he came. I took him to my office and politely told him that if it was too complicated to get hold of David Goodman in Hong Kong to make any changes, then gradings would have to stay as they were. To reinforce the point, I then produced the RSM, who, most respectfully but firmly, told the Brigadier that his action would simply not be understood by any of the Warrant Officers concerned, and he strongly advised against it. The Brigadier withdrew and I dismissed the assembled Warrant Officers, much to their relief and mine! What a start!

As it turned out, the Brigadier was right about those gradings. The RSM himself was embarrassed to find that Goodman had recommended him for a commission. He told me most emphatically that he wanted no such thing! He was right too. A few weeks later, that Brigadier, who was a very keen horseman, came down to say farewell to the regiment. I thought it would be a nice gesture to provide him with a horse from the Garrison stables so that he could ride out of the barracks, in the way it is often customary in the Army for departing senior officers to be driven out on an unusual form of transport. I warned him beforehand that he would be expected to ride, and I believe he thought I was joking. Nevertheless, all went according to plan, except that when he had addressed the troops and was just about to ride away, the RSM called the parade to give the good Brigadier three cheers. The cheers, echoing around the barrack square, startled the horse so much that it reared and bucked and tried to throw its somewhat anxious rider off. I am happy to relate that the Brigadier held his seat splendidly, but he was not entirely amused.

Brigadiers could be the bane of a CO's life in BAOR. I found that I had three to answer to: my Brigade Commander, my Garrison Commander and my Divisional Artillery Commander. All three made demands upon the regiment's manpower and time, often conflicting demands too. We had to accept far too many commitments which led to 'over-stretch', in the contemporary jargon. On one occasion the Garrison Commander asked me at short notice to provide a demonstration of equipment for a party of visiting Members of Parliament from London. The demonstration would take place on an already promised regimental holiday. Not only had extra time to be found to polish up all the equipment to display standard, but the soldiers concerned had to cancel their holiday plans. It was the last straw on this occasion during a particularly hectic period of training and administrative commitments. I appealed to my Divisional Artillery Commander who agreed with me, and he took it to the Corps Artillery Commander who hesitated a few days, agreed with my sentiments – and then told me to get on with it! The Garrison Commander thought I was 'whingeing' and un-cooperative. I was furious because it mucked the soldiers about. We produced, needless to say, a super demonstration, and there was no hint of the soldiers' disgruntlement.

I harboured few illusions about the chances of emulating my predecessor's success in such circumstances. And that was before I heard of the Army's plans for 'Restructuring'. Influenced by ever-tighter Defence budgets, it was decided to dispense with a complete level of command in the 1st British Corps in Germany. Ignoring the lessons of history, the MoD narrowly came down in favour of abolishing the Brigade HQ level. Instead, Divisions were to comprise a loose association of battalion-sized formations grouped together as necessary as 'Task Forces'. 26th Field Regiment's future was to be one of two dissimilar mixed artillery regiments in General Support of a Division. It was to expand considerably, taking on 76 (Maude's) Heavy Battery RA, a nuclear howitzer battery with its attendant US Army nuclear ordnance troop, 'M' (Swingfire) anti-tank guided missile Battery of the Royal

Horse Artillery, and a large increment in technical personnel for the REME Workshop to support this diverse assortment of weapons. To complicate matters still further, 'M' Battery RHA was to have two separate chains of command. It would retain an allegiance to the rump headquarters of its original host regiment, 3rd Regiment RHA, for tactical matters while coming under me for administration. This was a recipe for disaster, and so it proved, with poor Louis Wilkes (younger brother of Mike) finding his loyalties often confused. The nuclear battery was to be commanded by Major Warwick King-Martin, a very practical and forthright officer, whose main difficulty lay in expressing himself in writing, which, considering the complex staff problems with which he was going to have to wrestle, could have been a major disadvantage.

My first task was to study the staff proposals for the composition and accommodation of the nuclear battery. I wholly disagreed with the staff proposals! The idea that the battery could be manned by drawing people from all the batteries of the Royal Artillery held no appeal at all, as one could easily foresee a collection of everyone else's cast-offs. I worked with the Divisional and Corps Artillery staffs fairly amicably to get that plan largely altered. My accommodation plan, however, required the Garrison staff to alter their plan for major relocations, and the occupation of my splendid regimental headquarters building by the Garrison staff! I put my case for minimising upheaval and inconvenience to my sorely tried troops to the Garrison commander direct and he acquiesced. It was, however, not until later that I knew it was another nail in the coffin of 'unco-operative' Pughe!

I soon set about trying to balance the administrative nightmares through which the regiment was being put with 'fun' events. For instance, the regiment had at one time been renowned for its prowess at tug-of-war, and I restarted the inter-battery competition in this sport, which was to boost morale and hold long-term benefits when the regiment took part in international events. Inter-Battery boxing was revived, and I attempted to lay greater emphasis on sport and fitness. Indeed the whole regiment was required to go for a cross-country run at least once per week, which proved a shock for some of the less fit. I took part myself at the risk of being regarded a 'fitness fanatic' for I was determined to ensure that, whatever was thrown at the regiment professionally, we were healthy and fit enough to excel at it. I got the distinct impression that Alan Gordon thought that running was 'un-officer-like' and might 'alarm the troops', but it was only a pose and he took part as loyally as any with his long shorts and dignified stride. He was soon to leave the regiment, and we all missed him, but Andrew Cattaway took over Corunna Battery very competently, and, when David Gay arrived to take over Sandham's, Nick Bird moved to headquarters to become my exceptionally loyal and effective regimental Second in Command

With the reorganisation at its height I was told that I was to take the regiment for a four-month emergency tour in Northern Ireland. We were to return to the area of Armagh in which the regiment had served under my predecessor. This time, however, I foresaw the possibility of having an extra battery deployed. The nuclear battery would be formed and in station by the New Year and it should then begin its technical nuclear training. The US Army Ordnance Detachment, however, was months behind the play. I visited the US Army Ordnance HQ and, reading between the lines, I could tell that they would not be operationally ready to support my new battery for another nine months. It was only therefore necessary for me to get special dispensation from Corps to keep it in a conventional non-nuclear stance for its first year, and thereby have the option of taking it to Northern Ireland. 26 Regiment was also the first among Field Gunner regiments to have a female assistant adjutant – the lovely Lieutenant Gill Hayden. I obtained permission to take her to Northern Ireland with us – also a first – where she was to undertake some important operational and intelligence tasks most impressively.

Keeping my fingers crossed, I went to Portadown in April to do a preliminary reconnaissance of our operational tasks and area. The Brigade Commander gave me a very short interview from which the only impression I received was that he was possibly a sick and tired man. I spent much time, instead, with his Brigade Major, 'H' Jones, a like-minded officer of the Parachute Regiment, who was later to win a posthumous VC in the Falkland Islands.

Philosophising, we agreed that we were not beating the terrorists in Ulster, and instead of patrolling aimlessly, bumbling around in Land Rovers providing the IRA with ample targets, we should adopt less overt tactics to keep them guessing. In 1964, in his book *Guerrilla Warfare*, the EOKA leader General Grivas had pointed to shortcomings in British anti-terrorist methods in the 1955–59 Cyprus campaign. He said: 'It is only by constantly being alert and maintaining great stealth that the cats will be able to spot the mice and catch them at the moment when they emerge. We always stood in fear of the lurking cat.' I was mindful of this advice from so successful a terrorist as Grivas, and although there was no proof that the IRA followed EOKA methods, the principles, I considered, still applied. I was determined to go for stealth, and to set poacher against poacher.

At the back of my mind was the extra battery I was hoping to bring to the area, and I straightway offered him a complete battery trained in 'close observation', a scale of effort seldom, if ever, before devoted to this task by a single regiment or battalion. I had no idea where I would get all the necessary equipment needed for so many covert OPs, but I was excited by the challenge and opportunity. I felt certain that we could find, in a Gunner regiment, sufficient volunteers from among the well-trained artillery OP parties to provide a sound basis for my optimism.

I was not to be disappointed. Major David Gay, now commanding 16 Battery, was given the task to raise and train a complete battery of covert OPs. He sought advice from the SAS and 3rd Battalion The Parachute Regiment, begged, borrowed and stole the necessary equipment and radios, and got down to serious training at the beginning of May. The Standing Operating Procedures he devised and produced lacked any substantial precedent but were a model for many later to follow. Volunteers of exceptionally good quality for this exciting but risky role were not in short supply.

It is not easy to convert a Regiment of Gunners used to armoured warfare into skilful infantrymen in a few months. It is not so much a question of their not being able to master the weapon skills and fieldcraft, as one of instilling in them the infantry frame of mind. Out on foot patrol men must learn to react instinctively, as an infantryman does, to emergencies. This is not always achieved. I recalled that, in County Fermanagh in 1971, it was sod's law that dictated that my least adaptable Bombardier was the Patrol Commander when Corporal Powell was killed in the ambush not far from Lisgoole School. At the sight of blood his instinct was to dash to help the victim, allowing the terrorist a clear run to the border. In training, the correct reaction to an ambush had been impressed on him time and time again but it never became *instinctive* to him. An NCO who learns his profession as a self-propelled gun commander is not necessarily always the best man to lead a dismounted infantry patrol in action. However, it can be done and I trained my regiment day and night for three months to make them rank among the best infantrymen in the business. I nearly despaired of the young officers at times, but little by little we mastered rural as well as urban anti-terrorist tactics.

As a slight diversion from this important training, the regiment was tasked to participate in the massive parade for HM The Queen's Jubilee visit to BAOR. For this purpose we were 'loaned' to 4th Armoured Division whose GOC, Major General Nigel Bagnall, was later to become Chief of the General Staff. I regarded it as a great honour, and we worked hard between IS training sessions, to polish the guns and rehearse the mounted parade manoeuvres. I had never been on such a large parade of armour before, nor have I since. It was certainly a contrast to the 'Farewell to 4th Guards Brigade' parade on which I had led the regiment on first arrival, when the Brigade Commander and his headquarters staff rather quaintly rode about on horseback! Staff work for this larger and more ambitious wholly armoured event, however, as it affected 26th Field Regiment, was complicated by our being owned by one Division and being on loan to another.

Firstly there was the emotive subject of Jubilee Medals. The Regiment was given a quota of thirteen, and names were submitted up the normal chain of command. Somehow, however, the allocation was tied to a different chain, and not all those whom I had recommended eventually received one. In particular, Gunner Alfie Risden, the oldest serving Gunner in the Regiment (and probably in the whole Royal Artillery), failed to feature in the final allocation. I was rather upset, since in an idle conversation one day with this normally inebriated but loyal man, I had promised him some form of recognition for his 35 years service.

Having failed him with a medal, however, I promised him I would introduce him to Her Majesty on the great day. He was thrilled with the prospect and he almost vowed to stay sober for a few days beforehand! Yet it would not prove easy to get him an audience, as tickets for the Royal Enclosure had already been allocated by the staff. Fortunately, I discovered that a key staff officer concerned with the arrangements had been a student of mine at Camberley, and he 'fiddled' an extra ticket for me. The only difficulty would be concealing until the last possible moment on the day that my 'informal group' of twelve people would actually be thirteen!

On the great day – the 7th day of the 7th month of 1977 – early rain had damped the dust of the Sennelager Bowl down a little. The sun then shone, and Her Majesty witnessed one of the most glittering and impressive armoured parades many had ever seen. The parade ended with a magnificent drive-past, throwing up clouds of acrid smoke and dust into the eyes of the spectators. Those, like myself, who were obliged to ride with their heads out of the top of an Armoured Personnel Carrier, following in the wake of a few tank regiments, were covered from head to waist in black dust.

At the end of the runway I had to jump off my vehicle while it was still moving at considerable speed, dash through the line of thundering armour, and dive behind a bush where my driver/batman was pre-positioned. As I stripped off, he threw a bucket of cold water over me. At that precise moment, a helicopter zoomed overhead taking pictures! I then quickly dressed into my blue Full Dress uniform, jumped into the staff car and sped away to join Linda in the Royal Enclosure. I arrived breathless and hot, but was glad to find Gunner Alfie Risden, escorted by two stern-looking Warrant Officers, waiting in the wings.

Just before Her Majesty entered the enclosure, the two Warrant Officers propelled Gunner Risden forward to join my group – and it was

Gunner Risden meets Her Majesty 7/7/77

too late for objections! The Queen graciously spoke to each group in turn, but when she reached mine, Gunner Risden so captivated her that she spent nearly twenty minutes with us to the considerable irritation of the groups behind me. Nevertheless, I had fulfilled my promise to that great man, Gunner Risden, the salt of the earth in many ways, and I was content.

I was also tickled, myself, in commemoration of the Jubilee, to receive my second little medal ribbon! It was not awarded for any especially glorious deed, however!

And so we put our big guns away and returned to IS training. My Close Observation Battery exercised in the local countryside, quite contrary to regulations. But it was excellent practice for the OP parties to have to creep into a German village in the dead of night and get into the roof of a house or barn without disturbing dogs and cattle, there to remain undetected for days. We enjoyed the wholehearted support of the local population, and their generosity was not forgotten when we returned from Ulster the following spring. At about this time I lost Nick Bird as Second-in-Command as he was to be sent to an important Gunnery Instructor's post on well-deserved promotion. I had made his life quite difficult over the time he had so nobly supported me by sending him a veritable flood of pink memorandum slips day after day with endless requests and suggestions in them. When it came to his being dined out in the Mess he ended a most amusing valedictory speech by pulling out months' worth of pink slips that he had kept and torn up, and threw them across the dining-room in an unforgettable shower of confetti. I reckon he had the last laugh on me.

Somehow, in the early summer, Linda and I found the time to snatch a few days leave in England, to attend David's last Speech Day at St Andrew's School. He had been Head Boy in his last year and was awarded a scholarship to Wellington College. That day in the athletics he also won the sprint on stilts in an astonishingly fast time that probably stands to this day as a record.

I also found time, somehow in early July, to lead the regimental team in the Njimegen Marches. Not many COs do that, and I must admit to feeling my years after each day's 55 km speed march on hard roads. I would collapse into bed at 9 p.m. and stay there until 5 a.m. when we set out again. My team of fit young soldiers, however, would submit to two hours sleep, recover their strength miraculously and head for the delights down-town! I always enjoyed being with the lads, and the following summer I recall a weekend out in the Sauerland countryside with a small group of potential officers, leading them through a challenging physical course. Nobody could have doubted my paratrooper passion for exercise and the open countryside.

However it was not all plain sailing in that hard hot summer of IS training. Like many units, we had our fair share of 'negligent' discharges from rifles during the first few days of the final period of training, when blank rounds were first carried and the live-firing period on the ranges was intense. I had driven the regiment very hard and they were exceptionally tired when a spate of live 'ND's occurred. The normal rule was to give exemplary punishments to such offenders and place them in the guardroom for a lengthy spell. I was anxious, however, for such people to obtain more training, not less, and for them not to miss the final crucial days' exercises.

So I was more lenient than people expected, but for the first, and last, time in my Service, I had a major sense of humour failure when I discovered that within days a whispering campaign had begun around the regiment that the only explanation was that the CO must have had an 'ND' himself! I called in the Majors and the RSM and expressed my dismay over this and they swiftly dealt with the rumour-mongers. I can only say in hindsight, that my attitude was probably in the end effective, for we had no 'ND's at all in the whole of our four months' operations in Northern Ireland, a record many units might envy.

So at last we went to Northern Ireland, leaving some REME personnel and the two Quartermasters behind to prepare for the arrival of the fifth battery while we were away. On arrival at Aldergrove airport I was met by a staff officer. He had been sent by the new Brigade Commander to tell me that I was to use the additional troops that I was bringing to man a Permanent Vehicle Check Point on the border at Aughnacloy! That was not the role for which I had spent months of hard work training my covert OP parties. As the nuclear battery would be fully stretched providing the Maze Prison Guard force, and I required one battery at Portadown and another with regimental HQ at Lurgan, there was no fat to spare for a new task requiring 25 men at no notice!

Nevertheless, the hallmark of a good operational commander is flexibility in the face of the unexpected so I acquiesced. I knew that it would take some time for the RUC to devise sufficient tasks for all my OPs anyway, so there was no real difficulty in sending half the covert OP force to Aughnacloy for a while. They took turns with a few men from the Portadown battery after the first week, and after a month or so, the success of the covert OP operations and their popularity with the RUC and Special Branch was such that my plea for reinforcements was answered by Brigade. A prison near Ballykelly was to be closed and some Royal Signals personnel were given to me. I deployed them to guard the Maze prison, to relieve Major Warwick King-Martin's nuclear men of some of the boredom of that thankless task. So eventually the Aughnacloy task became easier to handle, being shared between the Portadown and Maze batteries. In addition Warwick was able to carry out some useful patrolling in the country south of the Maze, and also provide reinforcements for Belfast and Portadown on occasions.

Once or twice my covert OPs were 'compromised' by some mischance. Children playing in an empty house caused one such discovery. But, disappointed as we always were at the time, in several cases I feel sure their discovery unnerved the IRA and the vicinity of the compromised OP went quiet for the rest of our tour. Such was not the aim, however, and many an OP remained undetected for very long periods in some freezing attic or other, providing the police with invaluable evidence for later arrests; success which was not fully acknowledged by the Brigade Commander until many months after I had left the province and the regiment!

One covert operation I recall, however, was a catastrophe on the same scale of the Rosscor Bridge incident of my Battery Commander days. The Special Branch gave me a hot tip one night that a pub bombing was to take place the following night at a certain place in Portadown. They were so sure of the intelligence that they knew almost exactly when the deed would be perpetrated, the colour of the motor-cycle on which the terrorist would ride, and the direction from which he would come. Major David Gay duly set up a hasty ambush in the back of an old van which was parked opposite the target pub. There had been no time in which to find OPs in any of the occupied buildings in that street, and there seemed no better alternative to the van idea. The RUC promised to provide the 'long-stops' in case the terrorist made a run for it before we could stop him. David led the ambush himself and, in a deliberate display of nonchalance in case the IRA were watching me, I took off for a walk in the hills with the RSM, confident that all was as well as could be in the time available.

Twenty minutes before the appointed hour I was back in the Lurgan Operations Room and it began to lash with rain. The next report I had from David Gay was not the codeword for success that I had expected, but a muddled message saying a pursuit was being conducted as the man had got away. It transpired that the heavy rain had made the terrorist change his plan at the last moment. Instead of riding in on a motor-bike from the north he walked in from the south. He casually threw a grenade into the surreptitiously emptied pub while our ambush party were still looking north out of the confines of the van. On hearing the explosion, David's men leapt from the van and chased the terrorist through a crowded street of late afternoon shoppers, from time to time getting in an ill-aimed shot! To cap it all, the RUC long-stops failed to prevent the terrorist from making a clean getaway.

The only consolation from this disastrous affair was later to find a pistol lying in the road along the terrorist's escape route and spots of blood along the pavement, though these were rapidly dissolving in the torrential rain.

The RUC were as speechless with rage as we were ashamed. Their criticism of our bungling was in no way disguised, and for the only time in my tour, my excellent relations with the RUC were somewhat, and quite justifiably, soured.

Two days later, the RUC Superintendent came to me wreathed in smiles. The trail of blood had been followed up carefully, and many enquiries were made among local people. They led to the terrorist's hideout in a flat beyond the bridge in Portadown where two more suspects were found hiding too. Had we killed that terrorist, of course, these two suspects would not have been found. But professionally, it was small consolation for us, and I never lived to forget the tactical lessons from that botched ambush!

Again, it would be possible to write a complete book about that tour of Northern Ireland from November 1977 to February 1978. We were shot at and bombed and kept very busy. We tried every ruse in the book to corner the terrorists, but succeeded mainly in driving them to ground. We arrested a lot of people and made some sensational finds of weapons and explosives. Our final operation was a major cordon and search in Portadown, using a company of infantry as well as three sub-units of our own. This operation, at greater than battalion strength, was admirably commanded by my battery commander in Portadown, Andrew Catt-away, and good experience it was for him too.

Throughout the Regiment's absence in Northern Ireland Linda fulfilled the invaluable and demanding role of 'counsellor' to the worried wives left behind in Dortmund. She coped admirably with some awkward 'welfare' cases too, and kept me abreast of any problems in the Garrison that might affect the men's performance in action. The rear party also ran a driving course for the wives, much to some husbands' dismay. But it was short-lived as the car bought for the purpose somehow suffered a comprehensive crash just outside the barrack gates!

At the end of the tour the regiment received five awards, which was considerably more than most units received at that time. I was exceedingly proud of them and returned to Dortmund tired but very happy. I later wrote a book, under the *nom de plume* of Neville Hughes, as a tribute to the exploits of our Close Observation soldiers. It was entitled *Ulster Snapshot* and, though factual, for security reasons it was thinly disguised as a novel.

Sadly my happiness was not to last long back in the turmoil of a reorganising BAOR. I found myself in yet another Division under a new and dynamic General Officer Commanding (GOC). A Gunner regiment needs three weeks leave after an Ulster tour followed by a six-week uncommitted period in which to retrain men in gunnery. The GOC, for some unknown reason, felt that he could not wait that long, and while many of my men were still in England on courses, he called us out on a short-notice 'readiness' exercise. How we managed to direct the shells onto the unfamiliar Sennelager Artillery Range safely and without damage to ourselves or the local population remains a mystery to this day. But our half-trained gun crews managed creditably in the circumstances. The protests of the Gunnery staff and my Divisional Commander Royal Artillery (CRA) (a post reduced in the reorganisation from Brigadier to Colonel) fell on deaf ears.

We did have one pleasurable interlude, however, on return to BAOR. I was invited to send one of my Batteries to the live firing range in Canada. David Gay took 16 Battery there and performed magnificently. I flew over to visit his final exercise which was a thumping success, despite a spectacular fall in temperature one October day, when we were sweltering in shirt-sleeves one moment and two hour's later it was snowing. The Battery completed the visit to Canada with some adventure training at Banff in the Canadian Rockies, while I made off to the far north-west to visit my Uncle Neville Goss, a fine old soldier who had been badly shot up in the First World War, losing an eye in the process, and who had now retired to Victoria, Vancouver. It was an unforgettable excursion.

Back in Dortmund, our new GOC of the 3rd Division then came to a Guest Night in my Mess. He asked me how I felt about Northern Ireland, and I told him honestly that it was the best training for young officers and NCOs that was going these days. He frowned, and said that All-Arms training in Germany was more important really. I remarked that people's lives were at stake in Ulster, however, and men considered that more important. I thought that he might leave the table, he seemed so angry. He had not commanded in Ulster, although he had done so with distinction with the Parachute Regiment in Aden many years before.

He came again some weeks later, at my invitation to see something of our in-barracks training. He arrived at the Guardroom twenty minutes early and then expressed his dissatisfaction that nobody seemed ready to greet him formally. I had introduced a March-and-Shoot competition in the regiment, in which teams of 16 men from every sub-unit marched ten miles at high speed and then were required to shoot on the range at the end. Points were awarded for the teams' speed on the march and their accuracy at shooting. I invited the GOC to change into combat clothing, about which he had been previously warned, but which also appeared to annoy him, and we then travelled over the course in a helicopter. By mischance from overhead in poor visibility we only saw two teams marching, which further added to the GOC's displeasure. On the range subsequently, he seized a soldier's rifle from his shoulder as he was about to fire, and roared at him that he was holding it incorrectly. He stormed off the range and went back to his HQ breathing fire. Strangely, I don't recall his commenting on our principal activities at the time, namely preparing for the re-equipment of the gun batteries with 155 mm M109 howitzers and the taking of nuclear readiness tests by 76 Battery! Quite substantial projects!

Finally I asked the good GOC to attend our first Novices' Boxing Evening – always an evening of good fun and intense competitive spirit in any unit. I thought it would be nice if he shared the prizegiving with me at the end of each bout. That didn't please him; he wanted to do it all. I gave way to his wishes. At the end of the last bout he and I stood in the ring and announced to the regiment that the General would soon be leaving BAOR and that we should thank him for all the help he had given us. We gave him three hearty cheers and his scowls grew greater still when he was caught halfway through the ropes as the national anthem was being played. I never saw him again in Germany.

But I also continued to suffer misunderstandings with the Garrison Commander! I had especially asked the MoD to appoint an old friend of mine, Major Bill Winchester, as my new technical quartermaster. He had been my Battery Captain in Imjin Battery and he was a keen horseman and a live wire. I told him that I wanted him to take over the garrison stables when he had been in station for a few weeks, but to be sure that he didn't do so until he was wholly satisfied that the accounts were in good order. Imagine, therefore, my amazement when I was summoned from an exercise to explain to the Garrison Commander, a rather serious Gunner Brigadier, why I had given Major Winchester an order not to take over the stables! Stables can be an emotive subject in the Gunners, and many a good officer's reputation has been lost over them.

Some weeks later my adjutant was telephoned by a number of staff officers at Garrison HQ and divisional HQ asking for facts and figures about courts martial and petty crime. My regiment, particularly since returning from the excitement of Ulster operations to the peacetime frustrations of BAOR, had not behaved perfectly, but per capita, our 'crime' rate was very much less than any other unit in the Division. However, as we were the largest unit by far, we had the largest total 'crime' figures. In fact, of all the units I have ever met, 26 Field Regiment was one of the best behaved, happiest and contented regiments it has been my privilege to know.

Eventually I asked the CRA, a super chap called John Howarth, what all the fuss was about. The GOC had apparently been asking questions. Colonel John invited me to see him. He told me that he was about to write my annual confidential report. I had expected a high *Excellent* grading and an OBE. He told me the GOC was after my blood and wanted to give me at best a *Very Good* grading. Such a disappointing grading was supported by the Garrison Commander because he considered me 'unco-operative' at times! In fact, John Howarth bravely stuck to his guns, and gave me an *Excellent* grading anyway, but my prospects of reaching the rank of General were irrevocably damaged by written comments added by the GOC which amounted to my being 'damned with faint praise'.

I decided that I would anyway leave my regiment in a blaze of pageant if not glory. Keeping my fingers crossed that 'Colenso' Day in December would stay fine, I laid on a major mounted parade of the whole regiment followed by a Reception in the Mess, and large numbers of British and German guests were invited. The parade, with almost every armoured vehicle in the Regiment sweeping past the saluting base in fine style, though slightly under-rehearsed, went off very well. Major General Geoffrey Wilson, the senior Gunner at HQ 1 British Corps, took the salute and afterwards he wrote in a very kindly and appreciative fashion to me:

> Thank you for inviting Fay and me to your Colenso Day Parade and luncheon, and for asking me to take the Parade which was both a great honour and a real pleasure. The Parade and Drive Past was *outstanding* and all those who took part in it have every reason to feel proud of their achievement. As I tried to indicate in my address, however, you have so much to be proud of in what has been achieved by the Regiment in the past two tremendously busy years and I congratulate you on this.

Likewise, Colonel John Howarth wrote:

> What a splendid way to go! I congratulate you on arranging your departure to coincide with Colenso Day and holding of such a splendid parade to celebrate the occasion. I, along with everyone else, thought that the bearing of the soldiers on parade, their turnout and that of the vehicles and guns was quite excellent; well up to the standard we have come to expect from the 26th Regiment. Well done all of you.
>
> I will take this opportunity to congratulate you on your stewardship of the Regiment during your period of command. I know you have enjoyed it as I have enjoyed having the Regiment in the Divisional Artillery for the past months. You hand it over in very good shape.

Nice as these tributes were, they came too late. An even later tribute came some months later when Brigadier David Thorne, who had commanded the Brigade in which we served in County Armagh, saw me during a visit to HQ AFCENT, and rushed across the room to me and exclaimed: 'Neville! Good to see you. What a really super job your Regiment did in Ulster. Much of your work is only coming to fruition now! Well done indeed.'

Too late! The die was cast.

So! That was it! A marvellously successful and happy tour ruined at its end by someone who had known me barely six months. My only consolation was the loyalty of my officers and soldiers, whose side I had taken perhaps on occasions to a fault. But such a fault is one I gladly acknowledge.

Chapter 11

International Incidents

ONE CONSOLATION OF having commanded one's regiment successfully was to be given a fairly wide choice of subsequent employment. My last report had dashed my hopes of immediate promotion to Colonel, but when I visited the Military Secretary at Stanmore to lodge an appeal against that report, I was given to understand that there was every prospect that I would not have to wait long. In the meantime I could choose wherever I wished to serve.

Commanding a regiment is an expensive pastime, and most officers with a family and a mortgage finish their command tour £2,000 or more in the red. I was no exception. I needed a short period of financial recuperation, and a complete change from the narrow confines of the British Army. Family developments precluded opting for Hong Kong or somewhere equally far afield. I chose, therefore, to go to the Head-quarters of Allied Forces Central Europe, in Brunssum, The Netherlands. A NATO staff job was, in the British Army's eyes, neither the most glamorous of postings nor especially beneficial to one's career. This was an extraordinarily narrow outlook when NATO was the central plank of our Defence Strategy. But I was assured that things were changing in this regard, and indeed, neither my predecessor, Richard Swinburn, nor my successor, Roddy Cordy-Simpson, eventually suffered from the particular job I was to undertake, as both became Lieutenant Generals with knighthoods! Military Assistant to the Chief of Staff at HQ AFCENT was therefore considered if not a 'plum' job then certainly an important one.

A few weeks before the end of my regimental command tour, I set out to take over the UK MoD Hiring provided for me. It was in the small Dutch village of Houthem St Gerlach, near Valkenburg in Limburg, which is a province which the local people maintain is historically not in Holland, but is part of the larger Netherlands. The village lies in the rich fruit-farming area between Maastricht in the west and Aachen to the east, and hence the second language in this part of the Netherlands is not English but German. The area is often referred to as 'The Dutch Alps' as it contains the highest hills in the Netherlands – the banks of the River Geul valley fully 100 metres high! I did my reconnaissance and took over the hiring from an RAF administrative officer from HQ AFCENT. I looked round quickly and drove back to Dortmund where I told Linda that the house lay next to a railway, under the flight-path to Maastricht airport, and beside a motorway. 'All we need,' she said chuckling, 'is a canal going through underneath.'

It was almost prophetic, as a day or two later, we received a phone call from anxious administrators in Brunssum who reported that the entire lower floor and basement of the hiring was flooded! The same day I heard from our estate agent in Warminster that pipes had burst in our house there. To cap it all, it snowed more heavily that year in Houthem than ever before. The next day Linda's trip to the doctor to discuss a growing weakness and loss of feeling in her legs resulted in a provisional diagnosis of multiple sclerosis. I had a night having acute hyperventilation and shortly afterwards a duodenal ulcer was discovered in my somewhat stressed interior. For me that meant six months on Tagament pills and a total alcohol ban!

It was not altogether the most auspicious set of circumstances in which to start a new appointment. Neither was my first brush with NATO administrators all that happy, even over the simple matter of registering our Ford Cortina Estate car, AFC 97247, a process which took hours, waiting in a queue while a Dutch corporal took his time over filling in countless forms and issuing the required documentation. For someone having got used to having all such details done for one quickly by willing subordinates, this was a good lesson in humility. However, as time went by, this tour at AFCENT proved to be a valuable, interesting and significant time for me professionally and for the family.

My first concern was Linda's health. This loss of feeling in her legs, especially the left one, had been noticeable for some time. In fact she had first consulted the doctors about it when we were in Aldershot with the Parachute Brigade, but they dismissed it as a possible virus affecting the nerve endings. During our time with 26th Field Regiment the loss of feeling became worse, and it was accompanied by a considerable reduction in strength of the left leg. Doctors recommended physiotherapy, and we arranged for a PT instructor to supervise some exercises for her in the gymnasium. Poor Linda found these exercises quite impossible, for it was not just lack of muscle power, but a refusal of her muscles to react to signals from the brain. Although she laughed and made light of it this was really worrying.

Soon after settling in to Houthem, therefore, I arranged for her to have a thorough check up at the British Forces' Queen Elizabeth hospital in Woolwich, and after several visits, the analysis of blood samples taken, nerve reactive tests and a maelogram in the spine suggested that her problem was multiple sclerosis. While there she was referred to the National Hospital for Nervous Diseases in Queen Square, London for further tests. These tests took place in the summer, when the three boys were on holiday with us in Houthem. So while she was being examined in that depressingly Victorian hospital, I looked after the boys as best I could. I have to admit that cooking is not my forte, but the boys survived with only a few grumbles about lumpy custard and the unvaried menu from my pot of stewed and re-stewed vegetables and stewed fruit, both plentiful from our amazingly fertile garden. Linda said she would never go back to the National Hospital whatever happened, as she did not believe that she would get the disease badly enough in the first place, and in the second place she was determined to fight it all the way, and the atmosphere of that place was not conducive, in her view, to that approach. While many unfortunate people have succumbed to this mysterious disease, including many we have known, Linda, aided by her deep religious faith, has bravely fought off the worst effects for several years now, and she is a shining example in this respect.

The second family matter to deal with was the education and future careers of the boys, now that they were at Wellington. It was now 1979 and David, the eldest, was showing tremendous academic promise. He had secured a good scholarship to Wellington. A serious student, reserved, keen on classics and mathematics, one could see him becoming a university don, or an accountant. He was a determined lad who would do well whatever he chose. I did not think he was likely to be outgoing enough to obtain a commission in the Services. All three boys had received a first class grounding in classics and maths at Prep School, and our youngest, Jonathan, only just 12, would be starting at the Talbot House with the others next year. We had no doubts that he too would get to university as well. Paul Gilley, the boys' perceptive housemaster at Wellington, wrote in January 1984 that he considered Jonathan even to be the brightest of the three very intelligent Pughe boys. At that stage, however, I had doubts as to whether his physical prowess would prove sufficient to see him pursue an Army career successfully. Certainly if his reluctance to keep up on the long 'route marches' on which I regularly took the boys was anything to go by, he might not find Service life

entirely to his liking, his subsequent apparent enthusiasm for the CCF at
school notwithstanding. (Later he was to prove me wrong as he became
very sporty, a fell-and-mountain-walker and fitness itself!)

So my hopes of one of our sons following in the family Service tradition
rested with Richard, then nearly 15, thoroughly out-going, confident,
cheeky, socially aware, handsome, well-built and showing considerable
promise at all major team sports. Academically he was no slouch either,
and he too had been offered a small scholarship by the headmaster, that
fine man, Dr Fisher, soon after entering the school the previous year. I had
high hopes that I could talk to him and ask him whether he thought the
Army or the Royal Marines would be a good career for him to pursue,
even if only for a 3-year Short Service Commission. To say that I was very
keen for one at least of the boys to maintain the tradition was probably an
understatement. My paternal grandfather, father, and stepfather had all
been Royal Marines, as had my maternal grandfather, and three uncles had
served in the Army. I felt that the Service ethos was in our blood, but I was
not prepared to force the issue. All I could do was to suggest to Richard
that he might like to try for an Army scholarship, which would give him
the chance, if he eventually decided to go into the Army, of taking an
abbreviated form of the selection process for a commission. In the
meantime it would help me substantially with the school fees, which,
despite the Army Boarding School allowance and the small scholarships
the boys had won, were still not inconsiderable.

Richard went for a walk with me one day in Houthem, and readily
agreed to try for an Army scholarship. I was thrilled. Lieutenant Colonel
Paddy King-Fretts, the senior British officer in CINCENT's cabinet,
kindly arranged for him to go on a short attachment to the Devon and
Dorset Regiment to see what he thought about it. Afterwards, in
October 1980, I was sent a glowing report by the Officer Commanding
B Company:

> Richard Pughe is a very high grade young man who could make an
> excellent young officer. He is however rather young at the moment and
> although very keen to join the Army as such, he is on his guard against
> committing himself to a particular part or Regiment. He very much
> enjoyed his stay with us. He enjoyed the soldiers and they took to him.
> He enjoyed the company of the young officers who looked after him and
> would very much enjoy being part of a Mess with people of their kind. I
> feel certain that the Battalion scored very well with him but he wants to
> look at the Gunners as well.

That was a good start, and I was delighted that he enjoyed the introduction so much. He later went through the somewhat daunting process of interviews at Sandhurst, and passed with flying colours. The new headmaster at Wellington, Dr Newsome, thereupon wrote a nice letter to me saying how pleased he was, and he hoped that I would understand that, now Richard had been awarded an Army scholarship, he felt it necessary to remove the original small scholarship from him! I suppose that was only fair, and I should not have expected to have any of the boys educated totally free of charge.

At the end of July 1980 the last of the Pughe boys left St Andrew's School. It had provided the boys with a wonderful education which was to stand them in good stead for many years to come. I wrote a letter to the Headmaster, Rodney Maynard, expressing our profuse thanks. He replied as follows:

> It was a sad day on Saturday for us when we had to say goodbye to you knowing that there would be no more Pughe boys in the school next term but we are very grateful for your present of such a lovely painting by Turner and the picture now hangs already in Dublin dormitory . . .
>
> Secondly I would like to thank you for running and organising the Father's Match and entertaining us so generously afterwards; it was a marvellous day and we were certainly lucky with the weather. We shall miss Jonathan next term but of course he must leave and go on, but it will be funny not having a Pughe boy in the school and we think ourselves fortunate and lucky to have had three such delightful boys . . .

Family life at AFCENT proved to be superb fun, especially for the boys. Apart from the location being ideal for forays to the Moselle Valley and southern Germany, there were several British families at the headquarters, some of whose sons were also at Wellington. The families Petheram, Dickins, Bowen, Leonard, McQuiod, Dowdall and Bailey were particularly close, and others like the Kuuns had children of similar age to ours. When the charter flight touched down at Düsseldorf at each end of term, a large gang of teenagers would get off it, generally all good chums, and in high spirits. They would meet again throughout the holidays at the AFCENT sailing club at Roermond, where the boys became quite expert at racing 420s, and at countless parties in various tolerant parents' houses. There was ten-pin bowling too at Heerlen, the traditional Easter egg-rolling competition and all manner of diversions for them. Richard broadened his education in other ways too, while at

Brunssum, at one time enjoying an exchange holiday with a French lad called Stephan Creff, who, when he came to stay with us, showed he was a fine swimmer.

Lastly, on the family front, I was clear that we would have to take certain precautions for the future if Linda's health deteriorated more quickly. We agreed that it would be sensible to sell the house in Warminster and buy a bungalow somewhere. I immediately thought of the Aylesbury Vale area of Buckinghamshire. My parents had now settled in Cuddington, near Aylesbury and nearby was Stoke Mandeville Hospital, with its world-famous orthopaedic expertise. If a future posting took me to the MoD in London, this area would also be in relatively easy commuting distance. It was also centrally placed for the boys' school, Linda's relations in Surrey, and, hopefully, in future, Oxford University for the boys.

By about halfway through our time in Brunssum, therefore, we had successfully sold the Warminster house for over twice what we paid for it, and found a rather run-down little bungalow in the village of Granborough, near Winslow, for which we paid £85,000, most of which was mortgaged. We drove to and from Houthem and Granborough in our new Ford Cortina Estate AFC 97247 many times during the period of fitting out the bungalow. Leslie decorated the bungalow's interior expertly for us, and, because of the deplorable state of the garden, we called it 'Tumbleweed'. We were happy with this new venture, and grew to love the village and our neighbours. More of this anon.

Professionally, life at HQAFCENT was fairly humdrum. My job was to help the Chief of Staff, a charming little Belgian Lieutenant General who had won the British Military Cross shortly after 'D' Day, to interpret the directions of the German Commander-in-Chief (CINCENT, or in NATO-speak, 'SinkScent') in such a way as the staff could understand what to do. In fact, because the Chief of Staff and the then CINCENT did not see eye to eye on anything, it was left to me to write out the 'tasking' document after every meeting between the two. The 'tasking' would be distributed down through the relevant staff branches, where it would be discussed at length and be worked upon by the various staff officers of many different nationalities and levels of competence. Once the Branch Chief was satisfied the work had been completed, the responses or paper would be sent all the way up through various levels of command, be checked and signed off at every step on the way. At first I was constantly frustrated at the length of time it took to get anything done in the way of staff-work, and consequently to arrive at decisions. As time went by, one was increasingly surprised at how well the disparate nations represented there actually got on with each other and one could even take a sort of pride in the small progress made.

Language problems were, of course, not inconsiderable, but fewer nations were represented at HQ AFCENT than in NATO as a whole or SHAPE in particular. The French had a military 'Mission' in an adjacent building, as France was theoretically not part of NATO's military structure. They would visit the Chief of Staff regularly, however, and he, a Belgian, was able to converse with them fluently in French. I was not comfortable with my schoolboy French, but I did take steps to learn German, and this allowed me, later, at the age of 44, to sit 'O' Level German at the same time as Jonathan and we both passed quite well, he beating me by a short head. Whenever we had any language difficulties in my office, however, help was at hand on the shape of our wonderful Dutch secretary, Mvrw Bep van der Paas. Impressively, she could speak about six languages fluently and at the drop of a hat on picking up the telephone. Bep was also the possessor of a private pilot's licence and regularly flew small aircraft over to southern England, which she always admired.

After a while international politics dictated that I shared my office with two other staff officers. One was a Dutch Wing Commander who never did anything, and the other was a big American Lieutenant Colonel, Mike MacNamara, who was a source of much amusement and fun. 'I can speak English, *actually*,' he would say, 'and you will see everything's going to be tickety-boo.' He made frequent reference to a special English-American dictionary, and we pulled each other's legs unmercifully over our national differences. Perhaps the only occasion when he was not amused was after we looked after his Irish setter for a few weeks. These Americans evidently liked to see a dog well-fed, and the dog was, to a Briton's view, plainly fat on arrival with us, but sleek, with more classic lines, when he left. The MacNamaras must have thought we had starved the poor animal.

There was another American officer whose leg I could not resist pulling. He was a Brigadier General in charge of the Operations Division, an important position on the staff, and like all Americans, this man was very earnest and assiduous in his duties. He, like many, considered that the hours spent behind a desk were a fair measure of an officer's worth. His habit was to arrive every morning at around

7.30 a.m., often well before officers of other nationalities on his staff, and not leave again until 7.00 p.m. One day I noticed on his programme which he kindly gave me every week, that he would be away on a visit to another headquarters and would not return until late the following morning. When I left my own office at around 5.00 p.m. I dropped a note on his desk. He arrived at his office at 9.00 a.m. the next day, to find the note. It said, 'Urgent! The Chief of Staff was calling for you this morning at 07.45 hours and wanted to know why you were late!' The poor man came rushing up to my office asking to see the Chief of Staff to apologise. Although not renowned for his sense of humour, to give him his due, he saw the joke this time, and we became good working chums – provided I always tipped him the wink when the Chiefs were after him.

The daily life of the staff was dominated by CINCENT. There were two successive German Generals in this post while I was at AFCENT, both of them sticklers for detail and rather harsh in their treatment of their staff. The first of these appeared totally humourless, and he terrified staff officers when they were briefing him. We used to go some miles away into a nuclear-explosion proof bunker for exercises, and our dull routine there in a suffocating atmosphere heightened the tension when CINCENT was being briefed. One day he was interrupting and criticising successive officers, when he was faced with a normally placid and charming Scottish officer from the Intelligence Division. After the third time the Scotsman was interrupted by a really unpleasantly snapped question, he took a deep breath and said quietly, 'Sir, if you would mind keeping your questions until after I have finished so that you don't keep interrupting me, I should be very glad, Sir!' One could have heard a pin drop. Everyone in the room was astonished. Nobody had ever dared speak up like that before! The good German had the good sense to smile, and gently request the Scot to 'Carry on, please.' And it proved salutary.

I made some good friends among the more junior German officers on the staff. Oberst (Colonel) Klaus Bodenstein was the senior officer in CINCENT's personal staff 'cabinet'. He had been to the British Staff College at Camberley and was an Anglophile, but he was conscious of the importance of his position to the extent that he asked me once not to address him by his Christian name in the office! On another occasion, when the staff, encouraged by myself and other British officers, produced a solution to a problem which did not coincide with CINCENT's original guidance, Klaus called me in and gave me quite a rocket. He said that it was not customary to ignore a German commander's guidance in this way. I believe that he thought it was tantamount to mutiny! I replied that he should know, having been to Camberley, that in the British system, the staff were expected to explore every possible alternative and option facing a commander in addition to his guidance, and that we did not consider we were doing our job unless we did so! This was a typical example of the difference in approach between the two nations, and which twice in this century contributed to catastrophic wars. I am glad to relate that war did not break out between the nations on the staff, but Klaus Bodenstein and I resolved the matter amicably. Sadly, he was to die of stomach cancer a few months later.

Another friend in CINCENT's cabinet was Major Adam von Trott zu Solz, who, like our friend Berthold von Stauffenberg at Staff College, was the son of one of those officers who plotted against Hitler in July 1944 and who were subsequently executed. CINCENT's deputy was British, normally a 4-star airman, but it was a difficult appointment to hold, there being little to do with such energetic, detail-minded German commanders-in-chief. We saw four different DCINCENTs in that post during our tour of just over two years. Among our closest allies and friends was, however, a Dutchman, Lieutenant General Dirk Nederlof, who took over from our little Belgian as Chief of Staff. He and I compared notes about how to deal with duodenal ulcers, but, apart from that, he had a wonderful sense of humour and was a firm Anglophile, recalling always his gunnery training courses at Larkhill on Salisbury Plain after the war. When he left the headquarters some months after I did, he was delighted to be driven off in style in a gleaming Rolls-Royce which I had secretly arranged before I left. His wife, Maps, had been interned by the Japanese in Indonesia during the war, and they were a most interesting and cultured couple, who took the tragedy of a handicapped son bravely in their stride.

Linda and I took part in as much as we could at AFCENT. We attended the church on the base at Brunssum most Sundays, and when Polly Dickins was away, I had a go at playing the organ. I had had no training in this instrument, so it was necessary to play it by trial and error. After a little practice at which I would pull out a random selection of organ stops to see what they sounded like I managed to play some of the easier hymns. One can get away with fingering errors on a piano, but an organ reveals every 'bum note' quite starkly, and I certainly made plenty of them. However, I did improve, and by the time we left, I was able to play 'Onward Christian Soldiers' with speed and relish if not complete accuracy, which quite roused and amused the congregation.

All in all, we enjoyed our time in the Netherlands, but I was nevertheless impatient to catch up with my contemporaries who had been a DS with me at Camberley and nearly all of whom had already been promoted to Colonel. Brigadier Charles Grey, the senior British officer at HQAFCENT, kindly gave me every encouragement and some excellent reports, so I should not have been as surprised as I was when, in March 1981, we were given three weeks to pack up and report to the MoD in London as a full Colonel GS at last. Air Chief Marshal Sir Peter Terry, a recently arrived and most charming and popular DCINCENT, dropped me a note saying:

> This is just a line to say how delighted I am to hear that you are to be promoted shortly. This is excellent news , though the speed of your move to London may cause the same sort of domestic upheaval to which I've recently become accustomed! From what I have heard and seen your promotion is well merited and overdue, and I wish you the best of luck in what should be an interesting appointment in London.

I thought that was particularly nice of the Air Marshal, and he was right.

CHAPTER 12

Transatlantic Transactions

SUCH SHORT NOTICE of our move was not without its hazards. We had tenants in 'Tumbleweed', our house in Granborough, with whom we had an agreement to give them six weeks' notice to quit. It was touch and go as to whether they would leave in time for us to move back in. In the event, they did move out hurriedly the day before we returned, but left the place in an awful mess, rather, we felt, out of spite. We had subsequently to spend a lot of money in renovating the bungalow, and we added a bedroom for Jonathan by means of a fairly primitive loft conversion.

Linda was pleased, I think, to get back to England, and immerse herself in village life, where she made instant and numerous friends, as she has always done. Her MS condition was deteriorating only slowly, and she was in good spirits. It was certainly fun to be closer to the boys' school, and to be able to attend Speech Days and sporting events more easily.

My job in London entailed working for the Deputy Chief of Defence Staff (Operational Requirements) abbreviated to DCDS(OR) on the Central Joint staff at the Ministry of Defence. It was known as a 'purple' appointment and I shared an office with a Naval Captain, Richard Cobbold, and an RAF Group Captain, Brian Farrer. We worked directly to DCDS(OR) himself, a charming ex-cavalryman named Lieutenant General Maurice Johnston. Our main task was to oversee the application of the Defence Equipment Procurement budget, and see those individual Service equipment requirements which met our approval through the various committees. Step 1 was to steer it through the Requirement Committee and Step 2 was to get it approved by the technical and industrial committee. This process was time-consuming and bureaucratic, almost purpose-designed to build in delays in bringing much needed equipment into front line service. We sat in the eye of the storm of inter-Service rivalry too, which was not always comfortable, and our loyalties could be called into question.

Life was pretty humdrum, for all that, and I hated commuting daily from Granborough to Whitehall via the Leighton Buzzard railway line, or the charming but slow line from Aylesbury to Marylebone. There was no social life in the Ministry either and I missed the previous years' cameraderie and team spirit engendered by social gatherings with wives and colleagues, which in the MoD were notable only by their absence. On rare occasions, however, the tedium was relieved by a trip with the General to some equipment trials or a factory, and it was a pleasure to accompany him to GKN's production line for the new Armoured Personnel Carrier being developed for the Army, and later, on 16 March 1983, for the unveiling of the first of the new Challenger tanks from the Royal Ordnance factory in Leeds.

Family life, on the other hand, was very pleasant in Granborough. We really settled into the village life and enjoyed the community spirit there. Our neighbours, and families like the Emms, the Morrises, the Prodgers, the Evanses and Tillyards, really welcomed us and took us into their hearts. For the period from December 1981 to August 1982 I kept a 'Village Diary' and a glance at it today reminds me of how busy a lively village community can be. 'Tumbleweed' lay a stone's throw from the old village church. I tended the church garden, mainly weeding and planting roses, and I joined the Parochial Church Council. I also started a small choir from among the children of the village. It cost me 50 pence per child per attendance, but the parents almost doubled the regular congregation and it was good fun. I was also asked to help with the annual village fêtes, the proceeds from which were mainly devoted to meeting the cost of rebuilding the church tower. £40,000 had to be raised within three years, and for a village of fewer than 400 inhabitants, this was a considerable challenge. Suffice to say that the fêtes and other collections raised the sum required to supplement various heritage grants within two and a half years and the tower was duly rebuilt. It was good to see so many non-churchgoers contributing to this project too, realising as they did that it was part of everyone's heritage.

For one of these fund-raising events I was fortunate to secure the Royal Artillery Band from Woolwich. They came up on a Sunday and played in the Morrises' garden, which generated great interest and support from the whole village, as well as some amusement over the elaborate anti-IRA security precautions. The Band were kind enough only to charge a nominal fee for their transport costs and I stood all those hearty bandsmen a free beer in the Crown afterwards, contributing to a night of revelry the village pub scarcely ever forgot.

My help was called for in two successive years' fêtes. For the first, when I was considered still a relative 'newcomer' to the village, it was recognised that I was in the Army (although I always went to work in civilian clothes and the Morrises thought I was in MI5, or MFI as they called it!), and so I was asked to produce what the Army was supposed to be good at, namely tents and loos. Unfortunately, the fête was destined for the month of July 1982, and all the tents and most of the hessian which the Army possessed had been sunk in the *Atlantic Conveyor* off the Falklands. I contacted the American Air Force Base at Upper Heyford whose commanding officer, Jack Nelson, had served in AFCENT with me. A marquee was duly promised, but on the day of the fête, it failed to appear until halfway through the afternoon. Quite how popular I would have been had it been raining that day I dread to think. As for the loos, the only comment from our local farmer friend, Tony Emms, was that the amount of hessian I managed to acquire was only sufficient to provide privacy for Gurkhas. Tony was 6 ft 5 ins and he felt a trifle exposed.

The following year I was asked to run the whole show, and that included a dog show, a horse-show, all the usual stalls, bouncy-castles and so on. I also toured all the village pubs within a radius of five miles and invited them each to produce a tug-of-war team. That was easy to organise – just a rope and some tape – and it proved a big success, although some of the teams might have done rather better had they not enjoyed a substantial liquid lunch in their various pubs before the event. Tact, of course, was in demand in arranging the stalls. Everyone had their 'usual pitch' and I had to formally invite them all to do the same again that year, and woe betide me if I altered anyone's favourite pitch! We were very lucky with the weather and the fête was a howling success and raised £2,000 towards the church tower. Subsequent fêtes, I understand, after we left the village, and the financial objectives had been reached, were on a much smaller scale.

Other village projects we engaged ourselves in included rebuilding the wooden bus shelter just outside our front gate. Having obtained the necessary council permissions, and tactfully sought advice from Malcolm Newman, the village factotum, Brigadier Hank Bowen OBE, a good practical engineer whom I had known in Ulster and at AFCENT, came over from his house at Wallingford, and our two families totally refurbished the shelter for the princely sum of £100 (against a local builder's estimate of £250). It was a fine sight for the locals to see two senior officers labouring away in the noonday sun, their respective sons, I might add, getting rather high on Pimm's No 1 during the refreshment breaks! Repaired and painted, the shelter looked fine, but it was no real surprise to me when, a couple of years later, the County Council decided to supply a brand new shelter built of brick, considering, no doubt, that our effort was a bit of a 'bodge'.

I should also mention my DIY 'bodging' inside the house. Modesty, which is my only vice, forbids me from describing all the triumphs of woodwork which I accomplished there. We will pass over quickly my brilliant construction in our bedroom which we called an airing cupboard. I bought some timber and screwed it to the wall above a night-storage heater, deftly attaching to it some slatted or louvred doors. The doors did not quite meet in the middle, but once one had mastered the 'knack' one could open one of them quite easily. There was, I have to admit, a slight tendency for the other door then to swing out suddenly and hit one in the face, but by and large it was a huge success which I admired daily.

The other masterpiece, which the whole family remember with affection, was my corner shelf in the hall. I started with an old plank about 2 feet wide and 6 feet long. I should have, of course, started with a tape-measure, but I have always found them difficult to handle and normally superfluous when one is gifted with a good eye and a skill at guesswork. The trouble with a plank of that size is that it won't go into the corner into which you are trying to fit it as a shelf. The initial cuts or swathes with your blunt saw are therefore slightly problematic. I did, however, with much swearing and cursing, gradually whittle the plank down to manageable proportions, and sliced it roughly triangular. I then shoved it into the corner of the wall, which I at once discovered was not quite a right angle. This is, I have found over the years, quite a common problem with walls; they never are as square as they should be. However, I did have an old rusty plane, some half-used sandpaper and a chisel with a chip out of the blade, and armed with these instruments I ground down one side of the triangle to fit to the shape of the walls. Unfortunately I then found that I had shaved off the wrong side, so that when I slotted the shelf into the corner recess there was rather a large gap on one side. Undeterred I took it down and shaved off a slice from the other side, and tried again. This time, I found that I had shaved off a bit too much from the second side, and I now had to shave a bit more off the original side. I have now to explain that, as usual with my DIY projects, I found I was in a hurry and also in a temper. Nevertheless, with a couple more daring shots at getting the damn thing to fit snug into the corner, and the judicious application of a tin of plastic wood, the job was completed. My only sorrow was, that what had started out as a shelf on which to place several hats, scarves and a handbag or two, finished up as something on which you could just fit a pair of gloves. As I say, modesty demands that I do not mention other such carpentering, but the boys did award me the 'Master Bodgers' certificate.

If 'Tumbleweed's interior tended to suffer from my ministrations, its small garden flourished. Although the soil was heavy clay which made digging hard work, it was ideal for roses and I grew plenty. I entered some superb specimens for the annual village Flower Show in the Village Hall, greenfly and all, but was never allowed to win, as I hadn't been a resident for long enough. The lady who regularly won lived well outside the parish boundary, but as far as eligibility for the show was concerned, this was not a matter for discussion!

Quite a lot of my spare time at weekends when the boys were on holiday was taken up with teaching them to drive. David had a confidence problem at the wheel at first; he was alternately too nervous or excessively over-confident, with the result that he failed his test the first time. As someone who was not accustomed to failure, he was understandably mortified, especially as there was every prospect of Richard passing easily. In the event, all three lads passed in the right order of succession, and our old Ford Cortina was to be shared between them while we were away on our next posting.

Richard, meanwhile, was making a tremendous name for himself in the world of hockey. While a very severe mid-winter's snowfall must have disrupted the 1981/2 hockey season, both David and he were in the Wellington 1st XI that year, and we were able to watch matches at the school with great family pride. David, a left-hander, playing well on the left wing, and Richard, with a phenomenal long-range flick, playing left, centre or, as I had done, right half. Richard was clearly going to be exceptionally good, and in the spring of 1983 he was selected for an England Under 19 XI Trial. This took place at Bisham Abbey, and it was one of the big advantages of our being in the UK at this critical time in the boys' development, that Linda and I were able to watch the trial match. Richard did not play at his best, and was not subsequently selected, but he was definitely a name to be noted and was potential for the England 'squad'. He played at Bedford School for the South-Western counties and he subsequently went on to a good deal of representative hockey, as we shall see. He showed good promise at cricket too.

David and Richard completed their Wellington careers while we were in Granborough. David took four 'A' Levels, Latin, Greek, Maths and Further Maths and was awarded 'A' grades in all of them! These were stunning results but well-deserved rewards for application and determined, hard study. Needless to say, he had no difficulty in being accepted to the College of his choice at Oxford. He chose the one to which Linda's father had gone, University College, Oxford. We were very proud of his achievement. Richard also did well, achieving 'A' and 'S' passes in Greek, a 'B' in Latin and 'C's in Maths and Art. The combination of Maths and Art seemed fairly rare, and he was quite keen on becoming an architect at one stage, but I wondered if I should try gently to discourage that thought, bearing in mind the employment chances in such a career were not good at the time. In any case, I hoped that he was firmly set on the Army. Richard also sang with the choral society and studied the piano, reaching grade 7, but then he considered that he would not have time to take it further. I was very keen that he should not give up his music, as there was every sign of his being a really talented pianist. I strongly advised him to remember that one day he would no longer be able to play hockey and then he might be glad of the piano. I reminded him of the popularity accorded to anyone who could sit down and play the piano at a social gathering, and he sensibly decided to continue with periodic lessons without the pressure of taking further grade exams, and I was very happy to pay for them on that basis. How he managed to pack into his life all that he did was a mystery. Besides hockey and piano-playing, he was a promising cricketer, and he became friendly with a couple of girls who were now newly in the upper reaches of the school. He was always socially aware, and impeccably gallant to the girls, but I have no doubt that having girls in the 6th Form was a distraction to some, and one or two very talented boys were badly led astray at Wellington at that time.

David had left Wellington and was kicking his heels for a year waiting to go up to University College Oxford. Linda and I had hoped that he would find something adventurous to do in this 'gap' year, or at least a useful job, but he showed little inclination to do either, possibly because he had no money. We did suggest he advertised his availability in the local newspaper saying that he would consider any sort of job. He only got one enquiry – somebody wanted him to be a male nude model! He eventually found employment back at St Andrew's School as an assistant groundsman. Afterwards, in September 1983, headmaster Rodney

Maynard wrote that he thought David had 'found things difficult at times
. . .' but added, 'It seems that David has developed some very positive
ideas but fortunately he has not fallen into the traps that so many young
men of his age do.' We were not quite sure what Rodney meant by that,
for David was a tall, lusty, bronzed and very fit young man and he must
have been 'raring to go'. He devoted himself to long-distance running
at Granborough and he would go off every day in his tiny running shorts,
pounding the local lanes. He got to know the Morrises well, and their
15 year-old daughter Catriona. We very much liked Jenny and Catriona,
and David was able to share his addiction to a particularly cacophonous
brand of pop-music with Catriona. Although Linda was much more
tolerant of that than I was, David's departure for University that autumn
increased his maturity and put a timely end to my unworthy impatience!

My village chronicle started on 8 December 1981 but the entry for
Easter Sunday 11 April 1982 reads:

> After two days of cold winds from the north, the sun shone today and the
> countryside was quiet and yet alive. The church bells were rung and the
> church was full, almost to capacity. The Register recorded 65 people
> present, with a collection in excess of £53. Colin Beckett tells me that he
> delivered 105 lambs this year, of which 95 survived. Life everywhere
> overshadowed by the political and military crisis in the Falklands.

The chronicle came to an abrupt halt on 20 April 1982 on account of
that little problem in the South Atlantic. During the spring of that year
tension had been mounting between Argentina and the UK over the
sovereignty of the Falkland Islands and eventually, following invasion by
the Argentines on 2 April 1982, it became pretty obvious to everyone in
London that the endless parleying in the United Nations was leading
nowhere. We in the MoD were in no doubt that we would have to
deploy a full-scale counter-invasion force even if at the eleventh hour
the Argentines backed down and the use of force proved unnecessary.
The mood in the MoD, I have to say, was bellicose, despite the huge
challenges facing us in mounting an operation at such a vast distance from
the UK and remote from friendly airfields. Before long, plans became
preparations, and these became movement orders.

Lieutenant General Maurice Johnston sat at his desk waiting for a call
from the Chiefs of Staff to join their war committee. For several days
none came. He didn't say anything, but we on his staff reckoned that one
could not mount the sort of joint-Service operation envisaged without a

major input from the central equipment requirements staff. In due course, DCDS(OR) was asked to be present or be represented on the Chiefs of Staff Committee which daily, after meeting, dispatched the Chief of Defence Staff to brief the Prime Minister across the road in 10 Downing Street.

By the end of April 1982 much had been achieved by the MoD, although nobody reading the national press would have guessed as much. Notably clear, firm and unambiguous instructions had gone out to everyone in the MoD and in the major Naval, Army and RAF headquarters throughout the UK. First, Margaret Thatcher had given us an unequivocal mission: 'Retake the Falklands!' Everyone knew where they stood. Second, operational command was vested in the Joint Headquarters at Northwood; there was to be no interference from the MoD, only support, help and guidance when needed. Third, clear planning assumptions were issued: assume a three-week campaign with 10 per cent casualties in men and equipment, proceed at once to requisition civilian ships, so-called Ships Taken Up From Trade (STUFT), and use Ascension Island as a forward mounting base.

Our first job was to study the enemy threat to be faced, particularly from the Argentine Air Force which would have the advantage of being able to operate from bases on their mainland. The UK, on the other hand, possessed no Airborne early warning system to speak of and much would depend on the success of Naval Harrier jump-jet aircraft in a quick-reaction air-defence role, taking off from our Light Fleet Carriers *Invincible* and the aged *Hermes*. They would be armed with Sidewinder AIM (L) air-to-air missiles and, at the probable rate of engagement, it was clear that we would have to obtain more from the USA where the missiles were built. We studied the UK's proposed initial force composition and order of battle with a view to calculating what reserves of equipment we would need assuming the 10 per cent casualty rate. We consulted the three separate Service planning staffs constantly, and deduced that all manner of ships which were out of commission, being repaired or refurbished, would be needed.

We soon contacted the British Embassy in Washington DC and prepared the way for obtaining American help with two major pieces of equipment; Sidewinders and water-purification plant for Ascension Island. The latter was loaded and despatched within 48 hours of requesting it, and it played a vital role in the replenishment of men and ships there. The Sidewinders would have to be approved personally by

Casper Weinberger, the American Secretary of State for Defence. I spoke to his office myself and received the welcome news that approval was given for the transfer of 65 or so Sidewinders AIM (L) — which would have to be replaced in the US arsenal by the more modern AIM (M) version, so we would be charged the increased price of the (M) version! Beggars can't be choosers, and we had to accept, somewhat ruefully, the extra cost.

The joy of those heady days in April and early May was in being able to take far-reaching and important decisions with the full backing of Maurice Johnston and without interference from the Ministry's civil servant financial watchdogs. The deployment operation was able to get under way in a timely and relatively efficient way, therefore, although the general philosophy seemed to be: get the goods down to the docks, load them into the first available ship and get going! We watched the Ships Movement board daily and we were full of admiration for the way in which the Royal Naval planning and movements staff got the long convoy going. Inexperienced naval staff officers were learning their trade for real and rather swiftly. Mounting such an operation was wholly outside their experience, save those who might have been involved in the rather more leisurely Borneo operation in the early 1960s. Those officers retain my admiration to this day.

Naturally we were heavily engaged in the Ministry day and night for several weeks. Many officers of the operational staffs slept on camp-beds in the office corridors. I managed to avoid that discomfort, but on many occasions I caught a very late train home and a very early one in the morning, often sleeping exhausted on the train both ways. But we were kept going on adrenalin, and life, particularly after the landing on 21 May, was quite exciting. Of course it was frustrating too, not to be in the South Atlantic in the front line, but it seemed to confirm my darkest fears that glory was destined to elude me yet again. There would be no medals for the back-room boys.

As the campaign progressed, Maurice Johnston let us take his place from time to time in the morning Chiefs of Staff meeting. This was a highly interesting experience for me. My lasting impression, however, was the poverty of our intelligence about the Argentine forces on the Falklands. We received a little satellite surveillance data from the USA, less than we hoped for, owing to bad weather and inappropriate satellite tracking, and the front line tactical information obtained from the SAS patrols inserted behind the Argentine lines was insufficient to give an overall picture of the enemy strength. Not until the very last day of the war, when the Argentines surrendered, was a reliable count made of their numbers, a figure which General Glover, the Chief of Intelligence Services at the Chiefs' Meeting, released to the accompaniment of muffled cheers. The figures given showed that the Argentines outnumbered us by about ten to one, and locally about three to one. Conventional wisdom had it that one needed a superiority of three to one to conduct a successful attack. In this extraordinary campaign the defenders held that superiority but still lost when faced with the determined and professional forces of the UK. Later, when I went to the USA, the most frequent question I was asked concerned these numbers. 'What was the secret weapon you guys had down there that enabled you to beat 'em with such inferior numbers?' My reply was always the same: 'Our secret weapon was the quality of our soldiers.' My interrogators never seemed fully convinced, however.

Possibly the two most satisfying aspects of the campaign from my point of view were firstly to be able to feel less alarmed about ships being sunk than the press seemed to be because we knew that our calculations had been based on that sound planning assumption of 10 per cent casualty rate. In the event, only in ships did we come near to that figure, whilst in aircraft and men on the ground the losses nowhere nearly approached that rate. Secondly we had established a good liaison with the Pentagon both directly and through our Embassy in Washington, and this was to act to my personal benefit later.

My Granborough village diary seems to have been resumed on 29 August 1982, when life returned to normal. At the MoD, after being involved in many post-action reports and analyses, our attention was turned to reorganising the Ministry. The Falklands campaign had perhaps given some impetus to a reorganisation which had been constantly shelved over the years since the Mountbatten/Healey reforms in the 1960s. The thrust, as then, was to try to break down individual Service rivalries and form a larger Central Joint (or 'purple') Staff at the expense of individual Service staffs.

In an atmosphere of secrecy, Maurice Johnston peered over our draft diagrams and papers. We worked hard into the night, knowing that many of our proposals could meet with dismay or resistance from Single Service staffs and chiefs. Nevertheless we were content after using our best endeavours, that the new shape of the Central Staff was right, provided always that professional flexibility and common sense prevailed.

We were asked to report to the sixth floor office of the Secretary of State, The Rt Hon. Michael Heseltine. The rumour was rife that he was a trifle dyslectic and might not have read our voluminous papers. The meeting was memorable; set for 10.00 hours it lasted barely half an hour, during which time Mr Heseltine outlined his plans for the necessary restructuring. He made no reference whatever to the papers we had submitted, and paid little heed to muffled voices of concern among senior officers present. At the end, it was clear that we had our instructions, and that was that. I am glad to say that Mr Heseltine's ideas coincided in quite a number of respects with ours. Personally, I believe that he was wise to conduct the meeting in the way he did. Any other way, even the more traditional staff briefing method, could have resulted in argument and lack of clarity. There may be occasions when dyslexia is an advantage.

With this work completed, I became very bored at the Ministry. I became sufficiently frustrated with office life that I decided to answer an advertisement I had seen in the Appointments page of the *Daily Telegraph* and apply for the job of Practice Administrator for a firm of London architects. I visited the firm and was much taken with their charm, their interesting work overseas, and the need to sort out their chaotic manner of operating. They offered me the job after one visit, and I was very much in two minds as to whether to take it or not. Attractive though the salary was, it would still mean working in London and commuting daily, so I decided to contact Brigadier Tony Mullens at the MS postings branch at Stanmore to see what the future held for me in the Army before I made up my mind.

In our initial telephone discussion Tony said that I was not on the promotions list and the job I was pencilled in for was Defence Adviser, Singapore. It sounded attractive; my mother, Leslie and my sister Maggie had all been to Singapore at one time or another, and I had never had a posting east of the Persian Gulf. The boys would enjoy it in the holidays too, although it was a long flight. The big disadvantage, however, was the probable effect on Linda of the humid heat of Singapore. To be honest, too, I did not think that it was a terribly prestigious appointment, and the response I received from the present incumbent, an RAF officer, when I asked him what the job was like, was not very encouraging.

I then went to see Tony at Stanmore and told him that I could not take the Singapore job, and unless he had anything better for me, I was going to leave and become an architects' practice administrator! Tony said:

'Ah! Now let me see. Something has just come in this morning.' He shuffled some papers and then looked up over his desk with a whimsical smile.

'How does Assistant Military Attaché in Washington DC grab you, Neville?'

'What?' I cried, scarcely believing he was serious.

He said that, strangely enough, it was proving difficult to find full Colonels to fill the appointment because of school fees and other family reasons.

'I'll give you 24 hours to think about it, if you like,' he added.

'No need,' I rejoined, 'I'll take it!'

My flirtation with the architects' practice was concluded and the job went to a Gunner colleague of mine in the MoD at a slightly improved salary! Linda was as excited as I was about the idea of a couple of years in the great USA, and Richard would be having his 'gap' year while we were there, so the prospect pleased the boys as well. We began hectic preparations. We prepared the bungalow once again for letting. The locals said. 'Don't you let in the Americans. They bombed us in the war and wrecked one of our thatched cottages!' I said I thought it must have been a mistake and the Americans at Upper Heyford were a decent bunch nowadays.

We were then required to go on an Attaché indoctrination course. I say 'we' advisedly, as wives were invited to attend some of the lectures in London. Notably, they attended a wonderful talk given by a recent Russian defector. The story was that this Russian colonel had tried to defect to the British during an Embassy party in Geneva. The wife of the British Military Attaché there had apparently not taken the man seriously. Indeed, it was said that in reply to the Russian's opening gambit that he did not think very much of Mr Kruschev, the wife merely giggled and admitted that she wasn't very keen on our own Prime Minister either! Puzzled and frustrated, the Russian colonel then approached the French Military Attaché's wife, who, evidently rather more alive to diplomacy and espionage intrigues, made the necessary arrangements for the colonel to come across. No doubt the French were subsequently disappointed that the UK was his preferred and eventual destination.

It was certainly sensible for wives to take part in some parts of the course, and for some the training must have paid off. It certainly proved valuable to Linda, as we shall see.

While on the course, we met a charming couple from the Royal Marines, Colonel Andrew and 'Tiggy' Whitehead, with whom we immediately struck up a friendship which was to burgeon in Washington and remain close ever since. Andrew was to be the Chief of Staff to the Defence Attaché in Washington, Major General Tony Boam.

The course included a visit to the Defence Intelligence Centre at Ashford, in Kent. There we were taught the rudiments of clandestine photography. We thought that this skill was more appropriate to those unfortunate officers being sent to communist countries, the Cold War still being intense at this time. We were also instructed carefully in how to encourage and handle Russians who appeared to want to defect to the West, and watched films on how their NKVD spies operated in the UK. We thought all this was fascinating, but we did not really see how all this could apply to the diplomatic life in the capital of a friendly nation like the USA. Linda and I were soon to find out.

Chapter 13

International Intrigues

Washington DC in August is a hot and humid place, at times not much better than Singapore, but its climate is more changeable, winters especially so. I flew there ahead of Linda, who stayed with her mother in England sufficiently long to see David into University College, Oxford. Pickfords had packed our belongings at Granborough, and much to our concern had, among their team of packers, a Cambridge University undergraduate doing a fill-in job in the vacation. It was a pity that we didn't object at the time, because on arrival in the States, our boxes were tossed around by American airport transporters more used to dealing with large containers than small boxes. When I started to unpack I discovered that the heavy mahogany canteen of cutlery which the Cambridge lad had packed at the bottom of a crate full of china had been upturned, resulting in the heavy canteen crushing a high proportion of the china now underneath! I suppose bold letters on the crate saying 'This Way Up!' might have helped. Replacement china and glass were expensive in the USA.

I took over Foreign Office Hiring No 6221, Loch Raven Drive, McLean, Virginia, from Colonel Brian Pennicott and his family of five daughters. They were very sad to leave. It was a nice family home on two levels, the lower level having a fair-sized 'family room' in the American style with adjacent bedroom and bathroom. The spacious garage was accessed from a slope down the side of the house, and upstairs were the drawing room cum dining room, kitchen, and two bedrooms with attached bathrooms. The garden, or 'yard' as the locals call it, was overlooked by a splendid wooden 'deck' reached from the drawing room. The view was mostly trees and coarse grass, and I vowed to grow some roses there if I bust with the effort. I noted the fly-screens over every external door, and the steady hum of the air conditioning battling with the sticky heat. My handover/takeover with Brian was quickly completed and the next step was to get mobile. Brian was not bequeathing me his huge old estate car. Cars were always a problem for short tours in the States. New cars did not hold their value at all, and second-hand cars more than three years old were wrecks. It took me some time, therefore, to find two suitable cars to buy. The larger was a nice, comfortable Chevrolet, and the small one was the Chevrolet Chevette model. We found out later that this smaller machine could only go up hills or have the air conditioning on, but not both at once! It nevertheless proved to be a useful run-about for Linda and, during holiday times, the boys.

My first official engagement was to take the salute at a War of Independence re-enactment on the Mall in Washington – a strange introduction in many ways for a British officer! Linda arrived in September and at once enjoyed the heat, now rather drier than it had been in August. We joined the Highland Swimming Club nearby, which Linda, despite an increasing limp, could reach on foot. Few people seemed to walk anywhere in the States, but she set a super example. Walking down our tree-lined road and round the corner past Kellogg Drive – where she had hoped to live because of the name – gave one theoretically a rare chance to converse with the neighbours. Seldom, however, did we achieve any sort of conversation with them, as they would get into their air-conditioned car from inside their air-conditioned house and drive out through the automatic garage door, sometimes offering a cheery wave in our direction but little more. Our near neighbours on one side, the Haywards, were British employees of the World Bank, while more immediately on the other side lived an elderly American couple, Henry and Mary Damminger. He was a chatty fellow and grew the most delicious and huge sweet tomatoes – invariably pronounced the British way for our benefit – but his wife was obese and very poorly. She had sadly done so little exercise in her life and so seldom been out of air-conditioning or central heating that her metabolism had gone wrong. They made us feel welcome, however.

We joined the local Neighbourhood Watch which entailed patrolling the adjacent cherry tree lined avenues in one's car complete with radio. The neighbours took it very seriously. We also met a retired US Marine Corps colonel, Brooke Nihart, and his wife Mary Helen, who lived just a few 'blocks' away in Kellogg Drive, and who kindly let us use their private swimming pool from time to time. Brooke ran the US Marine Corps museum and was very widely travelled on the international military museum net. Mary Helen was an absolute scream, and had unrestrained views about successive occupants of the White House and the top echelons of the Marines. Long after we left the States, she would write long letters to us, vividly and trenchantly commenting on the latest scandals in Washington and the Corps.

Independence re-enacted, Washington, 1983

Other local Americans who were hospitable to us included Mike and Julie McNamara, with whom we had been stationed in Brunssum, and Al Davis, the 'realtor' through whom we obtained housing for many on the Embassy staff. Al took Richard sailing in his chartered 5 sq. metre yacht berthed at Annapolis, Richard soaking up the sunshine ('under-arm tanning') out in Chesapeake Bay and quickly learning the ropes of a larger boat than he had sailed in hitherto. On one occasion Al took Linda and me along too, and we asked to sail right across the Bay to Oxford, Maryland, where we had an unforgettable crab supper on trestle tables covered in brown paper. A nasty wind-versus-tide choppiness beset us on the way back, and poor Linda was horribly seasick. But all these excursions helped us learn about the great United States and her kindly people.

Prior to departure for the States I had purchased a book called *Coping With America* by Peter Trudgill. It was a most amusing commentary on the differences between the American way of life and that of the Europeans, and yet, while extremely funny in places, it nevertheless provided a serious insight into those differences. It should have been compulsory reading for all members of the British Embassy. The first edition of this book explained meticulously the hazards of, for example, the quaint banking system to be encountered in the USA, viz:

> If you do open a current account (US: checking account) at a bank, you will encounter what one British journalist has described as 'America's extraordinarily rudimentary banking system'. Some have only one branch. One consequence of this is that it is not usually possible to write a cheque (US: check) for cash except at your own bank . . . Paying for things by cheque is much more difficult . . . Many businesses, especially petrol (gas) stations, and some restaurants simply will not take cheques at all – you will see notices proclaiming 'NO CHECKS'. It is also quite difficult to use cheques in states other than the one in which your bank account is located.

And so on. This was all good advice, but in our experience it very considerably understated the problem. We joined Rigg's National Bank, which was anything but national, and it was incapable of rigging up a simple standing order. Some gas stations would not even take cash, the individual petrol company's credit card being the only form of currency they recognised. To get hold of these, and indeed to open a bank account anyway, one had to produce one's US 'social security number'. Conversely, one couldn't get a social security number unless one had a verifiable source of credit in the country. This total log jam could only be defeated by inventing a social security number which would fit the organisation's computer programme. We quickly found that my British Army Service Number, 445950, fitted the bill perfectly if one added three noughts on the front. We employed this ruse over and over again, and it worked every time.

The same device had to be used to acquire a driving licence. One was obliged to queue (US: stand in line) at the McLean driving permit office, while gormless looking clerks plodded away in the heat, stopping every now and then to insist very rudely that you stand behind the line painted on the floor in front of their counter. Talk about little town Hitlers! The time they took to accomplish such mundane procedures bore no relation to the complexity of the task. Scant regard was made to car insurance, for example, and in down-town Washington DC insurance was not obligatory anyway. This had the effect of raising the cost of insurance premiums in all the neighbouring districts. The bureaucracy we encountered was sufficient for me to write to Peter Trudgill and suggest that he included a special chapter on it in the second edition of his book.

It all said something to me about the average intelligence or standard of education of clerical people in the great USA.

In all this one obtained no help whatever from the Embassy. The policy was clear: domestic matters, apart from housing, were up to the individual, however difficult for newcomers. Likewise, the Embassy took a traditionally hard line over 'diplomatic immunity' when it came to minor offences like traffic accidents. One hot day I parked my car for two minutes on a double yellow line outside a store in the old part of Alexandria to collect a book I needed for my job. I was 'on duty' and most nations' diplomats would have claimed immunity, but the police were onto me in a flash, and I, following British Embassy policy, was duly fined quite heavily. I have to say that I did not feel resentful, and I still believe that the British are correct to be above reproach in the way these matters are handled in foreign countries, which is in marked contrast to the behaviour of many foreign diplomats in London.

The British Embassy, prominently situated halfway along Massachusetts Avenue, disappointed me. I had imagined that the USA's closest and greatest ally would have a superbly grand and prestigious building as its Embassy. Instead, it boasted a 1960s style functional concrete and glass office block, plain by any standards, notwithstanding the superb statue of Sir Winston Churchill on the sidewalk outside. Only later was I able to enjoy the grandeur of the adjacent British Ambassador's Residence, a wholly more appropriate place. Sir Oliver Wright was our Ambassador throughout my tour. After a tour in Bonn he had retired to run the Anglo-German Königswinter Conference among other things, but he had been brought out of retirement by Margaret Thatcher for this appointment in 1982. It was at once evident that we were going to be extremely fortunate to have this genial and experienced diplomat as the UK's representative in the States. He strode the international stage like a colossus, with great panache too, with Lady Wright involving herself closely in the Washington theatre and social scene. They were immensely popular, not only with the Embassy staff and the British community in Washington, but with all the other nationalities there, including our hosts.

One of the many reasons for the universal respect in which our Ambassador was held was our ability to wallow modestly in the after-glow and euphoria of our success in the Falkland Islands campaign. The stock of the British could not have been held more highly than at this time. It was by no means an uncommon sight in the first few months of my tour to see queues of young American youths outside the Embassy endeavouring to sign on to the British Forces. Only when they were told that they would have to forego American citizenship to do so were they deterred. It was flattering, but there was widespread interest in the UK's achievement, and I was called upon to contribute to spreading the word about our victory. 'What was your secret weapon?' I was often asked by audiences nurtured in the application of overwhelming force. 'The quality of our soldiers,' was my invariable reply. The more I saw of American soldiers during my tour in the States, the more I realised how much they had to learn from us.

My immediate superior officer in the Embassy Defence Staff was Brigadier Stephen Stopford, a most charming cavalryman, who at once decided that the best way to operate with me was to regard the post of Military Attaché as virtually shared between the two of us. He had inherited the duties of the former Technical Military Attaché, so he certainly had more than enough to do on that side of our business, including helping in the important equipment export drive by the Defence Sales teams in the Embassy and in the UK. This left me with a roving commission, dealing with purely Army operational matters, liaison with the Americans and supervision of all our British Army Liaison and Exchange Officers widely scattered throughout the States at American Army bases. That supervision not only included my having to write their annual confidential reports but also to ensure that their families were being looked after by the Americans properly, including medical cover. This meant that Linda was able to accompany me on all my visits to these officers at Her Majesty's expense, and she fulfilled a very important role in this regard. One only has to look at a map of Texas to see the remoteness of the huge American Army base there at Fort Hood. The British liaison officer's wife there was the only British woman for four hundred miles in every direction and to survive in such a desolate place called for a level of self-sufficiency few could fully appreciate without seeing for oneself.

The size of the USA was brought home to me early in the tour. It was my first visit to our Liaison Officer at Fort Benning, the American Infantry Base in the state of Georgia. We flew there and were invited to a cocktail party at the home of a local multi-millionaire in the 'city' of Columbus. He was a typical southern states American with a fine southern drawl. In conversation I tried to deduce how he had made his millions of dollars. I mentioned oil, the Persian Gulf and covered half the globe in search of what the source of his wealth might be. As his eyes were glazing over he interjected:

'Gee,' he said, 'you Europeans do know so much about the world, don't you? I made my bucks in bathroom furniture, and I've never been out of Georgia the whole of my goddam life!'

There was a pause during which I must have registered surprise. I was certainly lost for words.

'But then,' he pressed on with a knowing smile, 'Georgia is the size of the whole of France!' Whereupon he walked away leaving me gasping somewhat. I looked at an atlas when I got back to the base, and saw to my astonishment that one could fit the whole of Western Europe into Texas. We may believe that Americans are ignorant about the rest of the world, but some of us are not too clever about the USA.

The scale of the USA was a constant source of difficulties with the British Ministry of Defence civil servants responsible for pay and allowances. We seemed to have continual visits to Washington DC by these people on fact-finding tours at Her Majesty's expense. They seldom, if ever, travelled further west, but seemed to think that they could assess the budgetary cuts required quite easily from a pleasant weekend looking around the sights of the capital. I suggested that they should take a Greyhound bus or railway journey to Fort Hood, Texas, to see the extent of the country, but that could have been a two-edged weapon. They might have decided that there was so little on which to spend one's allowances in such remote places that the allowances could be reduced with impunity. But it did seem ludicrous that they insisted on making no greater allowance for an annual holiday road mileage subsidy for officers in American outstations than those in the close confines of Germany. As our officer in Fort Hood once said, 'My annual 600 mile petrol allowance gets me one trip to the beach – one way!'

The post-Falklands period was a good time for a British officer to be in the USA if only through being able to bask in the envy and admiration heaped on us. Supported by a number of people who were 'actually there', I was able to take part in presentation team analyses of the campaign for admiring American audiences. The effectiveness of the British 105 mm Light Gun in the campaign also boosted the chances of our sales team successfully persuading the American Artillery School at Fort Sill, Oklahoma, to buy it for their newly formed 9th Light Division stationed at Fort Ord on the west coast. Our sales team at Fort Sill was ably backed up by successive British Liaison Officers stationed there during my tour, first by Lieutenant Colonel Richard Craven, then by our old friend from 26 Regiment, Nick Bird. In every American base our Liaison and Exchange officers were held in very high regard, but possibly nowhere as highly as at Fort Sill. Sales, of course, were only a sideline for them, liaison over gunnery techniques and tactics being their principal responsibility. In most bases, however, the British officer was also prominent in many other fields, including teaching their hosts amateur rugby football. Our Exchange Officer in the American military academy at West Point was particularly successful in this respect, and much to the chagrin of the staff, cadets queued up to join his rugby squad. Americans often discovered that rugby had some important advantages for non-professionals over American football, if only in not requiring so much expensive gear to play it.

Back in Washington much interest was taken in the new British radio equipment too, and the Embassy staff included a Royal Signals colonel, Paddy Verdon. Establishing the same sort of liaison with the Pentagon was, however, not as straightforward for Embassy staff, and try hard though he did, in this case months of top level pressure was, frustratingly, not rewarded with a sale.

This period was also fascinating for an Attaché observing both the Defence and political arenas in the States. Ronald Reagan was President and he was having a marked effect on American morale generally. Although the shooting attempt on his life had possibly not done a man of his age much good, and there was every sign of impending Alzheimer's, he had an infallible touch with the American people, and struck a patriotic chord whenever he spoke on TV, radio or in public. He asked them to 'walk tall' at a time when post-Vietnam depression still gripped the country. Every ounce of his undoubted leadership skills was needed when, on Sunday 23 October 1983, 242 US Marines were killed in a car-bomb attack on an American barracks in Beirut. This tragedy, coming so soon after the debacle in the abortive attempt to rescue American hostages in Tehran, caused national morale to sink to new depths.

I was sitting in my office the day after the Beirut bombing when the telephone rang and I found myself talking to Senator Edward Kennedy. He wanted a few tips about how the British defended fortresses in Internal Security operations. I thought this a bit rich, since he had been a persistent critic of British efforts in Northern Ireland over many years. However, I answered his questions as objectively as I could, and mentioned some of the devices and tactics which we had used effectively for some years there. He was, of course, a Democrat, and I reflected that his interest may have been born of an intention to berate the Republican Administration over laxity. If so, many might believe such criticism well deserved, sixteen Americans having lost their lives in the bombing of the US Embassy in Beirut the previous April and two more Marines having been killed there as recently as 6 September.

Ronald Reagan became personally involved in the ensuing emotional outpouring of the nation's sympathy with the families of the dead Marines, and he certainly knew how to capture the mood of his people, although, as he admits in his autobiography, he found it difficult to explain to the parents of dead Marines why American forces were in the Lebanon in the first place. 'Bud' MacFarlane, the National Security Adviser at the White House, was a former US Marine Corps officer, and his reaction was perhaps more typical. I attended a lecture which he gave in a down-town Washington hotel just days after the latest outrage, and his was typically unsubtle: 'We'll go and bomb the hell out of the bastards,' he yelled, thumping the lectern. 'I'm ordering the US 6th Fleet to bombard them!' This bellicosity was met with unrestrained applause. I had the temerity to ask a question.

'Sir,' I began tentatively, 'can you identify individual terrorists with sufficient accuracy to make large naval guns effective against them?'

There was a stunned silence.

'Of course!' he barked. 'Next question.'

Whether my question was heeded or not, I was told in a most secretive fashion the next day that the American army was flying out special locating radars to the Lebanon. Within two more days the battleship USS *Missouri* was firing its huge 16-inch shells into the hills beyond Beirut, much to the satisfaction of most Americans. Later, I asked my informants in the Pentagon what results had been achieved. Coherent answers came there none – not surprisingly. I was soon invited, however, to give a talk to a Pentagon Study Group about our experiences of internal security operations in Northern Ireland, something which I found rather difficult without a comprehensive library of photographs and slides to hand. I enjoyed the experience, however, and afterwards received the following letter:

Office of the Secretary of Defense.

Dear Colonel Pughe; Please let me tell you how much your presentation to the Conflict Environment Task Force was appreciated. After several months of grinding through innumerable briefings it was sheer joy to hear of your personal experiences in urban control situations. While we had been slowly concluding many of the things you described, your discussion brilliantly focussed our thoughts and put things into perspective. Hearing directly from people who have served under such trying conditions has added a new dimension to our work. We are grateful. Thank you for helping us.

The Defence Staff in Washington had established good working relationships with the various Service staffs in the Pentagon. One had to develop trust and friendship with individual officers in order to break through an almost impenetrable and infantile shroud of secrecy cloaking almost every operational and policy matter. The boot was on the other foot, however, when it came to the Americans wanting to learn more about our Special Forces operations in the Falklands campaign. We had a former member of the SAS on our staff in the Embassy. He was a young major who had distinguished himself to a quite outstanding degree in the South Atlantic, and he was, like so many courageous men, modest and diffident to a fault.

One day the SAS major popped his head round my office door and said that he had been called over to the Central Staff's operations centre in the heart of the Pentagon. He didn't know what it was for, but he thought some staff officer he knew wanted a quick bit of advice about something. 'I won't be long,' he said cheerily.

Four hours later our young major returned looking as white about the gills and as discomfited as I ever saw him. 'Whatever's the matter?' I asked.

'The few quick questions I was expecting turned out to be me giving a full-scale briefing to the Combined Chiefs of Staff and Secretaries of State for Defence, including Casper Weinberger!' The poor young man had had to give a presentation on his and other Special Forces' experiences in the Falklands without any preparation. He did it brilliantly, of course, and the Americans were mightily impressed.

Such openness was, however, far from reciprocated when it came to seeking information about the US operation in Grenada. In late October 1983 the Americans became worried about Cuba-inspired anti-American feeling in this small island, principally because there were 800 US medical students there, who they felt were potential hostages. Ronald Reagan described his approach to the problem graphically in his memoirs:

We agreed that the operation would have to be mounted under conditions of the strictest secrecy ... If there were leaks, the result could be war between us and Cuba ... We decided not to inform anyone in advance about the rescue mission ... Grenada had been a British colony for almost two hundred years before it won independence in 1974, and was still a member of the British Commonwealth. We did not even inform the British beforehand ... Frankly, there was another reason I wanted secrecy. It was what I call the 'post-Vietnam syndrome', the resistance of many in Congress to the use of military force abroad for any reason, because of our nation's experience in Vietnam ...

None of us in the Embassy knew of military preparations at this stage, but by the afternoon of 24 October, Captain David Parkinson, our British Parachute Regiment Exchange Officer at the American Airborne base, Fort Bragg in North Carolina, telephoned me to tell me about a major and imminent deployment by the Division for an assault on Grenada. He asked if he could go too! When we in turn reported to London I asked whether he might be allowed to take part, but the answer was a very abrupt negative. I think that our calls on both the military and diplomatic nets created some excitement in London.

Ronald Reagan later stated:

Just before nine [p.m. 24 October] I was called out of the briefing to take a call from Margaret Thatcher. As soon as I heard her voice, I knew she was very angry. She said she had just learned about the impending operation ... and asked me in the strongest language to call off the operation. Grenada, she reminded me, was part of the British Common-wealth, and the United States had no business interfering in its affairs ... I had intended to call her after the meeting, once the operation was actually under way, but she'd gotten word of it before I had a chance to do so ... I couldn't tell her that it had already begun. This troubled me because of our close relationship.

Thus international political disagreement threatened to undermine all the work we had been doing in the States in an effort to improve mutual trust and confidence between our respective nations' armed forces. We found that our former friendly sources of information in the Pentagon faced us with tight-lipped smiles when we asked about the Grenada operation, and they said that we would be briefed 'in due course taking NATO allies in alphabetical order'! It did not escape our notice that under this policy the UK would be last to be told what was happening, so I took off post-haste for Fort Bragg. There I met some chums from the 82nd US Airborne Division, who rapidly filled me in on every detail of the operation, for which I was extremely grateful.

Grenada was a watershed for the Americans. It was not a well-executed operation by any standards, but against a small number of lightly armed Cuban opponents, the might of the United States quickly prevailed. There were casualties, principally, it transpired, through accidental friendly fire and 'gung-ho' helicopter flying leading to crashes. It seemed to us that more medals were distributed than numbers of soldiers taking part in the battle. But it was a very significant victory in terms of restoring the morale and self esteem of the US Forces. We British were soon forgiven for our national opposition to the operation, and good relations were quickly restored with the Pentagon.

There are people who believe that the life of an Attaché consists of one long round of parties. An Attaché's task was sometimes described as 'Destroying one's liver for Queen and Country'. I cannot deny that the requirement for entertaining as many as possible of the large contingent of foreign representatives in Washington and out on the bases presented a heavy load on our stamina and purse. Much business was done at social gatherings, and during this Cold War era, some important contacts were made with representatives of countries behind the Iron Curtain, of which more anon.

Strangely enough our contacts with our American hosts were not as fruitful or as close as we had originally envisaged. The Americans were very secretive, and no officer below the rank of Colonel was given authority to disclose any sort of information. It was an uphill struggle to obtain even some mundane information from people purporting to be the UK's closest allies. This was very frustrating at times, for the principal task of a Military Attaché is to advise both our Ambassador in the foreign capital and the Ministry of Defence in London on the military capability and intentions of the host nation, and therefore to spare no effort to find out as much as possible about those capabilities. One is a sort of legalised spy. To carry out such a task in the USA should have been simplicity itself, but that was far from the situation. Admittedly the covert photography skills which we had been taught at Ashford were not required in America, and Andrew Whitehead and I were only able to put those skills to good use by holding a running contest on who could snap the largest female bottom during our tour. At a time of widespread obesity in the States this was no mean contest. We named this artless competition 'The Backside of America', which Andrew eventually claimed to have won by producing a shot of the rear end of a hippopotamus!

We tried to make more social contacts with Americans and went to the local Episcopalian church in McLean. The service there was similar to a very traditional Church of England mattins, but it was lively and well attended, at least by white people. We were soon asked to contribute a tenth of our income to the church, which we declined to do. We were always amused by the hearty end to the services there. The 'pastor' would give us his blessing and send us on our way with a shout of 'Go in peace and praise the Lord' and the congregation would shout back 'Alleluyah!' Nobody really welcomed us there with open arms, however. On special occasions, like midnight communion on Christmas Eve, we went to Washington Cathedral. This magnificent twentieth-century Gothic building was nearly completed while we were in America, having taken the requisite twenty-five years to build, under the direction of a British stonemason. The choir was of men and boys on the English cathedral model, though the trebles were not quite as strong. Still, it was a brave copy.

On our first Christmas Eve there we came out of the service into a night air temperature of −16 degrees Celsius. With our breath freezing in the air, we rushed home, and the next morning our pipes burst in the kitchen. Christmas Day was not the time to find a willing plumber, so we turned the water off, and the boys spent the day ferrying buckets of water to the house from our neighbours, the Haywards. It struck us that the thin wooden walls of Washington houses were not designed for such cold conditions.

The church, however, which fascinated Linda most was the Mormon Temple on the northern section of the Washington Beltway, or ring-road. This fairy-tale, multi-pinnacled, shining edifice looked to me like a fantasy from Walt Disney, but there was something mystic about it which captured Linda's imagination. She visited it once with Julie McNamara, but came away predictably disillusioned, not only because she could not accept the Mormons' claim that the founder of the sect, John Smith, was Jesus Christ in His second coming, but because one could only gain access to the Temple's interior if one was a paid-up Mormon and contributed a sixth of one's income to the building of more temples. Even then it was difficult.

In the diplomatic circles of Washington, we found that we were less on the same wavelength with our American hosts than with certain

European colleagues and Attachés from the old Commonwealth countries like Australia, Canada and New Zealand. It was probably a reflection of the cultural difference. Our closest friends turned out to be the Assistant Military Attachés of West Germany, Oberstleutnant Jürgen Arbeiter and his charming blonde wife Heidi, and of Australia, Lieutenant Colonel Roger Wainwright and Tina. We included our French colleague, Alain Faupin, too, as well as a number of others in forming a close circle, among which information on our American hosts was often swapped. The Washington Association of Military Attachés was a body worth while joining, and the regular luncheons prospered under the chairmanship of an Australian, Brigadier Ray Sutherland. At these events one had a good opportunity to get to know the Attachés from hostile countries like Hungary, Czechoslovakia, Poland, Roumania and Russia.

One annual event which the Association organised was a skiing trip to Jack Frost Mountain in Vermont. The piste there tended to be hard and icy, and the runs short and steep, but during our first winter in Washington we were able to take Richard along with us. There he met Francesca, the beautiful 16 year-old daughter of another of our favourite German couples, Ulrich and Jutta Quante. Richard, who had never skied before, stayed with the basic class for the first day, but then, having met Francesca, he chased off after her. She was an accomplished skier, and Richard thereby learnt very fast indeed. Within a couple of days he was speeding down black runs very competently. Being a natural athlete doubtless helped, but I am sure the sex-drive had something to do with it! Surprisingly, nothing further developed from that initially promising friendship.

I enjoyed more skiing both in December 1983 and again the following year when we visited our two British families in Fort Carson, Colorado. We added a long weekend's leave to our visits, and drove up to Breckenridge in the Rockies, staying in an apartment leased by one of the two couples. In many an expert's view, this resort is far better than the more popular places like Aspen and Vale. It was certainly quiet and I never had to queue for a lift. During one long chair-lift haul I sat next to an American who, as they always do, got chatting:

'Where did you learn to ski?' he asked.

'In Germany mostly, but also in Norway,' I replied.

'Gee, are there mount'ns in Norway?' he asked with a look of considerable surprise.

Here, far inland in the Rockies, the snow was dry and powdery and I had several long runs almost to myself. The views eastwards across the plains of North America were stunning in the bright, clear weather. Linda, meanwhile, enjoyed the shops in the small, mock-Bavarian town of Breckenridge, although she had great difficulty in keeping her feet in the snow and ice there. These two short spells of skiing were quite the best of my life.

At one period in our time in Washington there was a spate of films on American TV dealing with India during the Raj. These films included *A Passage to India* and *Jewel in the Crown*, which tended to feed the Americans' ever ready anti-colonial appetite. One day Linda and I were hosting a 'Commonwealth Lunch' at Loch Raven Drive when the Indian Attaché described how often he had been asked by Americans recently, 'Don't you Indians hate the British?' He told us, charmingly, that he had had to explain to the Americans that people in India had much to thank the British for, notably for the infrastructure and civil service, and they shouldn't believe everything they saw in films!

There were several other sources of information about the American forces. For example, there was one officer on our staff in Washington, Major Jim Evans, who specialised in analysing the heavy Congressional committee reports and annual Armed Forces budget statements. He was permitted to attend many of the Defense (sic) Committee meetings in both the House of Representatives and the Senate. He became an acknowledged expert in this important field for which I was truly grateful as I found the bureaucracy of the Pentagon and the Capitol pretty tedious. Quite frankly too, such analyses were time-consuming, and I endeavoured to spend more time out of Washington than in it, visiting American bases and getting to know the country.

Linda and I were very fortunate to be able to combine work with pleasure, although we did take some leave from time to time, and managed to see nearly all the major National Parks and the well-preserved Civil War battlefields during our tour. What history the Americans have, they look after well. Most spectacular of the Parks from my viewpoint were Yosemite, the Grand Canyon, the Meteorite Crater in the Nevada Desert and the Petrified Forest, while for Linda, the additional thrill of visiting Mount St Helens in Washington State shortly after it had blown apart causing devastation to the surrounding landscape must have been the most remarkable experience.

Our side visits were not all quite so pleasurable for her, however. On one occasion in late 1984, a year of ceaseless visits, I had to go to Fort Irwin, a primitive camp at the US Army's tactical training area in the

Mohave Desert, in south-east California. Linda came too and we stayed overnight in a run-down hotel in the nearest 'city', Bairstow, a desolate former mining town miles from anywhere. I went off early the next morning with Richard Hoare, our exchange officer from Fort Hood, to watch the manoeuvres, leaving Linda to fend for herself. I felt especially anxious about this, as the car we had hired was not the most reliable machine in America, and had it broken down out in the searing heat of the desert, Linda would not have been rescued for some considerable time. As it was she visited Calico ghost town, a former silver mining settlement, way out in the desert, and thoroughly enjoyed herself. It said much for her typical single-minded resourcefulness. Meanwhile I had a fascinating time with the American army using the new laser target marker system, whereby full-scale battles could be simulated, 'hits' being recorded electronically. Richard Hoare had become closely involved in the development of these exercises, and it was impressive to see how the Americans would turn to this young British cavalry major for advice. He flew the British flag marvellously, and for his initiatives at Fort Hood and Fort Irwin I later recommended him for an MBE.

Back in DC, we also became expert travel guides for our many visitors from the UK, service and civilian. Among the latter came Linda's mother, also Caroline Weston, the Gordons and my sister Diana and her husband Christopher Everest, plus my sister Maggie from South Africa. We never tired of showing all our visitors the Air and Space Museum, the spectacular Great Falls on the Potomac River especially during the floods there in January 1984, the old colonial living museum town of Williamsburg and the numerous monuments of 'down-town' Washington plus our favourite, overlooking the wide sweep of The Mall from near Arlington, the intriguing giant statue depicting US Marines raising the flag on the summit of Iwo Jima.

One of our many visitors whom I had to escort on official visits to the US Army was the UK's senior Women's Royal Army Corps officer, Brigadier Helen Meekie. She was not at all the ferocious, masculine woman that our hosts were expecting. At a 'working breakfast' very early on the first morning of our visit, a group of sweating, hearty, American Army female officers asked Helen: 'Do you get your women up at dawn for their work-out, like we do?' Helen replied graciously: 'Oh, no. I ask our ladies to rise at 8.00!' There was muted laughter, but thereafter the visit went extremely well.

Richard had joined us soon after we arrived in Washington, and he quickly secured a job as a waiter in an 'old colonial' restaurant, Evans'

Farm Inn, on the outskirts of McLean. He was the only waiter whose skin colour and features resembled the 'old colonial' waiters of British descent which the costume-type uniforms tried to portray. He looked fairly comic in his wig, breeches, white stockings and buckled shoes. He worked hard there, only dropping a huge tray-load of dishes on one occasion I recall. He earned sufficient money doing this job for six months to be able to see many of the finest sights in the States thereafter. A generous US Marine Colonel wanted his sports car, a Datsun 280 ZX, driven from Quantico, the Marine base on the east coast, to Camp Le Jeune near San Francisco on the west coast, a distance of some 3,000 miles. He was asked to complete the journey in ten days, all legitimate expenses paid. That was quite an experience for a young man to have, although he would have preferred not to have done the journey alone.

Richard stayed with us for most of his gap year, having already selected which University he wished to attend. He had been much taken with Durham, especially Collingwood College there, but he realised that he had more chance of gaining national recognition in hockey if he went to Oxford or Cambridge and got a Blue. He had therefore been up to Cambridge and obtained a place at Fitzwilliam College. On 19 January 1984 Paul Gilley, the boys' housemaster at Wellington, wrote to me saying how pleased he was over this. He also said that he thought Jonathan's work in the Lower Sixth was impressive. He would be taking the Oxbridge exam in the winter term of that year. Meanwhile, Richard returned to England to convert the Army Scholarship which took him through his schooldays into an Army Cadetship to see him through University. He passed with flying colours and went for a pre-University three-week course at the Royal Military College, Sandhurst. At the end of this short course, he sent me a photograph taken of himself standing proudly in uniform on the Old College steps. He looked all set for a successful career both at Cambridge and in the Army. He would join the Cambridge University Officers Training Corps, and enjoy a series of attachments to regiments in his vacations, useful opportunities to learn more about soldiering and which took take him to Canada and Norway.

In the States, the only road journey of any length which Linda and I did was from Colorado Springs, east of the Rocky Mountains, across the Utah and Nevada Deserts, via Salt Lake City and the Sierra Nevada, to Los Angeles. It was substantially boring to drive 1,300 miles through so much featureless desert, even allowing for the State boundary sign on entering Utah – a small wooden board shot through with bullet holes. The car we rented was too small for any sort of speed through the mountains too, although we were stopped by the police in one almost deserted village. 'Sir!' he drawled, 'do you know that you were doing 30 miles per hour in a 25 mile per hour speed zone? And it's rush hour too!' We were let off with a stern caution. In subsequent vacations, David and Jonathan joined us in the States and they drove with varying degrees of success. In August 1984 when we drove up to Quebec for a holiday in a remote log cabin on Lac Serpent, David managed to damage the larger of our two cars when trying to negotiate a bend on a loose shingle track rather too fast. Jonathan, on the other hand, later in Washington DC, drove into the car in front of him when his attention was momentarily distracted by a gorgeous looking girl on the sidewalk. For both of these accidents I took personal blame, with the result that I had the utmost difficulty in renewing my insurance cover for the last six months of my tour. Most embarrassing.

By air, however, Linda and I travelled everywhere, and we saw 32 different states by the time our tour ended. Our most memorable flights were those in small aircraft between the larger airports. In May 1984 we visited Fort Huachucha on the border with Mexico and flew back to Phoenix in a small propeller aircraft run by Sunset Airlines. I think it was only one of two aircraft they possessed. The man who checked our ticket at the booking-in counter in the hut which passed as a terminal also turned out to be the pilot and baggage handler. He put our luggage into the space where I thought the engine should be, and after strapping us in behind his seat in the cockpit, we bumped down the runway and took off northwards. We flew low over the place in the desert where the US Air Force parks thousands of spare fighter and bomber aircraft, the dry atmosphere preventing rusting. We steeply descended to take a closer look at some flowering cactii, and lurched around in all manner of air pockets. After a while I noticed a red light appear on the pilot's dashboard. He had said that he had only flown for this airline for a fortnight, and I was on the point of drawing this light to his attention, when the engine started spluttering, and we began to lose height alarmingly. I clutched Linda's hand as though it was our last moment on earth, but scarcely had I begun thinking of ending up as white bones in the desert, than the pilot switched over to the reserve tank, and the engine spluttered into life again. We were glad to reach Phoenix, a city I otherwise found quite dreadful.

Another such flight took us from Atlanta, Georgia, to Fort MacLelland, Anniston, Alabama, the home of the US Army's Nuclear, Biological and Chemical Warfare School. We flew in a Dash 7 propeller aircraft through a very turbulent thunderstorm. We lurched around the sky, descending in a stomach-churning series of drops and banks towards the tiny airfield accompanied by spectacular flashes of lightning and pelting rain. There being no covered walkway, we got wet through as we ran from the aircraft to the diminutive terminal building. There we were met by the local British Exchange Officer. He welcomed us and said:

'Well, if you think that journey was awful, I'm afraid to have to tell you that worse is to come. The Army transport I ordered from the base has not arrived and we shall have to put up with second best.'

With that he gathered our bags and led us outside into the dimly lit forecourt and torrential rain. There on the threshold stood a gleaming Rolls-Royce with a small Union Jack on a masthead on the front wing. Beside it was the 'chauffeur' who was introduced to us as 'Colonel, retired, Farley Berman, anglophile and owner of eight Rolls-Royces', who would be our chauffeur throughout our stay. The Colonel was a colourful character, and his wife had been in the French Resistance. The next day he showed us round his heavily guarded private museum in the basement of his house. He had a remarkable collection of wartime memorabilia, including some of Goering's silver, and other German trophies which he said he had 'liberated' while he was with the US Control Commission in Germany in 1945. Every now and then the tour of weaponry would be punctuated by a loud bang as he squeezed a trigger on a pre-loaded cap as if by chance. He was a real showman and his generosity was remarkable.

The opportunities for travel which our tour in the USA afforded remain among our fondest memories. Not only could we visit the US Army bases in far flung places like Fort Leavenworth, Kansas, and Fort Knox, Kentucky, but we often used those visits as stepping-stones to a further few days private touring, as for example when, around Easter 1984, we went on a duty visit to the US Army Aviation Centre at Fort Rucker, Alabama. Outside the Officers' Club was a vast illuminated sign saying 'Welcome Col Pughe Assistant British Military Attaché'. From there, accompanied by Jonathan, we drove to a ranch at Umatilla, near Orlando, Florida, where we called on an old friend of Linda's family called Nancy Williamson. Jonathan and I were offered a ride on horseback while we were with her, a chance we jumped at. Although I had not ridden for some years and the stallion I was given was not used to the weight of a fully grown man, it behaved impeccably and I thoroughly enjoyed the ride. Jonathan, who claimed that he knew what he was doing, had something rather less pleasurable, as, after a few reluctant strides, his mare took off at high speed for the stables, stopping suddenly on arrival and throwing Jonathan precipitately over its mane. My laughter ceased abruptly as I saw Jonathan pitch forward and hit his unprotected head on the top of the lower half of the stable door. He fell and did not stir. We all rushed over to him and after a few moments' panic, we were relieved to see him move and get to his feet, dazed but undamaged. Luckily we were able to continue our tour with a fascinating canoe trip through the Everglades, and an unforgettable visit to Disney World and the Epcott Centre, Jonathan sporting a huge lump on his cheek, looking for all the world like some sort of chipmunk. I do not believe he ever rode again.

On another occasion in the summer of 1984 when David and Jonathan had flown over from England for the holidays, to join Richard and us, the four of us men went white water rafting on the rapids of the River Shenendoah. It was quite exhilarating but safer than it looks in the hair-raising photographs. Linda was disappointed not to be able to be with us in that raft, but I was concerned that she was simply not strong enough to take the sort of physical battering involved. Later that summer we all went north into Canada via the Niagara Falls, and stayed with friends in Ottawa. From there we went to Kingston and stayed in the old Fort Frontenac, then used as a senior Staff College. There, on the placid waters of Lake Ontario, we sailed for the Royal Navy against the Canadian Forces. As we were in familiar boats, the same type of 420 we had sailed in Roermond, we did well, and won the competition.

Linda and I managed two more visits to Canada during our tour in the States. We had the pleasure of having to visit the British Army family at Fort Lewis, in Washington State. On our first visit there in May 1984 we quite forgot that we needed passports to travel from Washington State to Vancouver, but around 4.00 p.m. we telephoned Richard who was left behind in Mclean and asked him to find our passports and take them to the nearest Federal Express office. He did so, and those documents were with us by 9.00 a.m. the next morning, a distance of over 3,000 miles. That was impressively good service, and it cost just $10.00. We sailed up the Puget Sound and berthed alongside Queen Victoria's statue in Victoria, the most British of towns in Canada. American tourists pushed and crowded expectantly to the head of the gangway, but a stentorian command came over the public address system: 'All those with *British* passports please go to the front now!' It was good to feel so much at home, and to see the envious look on the Americans' faces!

In Victoria we visited my uncle Neville Goss and Aunt Eve. He was a fine old veteran of the First World War, having been shot six times and lost an eye in France. Although he had some difficulty in recognising me at first, it was wonderful to find him in such good form. We were given a tour of the Buschart Gardens and the Bay, after which my uncle handed over numerous family relics and artefacts to me. He and Eve never had children of their own, and I believe that he was fond of me, his namesake. When Linda and I visited him the following year, his health had deteriorated dramatically, he was in a veterans' nursing home, and was unable to communicate with us. Sadly, we did not have a chance to see him again before our tour came to an end and he died just before Christmas 1986.

Our travels beyond the boundary of the USA extended to Mexico too. When we visited Lieutenant Colonel Mike Bremridge at Fort Bliss, El Paso, New Mexico, in May 1984, he and his wife, Paula, took us across the Rio Grande to Cuidad Juarez. There Linda espied an onyx stall, and she immediately fell for some finely carved solid onyx bulls about a foot long and six inches high. She bought two at once and we lugged these heavy ornaments back to Washington. Six months later Paula took Linda again across the border to buy another one, and the three, in different colours, are among her proudest possessions to this day. Mike was a model Liaison Officer; tall, slim, grey-haired but fit, he could run every American on the base off their feet, and was renowned for this, as well as having the best garden on the base – not quite so difficult. He must surely have been fitter than I was, because my brave efforts at taking the annual fitness test by running along the tow-path of the Potomac ended with my brushing against some poison ivy, which made me quite ill for weeks, and left me with a permanent allergy to ivy of any sort.

But a journey even further afield took place in that exciting year of 1984. The office of ABCA, the Quadripartite Alliance between America, Britain, Canada and Australia, was situated in Washington. Our small British staff there came under the Military Attaché's supervision, and Stephen Stopford and I attended the monthly conferences of the four nations' representatives. In many ways this forum had greater potential than NATO for the harmonisation of military tactics and standardisation of equipment. Commonality of language aided the production of agreed Standing Operating Procedures in a more timely fashion than NATO could dream of. Nevertheless, we always felt that ABCA was treated as a poor relation of NATO by our Ministry of Defence, with one exception: the biennial ABCA conference. This meeting alternated between the capitals of the four nations, with New Zealand being included as an 'observer nation'. It was our good fortune that it was the turn of the Australians to host the conference in November 1984, and wives could accompany their husbands at their own expense.

We flew to Sydney and stayed in a fine hotel in Manly directly overlooking a majestic surfing beach, where young Australian lads spent the whole day riding the long South Atlantic rollers. We were met by Alan Batchelor, who had been a subaltern with me in 33rd Parachute Light Regiment in 1960. He was now approaching retirement from the Australian Army, and he spared no effort to make our stay memorable, showing us round the flora and fauna of the Northern Beaches and many of the fine sights of the Sydney area. Most treasured of my recollections, however, was our first journey by ferry up the long sweep of Sydney Harbour in bright sunshine to the accompaniment of hundreds of small boats. I could then see just what it must have been like for my father in 1945 when he sailed in to Sydney on HMS *Indomitable* after surviving the horrors of Japanese kamikaze attacks off Okinawa. Alan Batchelor, always a fanatical cross-country runner, was preparing at the age of 54 to run around Australia. He subsequently achieved this remarkable feat. It took him three months and he raised over $1 million for cancer research.

After a night in the Argyle Tavern in The Rocks area of the city, during which Linda became closely acquainted with an affectionate young koala bear, and it rained so heavily that cars were washed down the street outside, we flew to Auckland. There we hired a car and spent five days touring the north island. We stopped overnight at Rotaroa where I found the sulphur fumes quite unbearable, had a day in Wellington, visited relatives of our life-long friends, the Westons, saw captive kiwis by infra-red light, and stayed in the magical sub-tropical surroundings of a lodge halfway up the snow-capped volcano, Mount Egmont. This short tour gave us a glimpse of what is, we have since always agreed, the most beautiful country we have ever visited. The variety of terrain and the somewhat antiquated atmosphere of the country were simply unforgettable.

If all this was not sufficient,1984 saw Linda and me engaged in the start of something altogether more intriguing than we had ever dared expect in the life of an Attaché and his wife in a friendly country like the USA. It all started with my regular six-weekly visits to the United Nations building in New York, to participate in the moribund Military Commission meetings. The meetings were attended by a small team of officers from the original Five Members of the UN Security Council: the United States, China, Russia, France and the UK. As, for obvious political reasons, there was never any prospect of agreement between the communist countries and the three Western nations' forces, the advice of the committee was never sought and so there was never any business to be done. We would meet, discuss the empty agenda, set a date for the next meeting, and take refreshments together, chatting amicably with members of the other teams. In April 1984 this farce was played out for the thousandth time since it was formed immediately after World War II. We posed for a group photograph, in uniform, as usual, but I had forgotten my khaki tie, so wore my Staff College tie and tried to hide this conspicuous sartorial mistake by the judicious use of my hand nonchalantly tugging at my throat.

The five nations were represented in different strengths, the Americans and ourselves invariably producing just one officer each, the French two, the Chinese two, and the Russians three. The Russian team included a young naval captain called Boris Morzhinsky. Although he seldom talked openly with me while his two colleagues were nearby, he did reveal to me that he had been an Attaché in London for four years and had thoroughly enjoyed the experience. Although Russian Attachés were normally trained members of the GRU, the military equivalent of the British MI6, and those posted to the Russian UN Mission in New York were almost certainly members, Boris assured me that he was a bona fide naval officer who had been to the Naval Academy in Leningrad, now St Petersburg. He seemed keen to establish his credentials with me, and I noticed that he sought me out with increasing intensity in the margins of each successive meeting, to chat informally. I began to like him, and we established a good rapport. I much admired his sense of humour.

As time went by there appeared to me to be every possibility that Boris was developing a certain empathy with the British and American ways of life, so I duly reported to our secret service people in the Embassy in Washington. They advised me to speak to our UN Mission representatives in New York after the next meeting. I did so, and the reaction I received at first surprised me. 'Oh yes,' they said, 'we know old Boris. He's a real card. Are you sure *he*'s not recruiting *you*?' I was advised, however, to develop the growing friendship more.

To do so was not easy, since we only met every six weeks and my suggestion to Boris that we met in Washington when he visited the Russian Embassy there fell on stony ground. I suspected that, with his background of prolonged service in the West, he was watched rather carefully and restricted in his movements. I was right. He even told me that, although his wife and 13 year-old son lived in the confines of the Russian block of apartments in New York, his 16 year-old daughter was held in Moscow. 'Doesn't that worry you?' I asked quietly one day. 'No,' he replied, 'she is looked after very well by her grandmother, and I am not concerned about her at all.'

Boris's English was excellent, so I knew that he chose his words with care. This response was of the greatest significance, and I again reported to my mentors in the British UN Mission building. They suggested that I pressed him for meetings outside our normal conference room, and I was very pleased when he agreed to meet me for a cup of coffee in a downstairs bar in the UN building after a meeting one day. He was clearly agitated about how to give his two colleagues the slip. But eventually, in a remarkable charade outside the front entrance of the UN building, he slipped away from his fellows at the very last minute as they got into the Russian Mission car. We then had a pleasant meeting in which he as good as told me that the British way of life held considerable appeal for him, and he was fed up with the Soviet Union. He pleaded, however, with me not to divulge this to anyone yet.

Unfortunately, it was my duty to do so, and my mentors thought that it would be a good idea to arrange an evening at the opera for him. I could not write to him, as letters would be intercepted, but I did manage to speak to him guardedly on the telephone. He seemed quite pleased about the prospect of an evening on the town, and to put him thoroughly at ease, I said that Linda would be with me. My UK UN Mission friends ensured that I made all the arrangements but they later picked up the bill.

We arranged to meet Boris in the foyer of the Metropolitan Opera House, where we were to see *Cavalleria Rusticana* and *Pagliacci*. We waited anxiously, and at the very last minute Boris appeared looking a little flustered, closely followed by a heavy, solid jawed man, who looked the archtypical Russian agent or bodyguard. Ignoring him, we took

(Left to right) Self, Mrs Morzhinsky, Linda, Boris: New York, 1984

Boris to some excellent seats in the stalls, and were not altogether surprised to see the bulky 'shadow' sitting three rows behind us. During the interval Boris said that he had obtained a car, which he would bring round to the front of the building afterwards, and we would go round to a favourite restaurant of his on the southern end of Manhattan. We were delighted, and when the show ended, Boris asked us to wait in the foyer.

As we did so, the theatre emptied fast, and when we idly looked up to the top staircase we saw to our surprise Boris earnestly talking to our friend the heavy shadow. Boris then came running down the stairs and moments later he appeared in front of the steps with a rather battered looking car. We jumped in, and then followed quite the most dramatic ride Linda and I had ever experienced. Boris said: 'Hold on tight. We've got to get rid of someone.' And we sped off into the night, along dark and dingy streets in down-town Manhattan, hurtling round corners with screaming tyres, for all the world like something out of a James Bond movie.

Eventually, we reached the southernmost tip of Manhattan, not far from Wall Street, and Boris appeared satisfied that he had lost his 'tail'.

We got out and he relaxed, leaning over the promenade railing, staring wistfully out to sea. 'My son and I often come here,' he said. 'It's like freedom. I hate the City. I sometimes long for the Ural Mountains where I was born.' We then got back into the car and he drove us to a nice little restaurant where we had a long chat and a super meal. Boris explained that he loved his country but hated the regime. All he wanted to do, he said, was to run a restaurant of his own, and that was something that he could not do in Soviet Russia under the communists. When we asked him if he wanted to 'come over' to the West he said that he was not quite sure. He needed time. Late that evening he drove us to the jetty from which we were going to catch the last ferry to Governor's Island, an oasis of tranquillity within sight of Wall Street across the water and where we were to stay as guests of the US Coastguard. Boris bade us a fond farewell, kissing Linda warmly.

Two days later my friends at the UK UN Mission asked me to attend a meeting with the FBI after our next Military Committee Meeting. I duly did so, and it was explained that, as we were on US soil, the host nation would now be taking over this case from the UK Mission. The FBI man, a foxy little chap, said that we had to give Boris some excuse for continuing to see me. I would have to pass him some low level classified information that he could pass back to his minders in the Russian Mission. I was horrified at such a suggestion. 'This friendship,' I protested, 'is based upon trust. We have a genuine rapport, he likes me and my wife, he wants friendship, and needs to feel he can trust me not to push him too far too quickly. We surely mustn't do anything to put the foundation of our rapport at risk?'

The FBI man pondered over his note-book. 'You must see that his latest escapade has put him at risk. I wouldn't be surprised if he was recalled. Unless we give him something useful to pass on, he could well be lost to us.'

I didn't like it, but was persuaded by that argument. So I duly arranged to have coffee with Boris after the next Committee Meeting. After our usual niceties and good-natured banter I casually mentioned a large NATO exercise that was taking place shortly in Germany. I had been given a few facts and figures about it. As soon as I spoke, however, I knew I had done the wrong thing. He looked shocked, and disappointed. He drank his coffee and left quite abruptly.

At the next two Committee Meetings Boris did not appear. Twelve weeks went by before I saw him again. We were now well into 1985.

He avoided me at the start of the following Meeting and I felt very depressed. Afterwards, however, I did manage to get a few words with him. He said that he had been back to Moscow, where he had been given a 'warning' about his behaviour. He smiled grimly and left hurriedly.

I then received a new instruction; I was to have lunch with some people from London and the FBI in an apartment just around the corner from the UN Building. I duly went and was welcomed by three people, only one of whom I had seen before. I was given a large a gin and tonic and I relaxed in a comfortable leather sofa. We then started lunch and I found myself almost uncontrollably chattering about Boris and all the conversations that he and I had had up to now. I was garrulous to a degree that, in retrospect, completely astounded me. My interlocutors asked me only an occasional question. I hardly needed prompting, and the entire lunch period, well over an hour, was taken up with my endless stream of chatter about Boris.

At the end of lunch the three men appeared satisfied that I had told them everything they needed to know, and one of them kindly drove me all the way to the airport, and saw me onto the plane for Washington. I fell sound asleep, and only when safely home in McLean did I stumble on the possibility that there had been more in that gin and tonic than I had bargained for. I did not relish the experience, although I could only have told the truth, which, since no defection had yet been achieved, must have been, for these people, quite prosaic.

Linda came up to New York with me for the next Meeting, and we met Boris in the downstairs coffee room again afterwards. He was really very forthcoming on this occasion. He told Linda quite openly that he would like to defect. He was not unduly worried about his daughter being a 'hostage' as she was well cared for, but he wanted time. 'Please do not rush me!' he pleaded with Linda. A few weeks later Linda and I had the rare experience of being invited to the Soviet UN Mission where Boris and his wife took the unusual step of having their photographs taken with us in the foyer.

I duly reported on these events, but no sooner had I done so than my posting order came through. I was to be promoted to Brigadier and, much to Linda's initial dismay, appointed to be Defence Attaché in Bonn. Furthermore, I was to return home to the UK at the end of September 1985 to take a six-month language course. This news was unwelcome to our friends in the Embassy and at the UN Mission, and

I believe that moves were initiated by the Foreign Office to have my posting delayed until the Boris situation came to a head. Nevertheless the Ministry of Defence evidently pressed for an early move, and my chance of glory in securing a defection eluded me.

So it was that, after I had written my end-of-tour report on the US Army, a report which Sir Oliver Wright admired and described as 'trenchant', and he had given Linda and me some apposite advice about the Ambassador and his wife whom we were to meet in Bonn, we threw a huge farewell party on 22 September at 6221 Loch Raven Drive. We found a larger house for my successor, Colonel Robert Ffrench-Blake, welcomed him and took our leave of Washington with our luggage safely stowed – this time in containers.

CHAPTER 14

Bonn Bombshells

OUR RETURN TO THE United Kingdom in autumn 1985 after just over two hectic years in the United States of America presented immediate disadvantages and some important advantages. Our first problem was the state of our bungalow at Granborough. 'Tumbleweed' looked derelict and dirty again, enough to cause my tired Linda dismay, despair and tears. Bravely she set about cleaning the whole place through once more, and within a few days, we had the family home looking comfortable again.

On the positive side we were welcomed back into the village again with open arms, and our return offered the opportunity for a Christmas together as a family again, our first such gathering for three years. Jonathan had now left Wellington, and I had received a remarkably moving letter from their housemaster Paul Gilley. He wrote:

> Dear Linda and Neville,
>
> The end of an era has arrived and I shall be sad not to have a Pughe in the House next term. Over the years the boys have served The Talbot admirably and have been a great credit to the school. Outside they have been splendid ambassadors for Wellington and it has given me much pleasure to oversee their progress and development here. I appreciate their friendship and I know they will come back frequently to keep me up to date with their plans and achievements. Jonathan has been a very good, loyal and efficient Head of House. Things have been done with the minimum of fuss and I should like to thank him for all that he has done for both House and myself. The place won't be the same without him . . .
> I would like to thank you both for being such supportive parents during the time the boys have been at Wellington. Between us I think we can be proud of what we have produced . . .
>
> With very best wishes,
> yours sincerely,
> Paul

No finer tribute to our three sons could have been written, and we were every bit as proud of their successful schooldays as Paul Gilley was. They had proved themselves to be strong contributors to the common good, as successful academically as on the sports field. The fact that all three boys were now at or about to go to Oxford or Cambridge Universities was another outstanding feat and a great credit to both the Prep school and Public school they had attended. Our financial commitment to their education appeared to have paid considerable dividends and had been worth every penny and every sacrifice.

Now it was my turn to be educated again. I was to have the best part of six months' private tuition in the German language to equip myself for my forthcoming role as Defence Attaché in Bonn. There I had no doubt that I would have to work in German, and I wanted to be really good at it. I rued the fact that I had not been taught German at school. True, I had taken 'O' level German when I was at AFCENT in 1980, but I was now nearly 50 years of age, and I needed every bit of the encouragement and skill dispensed by my tutor in Bicester, Laura Bond, the German wife of a British Army Officer. Despite my slowness, she did pretty well.

On 10 January 1986 I received a super telegram from my sister Maggie in South Africa. It said: 'Quoting WG: when you reach 50 take guard and set down for the century. Happy Birthday dear lad.' Nothing could have pleased me more than to have a cricket metaphor on this personal milestone. Linda then asked some of our neighbours and our closest friends, the Westons and the Dickins, to a party at home, and cramped as we were in that little bungalow, it was a wonderful day.

The winter and spring went by quickly, and we decided not to let 'Tumbleweed' when we went to Bonn but rather let the boys use it as a base. Besides, we had a notion that it was time we sold it and moved upmarket. Linda thought that her MS was not causing so much of a problem as we at first feared, and she would rather like to try a two-storey house next time. Our eyes turned towards the West Country. Devon was where I was born and grew up, but lovely as it was, it was a bit far away from the boys, and in summer it was too crowded. Dorset, on the other hand, especially around the little market town of Sturminster Newton, looked a good bet as far as house prices went. We started to look around in a desultory fashion before the time came to move, but no firm decisions were made.

Jonathan endured the first part of his gap year with us, taking on all sorts of short-term menial jobs, even counting screws in a nail factory in Haddenham! For the winter, however, he secured a job in Morgins, Switzerland, working in a restaurant at the foot of the main ski-lift. He was to find this immensely to his liking. Both his French and his skiing skills advanced quickly. We now had to buy a new car. I chose a Ford Escort 1.6 Ghia at discounted export price. The automatic gearbox of this vehicle caused us endless mechanical problems, and the steering was very heavy. The boys kept our old Fort Cortina, sharing it at University for a couple of years.

I began to prepare for a busy Attaché tour in earnest, and I was determined that life would be made as easy as possible for Linda. Fortunately, the Director Royal Artillery was now Major General Bill Cornock, an old friend of ours from 33rd Parachute Light Regiment days. Besides being the chief selector for the Gunners and Army hockey teams and keeping an eye on Richard's spectacular progress at this game, Bill had the last word in all matters concerning regimental manpower. Despite the shortage of manpower generally, Bill unhesitatingly supported my plea for a young NCO to be provided to be our house steward in Bonn. He suggested that I wrote to Robin Duchesne, another old Airborne Gunner chum, who was just finishing a tour in Cyprus, as he had had one Lance Bombardier Holmes as a house steward out there recently. I did so, and it was duly arranged that the good Holmes would transfer directly to me after reporting in to his parent unit, none other than 45th Field Regiment, then stationed at Hohne in Germany. Robin said, 'He's a good man, a Yorkshireman, but with a cockney sense of humour. Watch out for Friday nights, though!' I asked for him to report to me at our large Foreign Office hiring Im Etzental 15, Bad Godesberg, near Bonn, on the very first day in May when I would be in post.

In April I left for Germany. David Quayle, my predecessor in Bonn, had kindly arranged for me to have two weeks' language tuition with retired Generalmajor Alexander Frevert-Niedermein who lived at Swistal-Buschhoven, near Bonn. He had seen war service as a cavalry subaltern in the Wehrmacht, and had been captured by the British at Lübeck in 1945. He told me that he had been stationed in Denmark towards the end of the war, and when Germany surrendered, the Danes asked if his regiment would help them put down an uprising by communist rebels. Alexander agreed to help on condition that afterwards he would be allowed to ride his horses and carry his weapons into British captivity. He was successful on both counts.

Alexander held the British in high regard, and after joining the Bundeswehr when it was formed in 1949 and rising rapidly through the officer ranks in light armoured reconnaissance regiments, *Panzeraufklärer,* he secured a place at the Imperial Defence College in Belgrave Square, London, later to become the Royal College of Defence Studies. He was the first German officer after the war to do so. He and his gracious and charming wife, Sascha, loved London; they always had a good eye for quality and the aristocracy. Later, back in Germany, Alexander was selected to escort Her Majesty the Queen on her first state visit of the country. Such was the regard in which he was held by Her Majesty, that at the end of her visit she personally knighted him on the decks of the Royal Yacht *Britannia*. I was not aware of this until some days after I arrived for my language induction, when I saw the insignia of the KCVO and the citation proudly displayed on the wall of the Frevert-Niedermein's house. He rose to be the deputy chief of the German Army before retiring. He was a modest man with a wonderful sense of humour, and I knew from the moment I met him that we would hit it off in a big way.

As I had flown to Bonn, leaving Linda with our Ford Escort, David Quayle kindly arranged for me to have the loan of one of the Embassy Defence Section staff cars, a Vauxhall Cavalier, for my two weeks with Alexander. I stayed each night at a *Gasthaus*, 'Die Alte Post', in Essenich, a German village halfway between Bad Godesberg and Buschhoven. The splendidly Germanic wife of the landlord there had frightful difficulty pronouncing my surname. The vowel sound in 'Pughe' is unknown in German, so after a few gallant attempts, she said that she thought she would call me 'Mister Pee' if I didn't mind. This tickled Alexander's sense of humour considerably. He roared with laughter and called me 'Mister Pee' himself often thereafter.

By day and every day the Frevert-Niedermeins took me touring in their car everywhere within fifty miles of their village. They were not in their first youth, and it must have been very exhausting for them, but they never seemed to tire. We would speak German all day without a break, and it was I who found the days most tiring. Sometimes it would be ten hours' worth of German in a day, which, as everyone knows who has struggled to learn a foreign language at the age of fifty, demands much of one's concentration by evening. This charming couple entertained me splendidly, and I did arrange for some small monetary contribution towards their expenses, which was allowed under the rules governing these language attachments. They were embarrassed to accept it.

One day I was taken to the Bonn Rotary Club luncheon in the Hotel Dreesen, Bad Godesberg. Alexander revelled in telling me something of the history of this hotel, and in particular when it hosted a meeting between Hitler and Neville Chamberlain in 1938. It was said that Hitler was so nervous about that meeting that, before Chamberlain came across the river from his overnight accommodation in the Hotel Burg, Hitler was seen chewing a carpet. In Germany he was thereafter known secretly in certain circles as '*Der Teppichfresser*'. The guest speaker at the Rotary Club meeting was a German botanist whose chosen subject was rhododendrons. Just before he spoke I was introduced to the meeting as a guest, and Alexander asserted that I came from Surrey – England's most famous rhododendron area. The speaker said that he felt at a singular disadvantage as a result. Keen as I was on gardening, he need not have worried. My speciality was always roses.

The Freverts also introduced me to many interesting and distinguished people, explaining solemnly the difference between a Graf and a Freiherr, a Gräfin and a Freifrau. We laughed about America which Alexander had once visited, and where trans Atlantic computers could not deal with a long hyphenated name like his and people invariably pronounce the 'ei' in a name as 'ie'. 'They used to call me "General Nydermeen",' he chuckled.

As well as treating me to sumptuous German fare at restaurants and *Gasthäuser* during *Spargelzeit*, this time of the year when the German white asparagus was at its best, and showing me the local orchards in full bloom, Alexander plied me with gifts, mainly with military connections. He felt as if he were a Prussian, even if he was not born there, and he said that he never missed watching our annual Trooping the Colour ceremony on television. '*Hervorragend Präzision!*' he would say, and add with a twinkle in his eye, '*Fast preussisch!*' ('Wonderful precision! – Almost Prussian!')

This was one of the most valuable and formative fortnights of my life. The speed with which a rapport was established between the Freverts and me was quite remarkable. They also gave me a real taste for the language and what became an abiding interest in it. They started to teach me idioms and proverbs, which made learning the language great fun. I went on to develop this knack for unusual, and I have to admit sometimes rather old-fashioned, expressions, to the extent that I believe I became quite well known for so turning a conversation that I could introduce a few of my pet phrases or proverbs. At the last count I had accumulated over 350 German proverbs.

I was sad when my immersion in German came to an end, but I was longing to introduce them to Linda. So I returned the car and flew back to fetch her. She looked tired after packing up the house and saying goodbye yet again to our good friends in Granborough, but I could scarcely contain my excitement. If Linda still had reservations about this tour, she bravely and cleverly disguised the fact. We arrived at Im Etzental 15 in the third week of May 1986. The weather was fine and the setting was precisely as described so vividly in Le Carré's novel *A Small Town in Germany* which we had read assiduously. Linda's first impression of the house as we drove up the road must have been depressing for her. It looked for all the world like a German barrack block, with grills over some of the windows, and a very small front garden. Once inside, however, her fears must have been quickly dispelled. The hall and staircase were large and yet welcoming, the rooms spacious and well-proportioned. Although the Quayles had not used it as such, there was a separate wing for the house steward, who was due to arrive the next day.

'I'm sorry to tell you,' said David Quayle by way of a welcome, 'but in two days' time you have your first visitor, none other than General Sir Geoffrey Howlett, the Commander in Chief of Allied Forces Northern Europe!' To his evident surprise we both said, 'Excellent! And what fun!' Geoffrey had been one of the Parachute battalion commanders during my time as Brigade Major in 16th Parachute Brigade and I had never forgotten his kindness and advice to me then. I knew him as a fine cricketer and a really good sport, who would never stand on his dignity.

David said: 'I have arranged for him to stay at the Dreesen Hotel, if that's okay?' I looked at Linda enquiringly, and she at once knew what I was going to say and nodded. I said, 'Let's change that at once. We would like him to stay here. A hotel's so impersonal, and he's an old friend who won't mind if there's a certain amount of chaos here.'

We broke the news to Lance Bombardier Holmes when he arrived the next day, and he cheerfully accepted that it would be a 'nice challenge' to look after a four star general as his 'test guest'. Linda, he and the Philippino maid, Cincha, worked like fury for the next two days unpacking as fast as possible. Bed linen, towels and basic cutlery were sorted out, but few pictures were up and Linda had certainly not yet managed to put her impeccable stamp on the house to her liking. Nevertheless, I met Geoffrey at the airport from where he and his ADC travelled with me in my staff car incognito. We gave them a light supper as he requested, and he went to bed early.

The following morning the General came down to an early breakfast fairly informally dressed, which was in stark contrast to the display of pomp and circumstance beginning noisily outside in front of the house. There, motorcycle outriders and police cars were assembling in considerable numbers, giving all the neighbours cause to watch the commotion from their windows with growing interest. Finally Geoffrey Howlett was ready; he left the house smack on the second the German Army *Feldjäger* and civil police had agreed with me was necessary and the vast cavalcade made off down the road towards the German Ministry of Defence. It caused quite a stir, and made not a few neighbours wonder whether this was the style which the new Attaché was going to maintain!

We sped along the main roads towards the Hardthöhe, the German Ministry of Defence, on the outskirts of Bonn, driving straight through red traffic lights under the direction of countless police at every street corner. It was quite exhilarating, although Geoffrey spoke rather deprecatingly of 'all the fuss'. We arrived on time in front of the main tower block at the Ministry and admired the bearing and marching of the tri-Service guard of honour drawn up in the General's honour. The German Army band was excruciatingly awful, but it was soon over and I accompanied Geoffrey to upper offices in the building to meet the Secretary of State for Defence and other officials and senior officers. It was a most interesting and valuable introductory visit for me too.

Life at the Embassy soon got into a routine. Every Monday morning at 9.30 the Ambassador held 'prayers': a round table meeting of all the heads of sections. I must admit that I and my fellow Naval and Air Attachés found these meetings of little interest or value. Indeed, we considered they simply provided Heads of Sections with opportunities for 'point scoring'. Nothing of great international importance seemed to be discussed, and much of the hour or so spent at them seemed to be taken up with adjusting the fine wording of telegrams to be sent by the Head of Chancery, Keith Haskell, to London. Much of the more important business was done during the normal course of events during the week, as, for example, the formulation of briefing notes to London prior to a British Minister's visit to Bonn, or a despatch commenting on some erroneous newspaper report about the UK's economy and so on. Certainly we three Attachés seldom had much to contribute to the meetings that was of interest to anyone there, but occasionally the Ambassador himself showed polite interest in our brief reports.

Early in our Bonn days Linda and I were invited to an international horse show in Essen, which HRH Princess Anne was formally to open. She was accompanied by Captain Mark Phillips. The royal couple arrived an hour late, during which time the crowd was kept waiting with no explanation from the commentator save (in German) that the Princess had evidently not taken into account the hour's difference between German and British time! In fact the delay had been caused by fog at Heathrow, but the German crowd, unaware of this, greeted Princess Anne with whistles and boos. Linda and I spoke briefly with Mark Phillips whose anger was quite justified, and the embarrassment of all British present was acute. I duly reported the matter to our Ambassador, and I believe that Princess Anne quite understandably vowed not to return to Essen for some time to come.

Another early invitation given to us was to attend a NATO Musical Tattoo at a large outdoor stadium at Mönchengladbach. This remains in our memory as an especially amusing event. Each nation's military band gave a display in turn, and each successive band demonstrated their national characteristics to perfection. The British band marched stoically through pouring rain with precision and dignity. The American band stood in an informal circle and blazed away with jazz. The French dashed into the arena and played badly-tuned and noisy brass with élan. The Dutch Marines gave a colourful and varied display, but it was the Belgians who stole the show. They entered the arena mostly out of step, and certainly out of breath, making an increasingly cacophonous noise. This was made worse when they undertook the ambitious manoeuvre of dividing the band into two sections marching in opposite directions, thereby getting hopelessly out of time with each other. Finally, their corpulent drum-major finessed this excruciating performance by throwing his mace so high into the air that the band collided with him as he waited for it to descend. Undeterred, the drum-major then threw it so far in front of him that it pierced the ground like an Olympic javelin, to the accompaniment of roars of applause and comprehensive musical chaos!

Within a few weeks I found it necessary urgently to visit the German Ministry of Defence on the Hardthöhe to find out what was going on between the Germans and the French armies. There was rumour that they were going to form a joint Brigade and London was suspicious. I made an appointment with the Chief of an important politico-defence central staff branch, Leiter des Führungstabes III, or Fü S III for short. His name was Brigadegeneral Klaus Naumann, and I gathered that he had at one time attended the Royal College of Defence Studies, in London. With much trepidation I went to see him, and after a few polite formalities I stuttered my way in German through some leading questions on the German intentions regarding this Franco-German Brigade. Klaus listened patiently for a while, and then he drew his chair up closer to me, and looking me straight in the eyes said in perfect English: 'All right, Neville, now tell me what you really want to know'! I sighed visibly with relief, and he went on to tell me as much as he could about the plan, adding at the end that there would be formidable difficulties about joint and integrated command down to battalion level, that the only common language was English, and the British should not worry unduly about it as many thought it simply 'political froth'. I was tremendously grateful to him, and we kept in touch ever thereafter, even when he obtained rapid promotion to become the German Chief of Defence Staff and Chairman of the NATO Military Committee. It was not always as easy on the Hardthöhe, and we normally had to work hard in German for all information. Whereas our Foreign Office colleagues, I discovered, had a much easier time with their diplomatic counterparts, who nearly always discussed matters in English with them.

The Ambassador was Sir Julian Bullard, a very experienced and canny diplomat in the traditional mould. My predecessor, David Quayle, had apparently got on very well with him, David having a keen brain instantly recognisable, I suspect, from his having an Oxford degree. The Ambassador had had no difficulty in recommending him for promotion to Major General, which he duly and deservedly obtained. From the outset, however, I felt that the Ambassador did not hold me quite in the same regard. His appearance, with his beetling eyebrows, I must admit made me nervous. His formidable wife terrified me. Somebody said: '*He* looks fierce but isn't, and *she* doesn't but is,' which turned out to be a shrewd summary, but it took me a long time to feel confident in the Ambassador's presence, despite that.

Relations between the Defence Staff at an Embassy and the career diplomats is often uneasy. The Foreign Office is not above a certain amount of intellectual arrogance at times. It is not surprising that occasions arise when Servicemen may see matters in a different light or from a different perspective to diplomats. Servicemen are often decisive men of action, while diplomats are more sedentary, circumspect and trained to choose their words very carefully. We, like all Attachés, tried very hard to pull our weight as part of a team in the Embassy. But much depends upon the Ambassador himself, the Minister and the Head of Chancery, in addition to any members of the Chancery division who are appointed to take a special interest in politico-defence matters. In Bonn we were lucky in having a particular up and coming star in the Chancery division called Michael Arthur, and he and I established a good rapport early on in my tour. But even then, there was an occasion which in some ways typified the difference in approach between us and the diplomats.

There had been many months of discussion in the countries of western Europe about how to strengthen the politico-defence relationship, so that, if the USA should ever pull out of Europe, the combined strengths of the United Kingdom, West Germany, France, the Benelux Countries and a few others could be put to better use within the framework of the Western European Union. The problem was that the original WEU treaty was outdated, and a new one was required. The respective nations worked together over many months to revise the treaty and put more meat on the bones of the original. On the day the new treaty was signed, Michael Arthur came into my office waving the telegram. 'It's done!' he cried. 'It's signed and sealed. We've saved Europe!' He was only half joking, and I pulled his leg gently: 'Good heavens,' I said in mock surprise, 'I thought you were Neville Chamberlain for a moment. What's in a piece of paper?'

Michael looked somewhat taken aback, but he took it in good part, and spent some time lecturing me about the importance of the new treaty. I have no doubt he was right, and that he was justifiably proud of all the work which he and his colleagues had done to achieve it. But he also knew that I was right. Treaties are no good unless they are backed up with the necessary deterrent force. I felt that it was my job as the Defence Attaché to say so.

There have been rare cases in some parts of the world of a Defence Attaché falling out with the Ambassador himself. The root of the problem, if it ever arose, would in my view lie in a confused chain of command. It may not be clear whether the Defence staff's first loyalty is to the Ambassador or to the Chief of Defence Staff in London. It is a long-established practice that all nominations to Attaché posts on an Embassy staff are approved by the Ambassador personally before the MoD can publicly announce them. This is principally a courtesy, but does it suggest that an Attaché, an officer 'attached' to an Embassy, whose paramount duty is to serve, support and advise the Ambassador, once appointed, approved and in station, owes his first allegiance to the Ambassador and through him to the Foreign Office, or does he retain primary allegiance to the Defence staff in London to whom he is required to send reports on all Defence-related matters in the country to which he is accredited? (Both contribute to his annual confidential reports!) In the normal course of events this question needs no answer, as it is normal for Attachés either collectively or individually to discuss matters for reporting to London fully with senior Embassy staff, and occasionally with the Ambassador himself, as well as informing the MoD. The only possible difficulty could arise if there were a conflict of opinion between the diplomats and the Attachés.

Unfortunately, such a difference of opinion did arise on three occasions during my tour while Sir Julian Bullard, and his Minister, Nigel Williams, were in Bonn. On each occasion, I was treated generously by this experienced Ambassador. The first occasion arose when I had been in post only a few months. I noticed an article in a German newspaper in which Hans-Dietrich Genscher, the outspoken champion of détente with Soviet Russia, and the longest serving foreign minister in the West, appeared to me to be suggesting that NATO countries should reduce their nuclear weaponry. I was sufficiently concerned to send off a signal to the MoD on the Friday the article appeared. On Saturday morning I received a phone call at home from the Ambassador. 'Neville,' he said quietly, 'what have you been telling the Chief of Defence Staff? I really don't like being called up in the middle of the night by him unless there's a real reason for it.' I stammered a quick explanation of my actions, and Sir Julian said, 'Well, I've told him that I don't think there's anything really to worry about, but please come and see me on Monday morning first thing and we'll see what this is all about.' To say that I slept uneasily over that weekend would be an understatement.

I re-read the article carefully, and consulted my German dictionaries once again. I soon saw that I should not have worried too much. It was possibly all a matter of an umlaut. Genscher had used the conditional tense, and I thought he had used the indicative. The Ambassador was kind to me on the Monday morning when he realised that it was a small language problem, but he left me in no doubt that I should be more careful in future and consult the Head of Chancery, Keith Haskell, whatever the time of day, before despatching such a signal.

The second occasion for misunderstanding arose in November 1986 when the Prince of Wales and Princess Diana were to pay a state visit to Germany. One of the Prince's engagements was to be a visit to the

German Forces' university in Munich. This would be the first time a member of the British royal family had visited a Bundeswehr training establishment, and this one was an especially prestigious one. Keith Haskell asked me to help him with drafting a speech for the Prince. We divided the speech into two parts, the first of which was my 'Defence' oriented piece, the second was Keith's diplomacy and politics piece. I thought it would be appropriate for the Prince to start his speech by saying how pleased he was to be invited to this fine Bundeswehr university, and what high regard German officers were held in throughout NATO these days. I believed that this was unexceptional politeness. How naïve I was!

The royal couple came to the Embassy and Linda and I were delighted to have the opportunity to talk with both of them. While rumours of a possible separation were rife then, nothing occurred during their visit to suggest that divorce was imminent. Diana looked serene and elegant, but conversation with her was difficult, whereas the Prince chatted easily with everyone. The occasion was shown on German TV and the Naval Attaché's *Putzfrau* said she had seen and admired the Defence Attaché's elegant wife on the screen. 'She must be a "von", you know,' she said! The next day the Prince gave his speech at Munich and the British newspapers carried detailed reports of it under banner headlines condemning the Prince for his insensitivity in praising German officers on a day so close to Armistice Day, 11 November! I was stunned and very disappointed. Keith Haskell was furious and asked me to come to his office, which I did with alacrity. I found him sitting at his desk surrounded by newspaper clippings, holding his head in his hands looking very perturbed indeed. He then proceeded to blame me for what he termed a public relations disaster. I was none too pleased. I asked to see the Ambassador. Keith got in first, so that by the time the Ambassador's secretary called me to the office, I found Keith already there. The Ambassador, however, asked Keith to leave as I came in, which surprised me somewhat. 'Before you say anything, Neville, I'd like you to know that I consider the Press have got it entirely wrong, and you have nothing to feel embarrassed about.' He then changed the subject and we talked amicably about various other Defence-related matters for ten minutes or so. I admired the way Sir Julian handled this matter, for he certainly did not want any discussion about it which might reflect on his loyalty to his Head of Chancery. He was a wise man, and I was mightily relieved.

The third occasion when relations were strained, was, however, altogether more serious, and it occurred much later in my tour, towards the end of 1987, I believe. It involved Herr Genscher again. This time he was more open than ever in a speech about *détente* and the need, in his view, to do away with short range nuclear weapons. This time there was no doubt about the language. My German had improved to the extent that I had taken and passed the Civil Service Interpreter examination, of which I was quite proud (the award was only '2nd class'!). My suspicions about his policy declaration were reinforced by a glance at the German Defence budget proposals about to be taken through the Bundestag. In them I saw no financial provision for short range nuclear artillery for the following year and beyond.

I discussed my concerns with Keith Haskell and Nigel Williams, both of whom dismissed my analysis as naïve. 'This is just diplomatic language,' they said condescendingly. I also consulted my fellow Attachés, but they were non-committal. I thought for some time about what action I should take, the Ambassador being temporarily away. I decided that this issue was of such importance that the Chief of Defence Staff must be made aware of it, so I despatched a clear signal to him and copied it to the Commander in Chief of the British Army of the Rhine General Sir Brian Kenney, and the UK Military Representative in NATO's Military Committee, Air Chief Marshal Sir Michael Knight. I knew both of these senior officers quite well, and I was encouraged by receiving appreciative signals from both of them the same day.

The following day Keith Haskell burst into my office, evidently furious when he had seen a copy of my signal. 'Why didn't you discuss it with me before you sent that signal?' he roared. I told him that I had discussed the matter with both him and the Minister and got nowhere. A day or two later, Sir Julian returned from his trip, and called for me. This time he was not amused. 'You had no business to send this signal on military channels without my approval,' he said. 'I don't agree with it, and you really must not do this sort of thing without clearing it with my staff first.' I was naturally contrite and apologised, but I knew I was right in my analysis, and brooded over the matter for some time afterwards.

My relations thereafter with Sir Julian were, I feel, a little strained, and the situation was not helped when Linda and I asked him to come to dinner with us. We went to considerable trouble to fix the date well in advance and invite other suitably senior guests. He graciously accepted but then, barely five days before the event, Lady Bullard rang to say that the head of the Bundesbank was coming to Bonn that day and they would like to have him to dinner, and therefore they would not now be able to attend ours!

Considering all this, Sir Julian's contribution to my annual confidential report in October 1987 was generous in the extreme. John MacMillan, formerly a fellow DS of mine at Staff College, was now Assistant Chief of the General Staff in London and he had the responsibility of writing my report from afar, picking up what he could from various sources closer to me. He wrote;

> Brigadier Pughe's relationship with his Ambassador and the FCO colleagues is excellent. And in his report the Ambassador comments favourably on his ability as a co-ordinator and his willingness to integrate the Defence Section fully with the Embassy.

Significantly, he went on to say that I reported promptly and perceptively to the MoD, keeping it informed on a wide range of German politico military issues. I was also asked by General Sir Brian Kenney and his successor Martin Farndale to keep in even closer personal touch with them on all matters affecting Germany and the Bundeswehr, which I continued always thereafter to do. The final endorsement of my actions however came with the arrival of the new Ambassador, Sir Christopher Mallaby, who had come straight from being Deputy Secretary to the Cabinet in Whitehall. His first words to me were very reassuring: 'Hallo Neville. Your information on Genscher and battlefield nuclears was received with much interest!' I said nothing, but surprise and relief must have been written all over my face. (Later, I read Margaret Thatcher's book *The Downing Street Years*, and at page 774, she refers to the matter, which was significant as my message reached her just prior to the important NATO summit in March 1988. She wrote of concerns about the German position: 'Mr Gorbachev had launched a very successful propaganda drive to win over German opinion to a denuclearised Germany. Within the Federal German Government I knew that Chancellor Kohl was still fundamentally sound on the need to avoid a "third zero" and denuclearization. Herr Genscher, the Federal Foreign Minister, by contrast, was not . . .')

If relations between the Defence staff and embassy officials could be strained on occasions, so also could certain difficulties arise within the Sections between Attachés. It was, to be fair, only an occasional problem,

With HM Ambassador, Sir Christopher Mallaby, Bonn, 1988

and it arose simply because the chain of command and relationship between the various Service Attachés had never been clearly laid down. My fellow RAF colleague, Colin Reineck, was an Air Commodore, and the Naval Attaché, first Mike Bickley then Bill Hutchison, was a senior Captain RN. We were therefore all of equivalent rank, and indeed Colin was theoretically senior to me. My job description failed to refer to my powers in relation to the other Attachés; I was not described as commander of the Defence Section. I deduced that I was really '*primus inter pares*' which meant that I could not give an order to my senior colleagues, and they could appeal to their single Service authorities in London if I tried to make them do something which they did not want to do. One example was attendance at periodic Investitures at the Ambassador's Residence on the banks of the Rhine. Linda would do the most magnificent and spectacular flower arrangements for these and afterwards have around forty or so Other Ranks and their wives for a sumptuous lunch at Im Etzental 15, which they always much appreciated. Our Naval Attaché, however, felt out of place at a ceremony which normally involved only Army and RAF recipients of awards, the Navy being thin on the ground in Germany. He asked me if he could be excused, but I knew the Ambassador's views and I insisted that Mike should attend. He did so without much grace, but he did not choose to challenge my authority on this. Normally I had to work simply through charm and persuasion. Because of the friendly working and social climate the three of us engendered, this seldom gave rise to any difficulties. A small administrative problem did, however, surface when Mike Bickley was handing over to Bill Hutchison.

The cause of this little problem was housing. The road, Im Etzental, contained several spacious foreign office hirings which were eminently suitable for entertaining. In previous years these houses had been occupied by the three senior Attachés, the Commercial Counsellor, the Defence Sales counsellor, the Head of Chancery and another senior member of Chancery. Mike Bickley's predecessor had, however, moved out at some stage and taken a smaller hiring near the Embassy. Mike and his family took it on, together with a wonderful *Putzfrau*, and enjoyed it there. It was, however, not as suitable for entertaining as the Im Etzental houses, and it seemed to me that there were several advantages in having the three senior Attachés close together. An Im Etzental house was becoming vacant at just about the time that Bill Hutchison was to take over from Mike, and I asked that steps be taken to return the new Naval Attaché to the fold. To cut a long story short, the two Naval Attachés between them thwarted my plans, and furthermore, when I challenged Bill on the subject, he threw a complete 'wobbler' and said that he was not obliged to take orders from me.

As it was purely an administrative matter, I did not rate it highly enough to make a serious issue of his objection, but it did, of course, present a matter of principle, which I felt, for the good of my successor, if no-one else, ought to be clarified. So I wrote to the Chief of Defence Staff, explaining how the *primus inter pares* situation could lead to problems, and asking that the authority of the Defence Attaché over the other Attachés be confirmed in writing. MoD staff officers wrote a series of prevarications and they procrastinated over the matter until well after I had left Bonn. Fortunately, there were no further incidents of the sort I have described, however minor, and all the Attachés in the Embassy were valued colleagues and good friends, remaining so to this day.

My first Assistant Military Attaché in Bonn was a Royal Tank Regiment Lieutenant Colonel called Gordon Gray. He was a most assiduous officer and a brilliant organiser. To him fell the organisation and running of the annual Attaché Ball in Bonn. The British generally are renowned in international Service circles as the best organisers of anything, but a Ball of the particular scale and standard traditional in Bonn was a considerable challenge. Theoretically a committee planned and executed the arrangements, but 90 per cent of the work, down to the most minute details necessary for a really successful event of this nature, was done by Gordon. Although he was steadiness itself in approach to life, never one to panic, he could be very quick off the mark when necessary. Twice in one month this attribute of his was in demand by the Embassy.

On the first occasion a confidential signal from Whitehall came my way calling for someone urgently to undertake a somewhat clandestine mission to a destination some considerable distance from Bonn. The precise details of this matter cannot, of course, be divulged even now. I called to Gordon who was sitting peacefully in his office across the corridor, and briefed him on the equipment he would need and the precautionary measures to take. He had just 2½ hours to reach the target, the description of which we had been given. To cut the story short, it is sufficient to say that he achieved all this with great dash and aplomb, although getting thoroughly prepared for the task was the probably the greater challenge in the time available.

No sooner had Gordon pulled off that little wheeze, than one day a Polish worker reported to the Embassy front door saying that he wanted to speak to the Military Attaché urgently. I thought Gordon was just the chap to take this interview on, and I was not disappointed. The Polish informant turned out to have some sensational information about several of his fellow-countrymen who were working with the British Forces in Germany and spying on us. Gordon did all the right things in his dealings with this man, and his work contributed to a successful swoop by the security services on the spies concerned.

For these achievements I recommended Gordon for the OBE which, I am delighted to say, he duly received at Buckingham Palace. When the time came for Gordon to leave the Embassy we threw a little party for him at Im Etzental 15, and because Gordon was madly keen on military bands, and one of the Tank Regiments had a Pipe and Drums band, I tried to get hold of a piper to come to the house to pipe Gordon and his wife Sheila away. I was told that the band was in France for a ceremony in connection with Cambrai Day, and I was about to be disappointed, when the Pipe Major said that he had been excused the

Cambrai event because his wife was expecting a baby. Gordon, of course, knew that this band would not be in the country, so it was a really pleasant surprise for him when I threw open the french windows and the Pipe Major in all his Scottish finery swept into the room. The noise of the pipes was deafening in a drawing room, however large, and I personally have always regarded bagpipes more as a weapon of war than a musical instrument. But that was an occasion to remember.

Social events at Im Etzental 15 were frequent and of a high standard. Lance Bombardier Holmes was a past-master at behind the scenes organisation and front line stewardship. He showed great flair. He would parade the small army of Philippino waitresses and cooks in the cellar before a major social event, and they giggled at being paraded and inspected for all the world like a military platoon. On other occasions, when just Cincha, our principal help in the house, was doing the ironing he would steal her handbag and hide it in the deep-freeze, or have her marching up and down the corridor with a broom over her shoulder, teaching her rifle drill. They were a super team, and provided us with wonderful support and a lot of amusement. There were times, I have to admit, when Holmes' future with us was in some doubt, mainly through his occasional bouts of heavy drinking, often at the Irish pub in Bad Godesberg. These bouts, as Robin Duschesne had forewarned us, generally occurred on a Friday evening, when he regarded he had a legitimate right to have a late night out on the town. His punctuality on Saturday mornings was therefore somewhat suspect. Most weeks this was not a problem for us, but on occasions when we had house guests or a social commitment on a Saturday, his rather rough appearance and highly charged breath were hard to stomach. I did have to warn him very severely on occasions and threaten to send him back to his regiment, but he took his fitness in hand, went out running with the Hash-House Harriers, and gave us renewed good service every time.

Bombardier Holmes, as he was always called, got on well with everyone, including our own sons when they came out to stay with us during their vacations. He was a real 'character', he had a great sense of humour, he was spotlessly efficient at his job, and he responded to being treated properly. He had a few typical turns of phrase which we shall always associate with him. When he had done especially well in support of one of our major social events I would congratulate him and he would turn to Linda and say chirpily: 'There you are, Mrs P. What did I say? We've come out smellin' of roses again!'

Sadly, when we left Bonn, Bombardier Holmes could not settle down to regimental life again, he reverted to his bad old ways, and was released from the Army. Last heard of, he had married a Yorkshire girl, divorced her six weeks later, and was then pursuing a pretty girl at the New Zealand Embassy in Bonn where he secured the rather unlikely job of security guard.

During the Bonn posting we became renowned for certain social events, notably the annual summer garden party which I instituted at Im Etzental 15. We invited about 150 guests to this event, all German working acquaintances and friends of all the Attachés. I managed to get the Royal Artillery Band to come over from Dortmund and play background music all evening under the shade of our apple trees. Our small army of Philippinos plied our guests with Pimms No 1, with which most were wholly unfamiliar, and a very agreeable atmosphere was generated. I gave a speech in German, standing on the balcony, overlooking the lawn on which all the guests were standing. I used every quaint expression I could muster, and made jokes in German, which even the most serious Germans seemed to find amusing. I claimed that the date I had chosen for the party was the anniversary of the last time that Great Britain was invaded – by the Dutch at Chatham in 1767 or thereabouts, an invasion which was repulsed by the British offering the invaders a cup of tea. This was, in fact, partly true, and it went down very well.

Those garden parties are among the most long remembered of our social activities at Im Etzental 15 by our German friends, even to this day. Possibly a less appreciated event, however, at least by our principal visitor, occurred in early March 1987. He was the British Army's Quartermaster General, and he wished to visit the German Ministry of Defence. He chose to do this on the Tuesday following Karneval and Rosenmontag, despite my having given him and his staff clear advice that this was normally a holiday in Germany. The Germans, not wishing to appear impolite, agreed to accept this visit, even though it must have caused several officers considerable inconvenience and loss of a day's holiday. I arranged, as was customary, to accommodate the good General at home and to have a dinner party in his honour on the Monday evening. I could not, however, resist asking the German officers whom we were inviting to wear dinner or smoking jackets as usual but with the addition of one item of carnival costume.

On that Rosenmontag evening, all the Germans joined in the spirit of the occasion splendidly; they all turned up with several items of carnival dress, masks, odd hats, brightly coloured wigs and so on. Even General Malecha, a fairly serious Prussian, and then Deputy Chief of Staff of the German Army, arrived with sundry bright appurtenances to his attire. Our British guest, conventionally dressed in black tie, strode downstairs to join the party in the drawing room shortly after all the other guests had arrived. The look on his face on seeing the motley assembly was a treat. I lent him my Arab headdress, which he sportingly wore, but his bread-and-butter letter of thanks later that week could not disguise a certain frostiness. It was, I think, a legitimate joke to play on him for being perhaps a little insensitive to German national customs and his staff apparently ignoring my well intentioned advice.

Linda coped with all these social events extremely well. Many of our dinner parties at home were conducted in a peculiar mixture of German and English, which turned out to be quite entertaining. There was one occasion when the guests at our dinner table on Linda's right and left were a Russian, Major-General Tcheremutjin and an Indian, Admiral Ravi Vohra, their respective nations' Defence Attachés in Bonn. Indian Attachés as a rule had difficulty with the German language, and one of them once explained to us that, as there were about 23 different languages for them to learn within India, it was stretching things too far to expect them to learn a European language which they would never use again after their tour in Bonn was over! On this occasion Linda, sitting between the Russian and the Indian, acted as interpreter. The Russian spoke no English and the Indian spoke some Russian as he had once been to Moscow for a Defence course. The conversation was therefore triangular; the Russian would make a remark to Linda in German, who, not confident in German, would put the reply in English to the Indian, whereupon the Indian would pass it to the General in Russian. Such situations and procedures made the international life in Bonn particular fun.

There were the inevitable cocktail parties and receptions, however, and one we attended early in our tour was at Rheindahlen when the Duchess of Kent was visiting the British garrison. We found her extremely charming, and we have a singularly amusing photograph which makes the Duchess appear as if she is curtseying to Linda rather than the reverse. Receptions however at various Embassies were less entertaining, and those at the largest Embassies were especially difficult. The problem lay with the numbers of people present, sometimes over two hundred, and the noise was deafening. The *lingua franca* was, of course, always German, and I well recall how impossible it was to understand what a Chinese or Japanese diplomat was trying to say in German against such an ear-splitting background. This could have had unfortunate consequences if one was faced with an Attaché from an Eastern bloc country asking if he could defect to the West! As it happened, none ever put such a request to me in Bonn, – at least as far as I am aware!

The only time I did have potentially interesting dealings with a Russian Attaché was towards the end of our tour. Colin Reineck, our Air Attaché, had left on posting to the UK, and he left me to continue a good friendship which he had developed with the Russian Air Attaché, one Leonid Miljutin. I held several clandestine lunch meetings with him and learnt that he was not looking forward to returning to the Soviet Union. He had enjoyed the good life in Germany, and in particular his Mercedes car, which, on return to his home country, would be replaced with a cheap Lada. One day he volunteered to come to our house and show me a video of what he described as an 'American Air Force training film'. The freedom which Russian Attachés in Bonn enjoyed was in marked contrast with the situation we had witnessed in the States. We had every expectation of a serious discussion with Leonid and his wife on possible defection. When they arrived rather furtively at the house, Linda took Mrs Miljutin into the drawing room for coffee, and I took Leonid into the study where we had set up the video recorder which we had borrowed from Bombardier Holmes. Leonid said little, but rather nervously started the video. When I saw the title I shrieked with laughter – it was the American Hollywood thriller film *Top Gun*! Leonid had a great sense of humour, but nothing came of his disappointment at the prospect of returning to Russia. He kindly presented me with a copy of the book which was taking Germany and the world by storm at the time, *Perestroika* by Michail Gorbachev.

Our opportunities for travel in Germany were very much more restricted than they had been in America. Wherever we went, however, we were given red-carpet treatment by the Germans. At every military base we entered we were treated to wonderful hospitality, formal presentations and lectures, and even a full scale tactical demonstration and parade just for me at the German Armour School. We were showered with gifts, and, of course, we reciprocated. We soon ran out of Wedgwood ashtrays and all the fine china and glass presents which we had bought in London before moving out to Bonn. Such protocol was very expensive, and no allowance was given to us for such things, the Foreign Office being understandably nervous of spending tax-payers' money on gifts to foreigners. One was given, however, a fairly generous entertainment allowance on top of one's salary, which had to be carefully accounted for. Gifts, nevertheless, could not be shown against it.

We managed to visit Jonathan in his beautiful mountain base at Morgins in Switzerland during our first summer in Bonn. We also achieved a short trip back to England in the spring of 1987 to see Richard get his second hockey Blue, after which Varsity match we met his strikingly red-headed girlfriend, Caroline Nayler. In October 1987 we took a pre-Silver Wedding anniversary trip to the northern undeveloped part of Portugal, where we got a severe dose of food-poisoning just in time to fly on to Vienna, where we naturally got to know extremely quickly every loo in that wonderful city. But in Germany my favourite visits were probably those on duty to the Führungsakademie at Hamburg, where we were made very welcome by successive commandants, Generalmajors Jörn Söder and Werner von Scheven, to Berlin on an Attaché tour and to the German Army's mountain warfare training centre at Mittenwald in Bavaria. Whilst there I went skiing on the Zugspitz and Linda and I found time to visit the Kloster Ettal nearby, which we both found such a moving experience that I cried. Visits to Münster, Munich and Hammelburg, as well as to the extraordinary Zentrum für Innerer Führung at Koblenz, where I lectured a disbelieving audience of German conscripts about the British system of voluntary Adventure Training, were also memorable each in their own way, and sometimes repeated. On the British net, Linda and I were also invited to visit British ships paying port calls at Hamburg or Kiel, the aircraft carrier HMS *Ark Royal* and the nuclear submarine HMS *Churchill* being two notable examples.

Professionally matters were moving ahead very much more easily in Bonn too. The new Ambassador, Sir Christopher Mallaby, proved to be very much in tune with Defence matters, and he regarded our Defence relationships with Germany as being of central political importance. When he first arrived in March 1988, he insisted that he be accompanied by the three principal Attachés and their wives when he went to the President's palace for accreditation. This was a super occasion and it was good to meet that gentle and intelligent man President Richard von Weizsäcker and see the gracious interior of the Villa Hammerschmidt. Sir Christopher soon suggested that I invite the German Chief of

Defence Staff, Generalinspekteur der Bundeswehr, Admiral Wellershoff, to have a working breakfast with just him and me at the Residence. This was a typical demonstration of support for me and my work which I greatly appreciated. His German was faultless too, and by that stage of my tour I could participate fully in such an hour's important discussion in German.

But the smooth and increasingly successful tenor of life in my professional world was badly interrupted by two less happy developments in the family. First Linda's limp was clearly getting worse. Indeed, one day she was stung by a bee on the back of the neck, and, for someone with MS, an affliction of the spinal column sheath, the sting was in a dangerous place. She then suffered a bad period of unsteadiness, requiring the permanent use of a walking stick, and her eyes were so badly affected that she had to give up driving for a while. She could just manage to walk down through the nearby park to the shops in Bad Godesberg, and we could also go for many a saunter on the flat path along banks of the Rhine, stopping for recovery for *Kaffee und Kuchen*, or often her favourite *Johannesbeersaft* at the little 'Weinhäuschen Am Rhein'. She would enjoy these forays enormously, and was determined to walk as much as she could manage. We were especially happy during our strolls along the Rhine, under some magnificent copper beech trees, looking across the river and its barges to the Drakenfels.

In the spring of 1987 the futility of man's attempts to constrain natural forces by hemming in the annual snow-melt between concrete walls led to dramatic floods along this great river. The Dreesen Hotel and many other buildings along the river banks suffered severe damage to their cellars and ground floors, but we never tired of the changing moods of the river and the constant shipping activity in its powerful current. There was one boat which caught Linda's fancy in particular. It was a floating restaurant built and decorated to resemble the open jaws of a whale or shark. It was called 'Moby Dick' and was really a comic sight. The Naval Attaché, Mike Bickley, thought it a vulgar monstrosity, so Linda suggested that we secretly booked it for a meal and trip up river for Mike's farewell party. This we did, and it was a great success. Fascinating as the shipping was, it was possibly the slow pace of life on the river that we found so pleasant; a restful contrast to the hectic life we were living.

The second blow came from our son, Richard. His letter was dated 20 October 1987, and it was a veritable bombshell. He wrote it at

Sandhurst after he had been there about six weeks. Richard had seen quite a lot of the Army while he had been up at Cambridge. As someone enjoying the comparative financial luxury for an undergraduate of an Army Cadetship, Probationary Second Lieutenant, he had been a part-time member of the Cambridge University Officers' Training Corps, and during his summer vacations he had been on attachments to both 45th Field Regiment in Germany and Canada, and then with 29 Commando Regiment in Norway. He had certainly gained a taste of life as a junior subaltern, with all its joys and pitfalls. We had no reason to doubt that he relished the experience, and my view was that, even if he only served the five years in the Army after University which was obligatory for an Army scholar, then it would stand him in good stead whatever he eventually decided to do with his degree, a 2/2 in Classics. His experiences in 45 Regiment included, incidentally, playing the very same grand piano in the Mess which I had played as a subaltern, and his time with 29 Commando struck a chord with a family with such a long tradition in the Royal Marines.

In his letter, Richard told us that he had decided after all that Army life was not for him and he was going to leave. His mind was made up and by the time we received the letter late on 26 October, he was evidently on his way. I wrote as objective a reply as I could, Linda cautioning me that it was his decision and he would have to live with it. All we could do was to offer help. I wrote, 'Do not worry what other people might think of you; do what is honourable and what you think is correct . . . Whatever happens we shall be wishing you, as ever, all the best in the world.' So the family Service tradition was to be broken, but we were sure that he would succeed in whatever he chose to do, and Linda and I would be proud of him for that. Service life might not be quite what it was anyway.

Richard quickly used his initiative well; he joined the accountancy firm Arthur Anderson in London, and after a couple of years passed the exams. During this time he married the lovely Caroline, their wedding being described elsewhere in this narrative, and eventually moved north to Yorkshire, near Caroline's parents. We are so pleased that he is happy and doing well, now an expert in Litigation Support Accountancy. Their two adorable children, Camilla ('Millie') Louise and Thomas (Tom) George, are accomplished sportsmen, and the former quite a musician. They are chips off the old block, but Tom and Jonathan's Charlie are, so far, the last of the Pughe line.

On 19 January 1988 Linda and I celebrated our Silver Wedding anniversary. We decided to do it quietly and we sneaked away to our favourite little *Gasthaus* in the Ahr Valley, the Hotel Zur Post, in a hamlet which delighted in the name of Müsch, just upstream from the wine growing village of Mayschoß. It was a friendly *Gasthaus* run by the Bauer family, which I had first come across when, as Secretary of the British Embassy Fishing Syndicate, I was both helping to stock our 5 km stretch of the Ahr and later rather unsuccessfully trying to catch trout we had put in there. On this occasion, in the depths of winter, it looked as if the place was closed when we arrived in the early evening. I had booked a room and nothing about being closed had been mentioned. We hammered on the door, and, after what seemed an interminable pause, the door was thrown open, and the whole Bauer family welcomed us with a shout of triumph. Inside we had the candle-lit restaurant to ourselves, a wonderfully homely evening and a quiet night's rest. The Gasthaus had indeed been closed, for the family Bauer was on holiday, but it was typical of their hospitality that they would not mention it over the telephone, but opened just for us on this special anniversary. A few weeks later we drove back to England, and met the three boys and their girlfriends for a celebration dinner in a restaurant of their choice in Covent Garden. It was a super evening, and all got on well with each other.

We secured the purchase of 'The Fieldings' in March 1988, Linda's brothers, Denis and Tim, as ever, respectively completing the legal arrangements and the survey. We were in no hurry to move in as we were not due to leave Bonn until the end of the year. We wasted no time, however, in driving across at every possible opportunity to get work done on the house, like having an extra banister put onto the stairs for Linda. I also slipped down to Poole one day while we were there, and bought an Amstrad word processor. I took it back to Bonn with me in the car and started to rewrite the first draft of my book about Northern Ireland for which the Ministry of Defence had originally declined to give security clearance. I had written that first draft on an old typewriter during our time at AFCENT but now, with a word processor, I was able to amend it in all the places suggested by the Ministry of Defence, renaming it *Ulster Snapshot* and changing all the names of personalities in it, including the author's, and I became Neville Hughes.

We quickly got to know the neighbours during our visits to Marnhull, and Ron and Pat Keeble soon came out to visit us for a long weekend in Bonn. We took them on the usual tour: up the Ahr Valley, across the Eifel, into the Moseltal at Beilstein, near Cochem, down river to the Rheinecke at Koblenz, a visit to the historic Schloß Ehrenbreitstein, and back north along the throbbing Rhine to home. This was a tour which we did repeatedly with visitors from all over the world; Al Davis and his girlfriend, who were with us in America, came on their first ever visit to Europe. They thought Germans were rather a solemn lot until they saw a *Weinfest* in the Ahr valley! Linda's mother stayed a week. The Gordons came down from Hohne and left their lovely dog 'Shadow' with us while they went on holiday. Friends from Granborough made the trip, Tony and Mary Emms, and Brian and Peggy Evans. Even Maggie stopped over via Frankfurt on a visit to England from South Africa. One Christmas holiday all three boys came out and joined in a riotous fancy dress party at the Haskells' house in Im Etzental. With the Keebles we went one evening down to the Weinhäuschen am Rhein, and stood in a glowering thunderstorm watching the lightning flickering against the sky behind the Drakenfels. It was very eerie, atmospheric and unforgettably Wagnerian. We adored having all these visitors, and relished showing them our surroundings.

In April 1988 I received a very unexpected and nice letter from the Ministry of Defence saying that I was to be put forward for appointment as an Aide-de-Camp to HM The Queen. I was also asked, rather comically, to own up to any discreditable conduct! My conscience was clear and I was evidently believed, as on 13 April 1988 I was able to drop a note to the Ambassador's private office saying: 'The Ambassador may wish to know that I have received a letter from the Military Secretary which states: I am writing to confirm that The Queen has been graciously pleased to approve your appointment as Aide-de-Camp to Her Majesty from 26 May 1988 . . . The announcement will be published in the *London Gazette* on 31 May 1988.' The Ambassador kindly replied by writing on the note: 'Congratulations!' The appointment was, of course, pretty gratifying, but I was in no doubt that it was purely honorary, and meant nothing except the addition of EIIR on one's epaulettes and the wearing of one's aigulettes on the other shoulder. It was, therefore, though an honour, an elusive sort of glory.

I was similarly honoured to be awarded a medal by Chancellor Kohl at the Kanzleramt. He gave a short speech of thanks for the British troops' efforts in Germany, in German, and he was then handed a cardboard box from which he proceeded to dispense silver medals depicting himself, and which for all the world looked like chocolates, or toy tokens, walking around the room as he did so. It was a rum sort of ceremony and not one which many might wish to emulate.

Every year students at the Royal College of Defence Studies, which is located at Seaford House, Belgrave Square, London, go on a tour of foreign countries. The course is divided into several groups, each group travelling to different continents. When the group touring Europe came to Bonn, the programme was arranged by the Defence Attaché working in close consultation with the German MoD's Protocol Section. My friends there were Oberst Christoph von Plato, whom we had known in Camberley when he was at the German Embassy in London, and Oberstleutnant von Heimendahl. Both of them were charming and efficient aristocrats, the latter being a relation of Sascha Frevert-Niedermein. During their visit to Bonn, the RCDS students were always entertained to a black-tie dinner at the Ambassador's Residence. By tradition, all German officers who had at any time been students at the College, also gathered at the Residence for the dinner. In 1988 Linda and I attended such a dinner as usual, and so naturally did Generalmajor Alexander Frevert-Niedermein together with twenty or so other German officers, all of whom we had got to know quite well by then. It struck me very forcibly on this particular evening what a very special rapport was engendered amongst the British and German officers present. The Germans agreed and said it was because they all regarded that year at RCDS as one of the most unforgettable of their careers, and one which they had valued for the rest of their lives. They all held fond memories and a really strong, almost emotional, attachment to the British as a result. Those who had also attended Staff College or other courses in the UK were even stronger in their affirmation of the special regard in which they held us.

I determined there and then to examine whether or not this feeling could be made the basis of a more formal association, adding to it by bringing in all German officers who had served directly with British forces, and British officers who had mastered the German language and served with the Bundeswehr. I tested my idea on my German friends, the Ministry of Defence NATO politico-defence desk holders and Sir Christopher Mallaby. All thought it an excellent initiative and encouraged me to get it going.

The last party but one to which we were invited in Bonn was at the house of Generalmajor Hanno Graf von Kielmannsegg. All the other guests were German aristocrats, all of them 'Graf und Gräfin' or 'Freiherr und Freifrau' or at the very minimum 'von' something. Hanno had been to Staff College, Camberley, and to RCDS, so he was acquainted with what he termed 'a typical British evening of games'. This was to be such an evening, and, of course, the conversation was in German throughout. It started with our being asked to pin a card on our backs which contained half a German proverb or idiom, and we had to question others to find out what it was and then find our partner to complete the phrase. Linda was rather good at that, and I had made a study of such things. The next game required all the ladies to hide behind a large bed sheet into which were cut small holes. They were asked to put their noses through the holes, and we men had to try to recognise our own wives' noses. This is not as easy as some thought it should be! Little by little the games became more complicated and as those present became more intoxicated and giggly, the explanations on how to play became less and less comprehensible. It was a hilariously entertaining evening, but Linda and I were absolutely exhausted by it. We should, I suppose, have felt honoured to be the only foreigners invited to such an august gathering. It was certainly one of our more memorable experiences.

Sir Christopher Mallaby gave a formal farewell dinner for Linda and me at his Residence, and I made a speech in German which Alexander Frevert-Niedermein said was far too long, probably because I had thanked him personally in it, and in his view far too profusely. I was allowed to select the other twenty or so guests, and so it was a wonderful opportunity to have a final social meeting with some of our closest and most senior German chums. It was a fitting finale to what had been a very happy and successful tour. Most gratifying of all, however, were the words written in my final report by Major General Charles Guthrie, then Assistant Chief of the General Staff, and later Chief of Defence Staff, where he said:

> Neville Pughe has a delightful, warm-hearted personality and a great gift for getting on with people. This has enabled him to establish a very wide range of contacts in the Bundeswehr. He provides a stream of reports on developments in German plans and tactical thinking, invariably accompanied by his own perceptive comment. He has developed a comprehensive understanding of the German armed forces and plays a key role in interpreting this for the MoD.
>
> His Ambassador clearly thinks very highly of him, reporting that he is well liked and respected both in diplomatic circles and with the German

authorities. He adds that, despite her ill-health (she has multiple sclerosis) Linda Pughe supports her husband exceptionally well, and they both play a very full part in the wider life of the Embassy. I, myself, have seen just how effective they both are and have never seen a DA in Bonn who has established warmer and better working relations with senior officers of the Bundeswehr.

I treasure this report, and seldom can anyone have been treated to such generous remarks about one's wife and one's own efforts. The report went on to recommend me for promotion to Major General, while recognising that the opportunities open to me were limited. And so it proved correct, but at least I was posted to one of the best Brigadier's jobs in the entire British army.

CHAPTER 15

Last Posts

M Y NEW POSTING was to Bulford, on Salisbury Plain. There I was to have a threefold job: I was Deputy Commander South West District, Commander Bulford Garrison, and Commander of the United Kingdom Element of NATO's Allied Mobile Force (Land). This offered the prospect of travel and fun, and my boss was Major General Tony Jeapes, who had been on the staff at the Staff College, Camberley, with me, and whom I knew well. He at once said that he would like to give me as much freedom as possible, and as far as the duties of commanding South West District were concerned, it was such a large command that he would like to share the job with me as much as he could.

'For a start,' he said, 'consider yourself solely in charge of the AMF(L) units, they are yours to train in the UK and Norway, and I shall not interfere. Just keep me informed of roughly what you are doing, and let me know if I can be of any help. In the District I would like you to take a special interest in the Cadets, both the Army Cadet Force and the Combined Cadet Forces at public schools. You go and do their annual inspections. Remember we have Royal Marines and Territorial Army in the District, and both need careful handling. Here on Salisbury Plain we have a major conservation project, and I am very keen on this. You will get involved, however, as Bulford Garrison Commander. Lastly, as Garrison Commander, please run the shoot. Any questions?'

I had none. It was as good a briefing as I had ever had, and I proposed to make the fullest possible use of the freedom it entailed. I did however add an afterthought: 'Tony,' I said a little hesitantly, 'there's just one thing. I don't want to sound ungrateful, and I am thrilled to have this super job, but Linda is not too well, and I would like to think that if a civilian job were to come up, I could leave the Army at three months' notice instead of the requisite six months'. Linda will be staying in our new house in Marnhull most of the time, but will come up to Bulford, to join me in our Beacon Hill House quarter from time to time. I hope that's OK?'

'Of course it is,' said the General, 'and I will write to the Military Secretary and let him know that I support your request for shorter notice.

I do hope, however, that you won't leave too soon. Both your predecessors left after only a few months, and we do need some continuity.'

The lovely Beacon Hill House under Kiwi Hill, which I was obliged to rent as there was no room in the Mess, was sparsely furnished to Army standards, and we put only the barest minimum of our own belongings into it. I stayed there most days during the week, enjoying early morning runs over hills directly behind the house, and supervising the gardener's efforts to make the large garden look good and be productive. Each weekend I returned to The Fieldings, 13 Ham Meadows, Marnhull, to join Linda. She had the use of our Volvo 240 GLT, which we had bought on the export market in Germany on 20 February 1988, and I travelled to and from Bulford Camp in the staff car, a journey which would take just three quarters of an hour. Linda settled into the quieter life of a country village extremely well, became very friendly with the neighbours, and she was thriving without having to endure the high pace of life that we had conducted in America and Bonn.

My job too progressed at a gentler pace. I even had time to complete my book *Ulster Snapshot* and get it published. I also wrote a series of short stories. Garrison duties were light and mainly administrative, as there was a very long-established staff at Garrison HQ, supervised efficiently by a keen Lieutenant Colonel. The Shoot ran itself too, and I was only required to take an interest in the rearing of the birds, protection of the coverts, and overseeing the accounts. I took pains to visit every unit in the Garrison, of course, including the primary schools, NAAFI and so on, and enjoyed that immensely.

My visits to cadets included a flight from Southampton to Guernsey to see Elizabeth College, which I much admired, and nostalgic returns to Blundell's School, Kelly College and Exeter School to inspect their CCFs. Linda came with me to Blundell's and we both hit it off exceptionally well with the headmaster, John Rees, and his wife, Carol. I was presented there with a fine print of a game of cricket on the school grounds, the school being well aware of my background and my having played there for Exeter School. I sent the Contingent CO a cheque, as presents should not really be accepted, and I was delighted to hear from him that a shooting competition cup would be obtained with the money, to be called the Pughe Trophy. Likewise at Kelly, my hosts took the trouble to dig into past school records and found the scorecard of the last match I played there. At Exeter School, I naturally, had a very warm welcome, and my day there was filled with fond memories. Mr Geoffrey Goodall, the headmaster of Exeter, wrote a very nice letter afterwards in which he said:

> ... how proud and privileged we all felt to have an Old Exonian as our inspecting officer on Field Day ... Thank you too for your very moving speech to the Contingent at their final muster. I watched their faces as you were speaking and there was an attentiveness, sincerity and brightness about them I too found touching. Who knows, one or two of them may emulate you in 30 years time or so.

I was really tickled over that letter, as it was the first time in my life that someone had suggested that anyone might wish to emulate me! One other visit to cadets, however, sticks in my memory vividly, and that was not to a public school but to a village hall in Lytchett Matravers in Dorset. There I was struck by the spirit of endeavour by the boys of the ACF, and more particularly by the enthusiastic support given to them by their parents, all of whom came to the inspection evening. If only more contingents were as well run as this one, so well supported, involving parents so much, we would all be better off and our future more secure.

My principal activity, however, during this posting was in connection with the UK units of the AMF(L). By a happy chance, the commander of this NATO force while I was at the helm in Bulford, was Generalmajor Peter Carstens, whom I had known in Bonn. He had had a remarkable career, in that he had attended RCDS and was a firm Anglophile, but was a member of the German socialist party, the SPD. Promotion in the Bundeswehr was normally unlikely for such an openly declared supporter of the opposition at a time when the Conservative CDU were in power. Not only was Peter a member of the SPD himself, but his wife, Heidi, was a fairly militant party worker. Despite this, his talent and charm were undeniable, and we became firm friends while he was at the Heeresamt in Köln in charge of German Army Training. He risked his career there on more than one occasion by publicly denouncing the level of commitment and poor standard of training of Bundeswehr conscripts. Rather than such outspokenness harming his prospects, however, it was good to see him prosper in spectacular fashion to become the first German to be appointed to command the AMF(L).

I lost no time in paying a visit to him in his new headquarters in Heidelberg, and Linda and I had a wonderful few days, enjoying the special atmosphere of the Heidelberg *Weihnachtsmarkt* whilst there. He

Commanding at Bulford, 1989

subsequently came over to Bulford to see something of my units, and he and Heidi stayed at our house in Marnhull, while his ADC found the Crown pub in the village quite an interesting experience. He was mightily impressed with our training.

My job was to ensure that the British units were trained for every role envisaged for the AMF(L), from winter warfare to desert survival. Winter warfare posed the severest challenge, but every year all my British units would go to the Voss area of Norway to work up their skiing and other winter warfare skills for six weeks before they joined the main AMF(L) exercise there. The British units comprised an infantry battalion, a Gunner regiment, a logistic regiment, a signals squadron, an armoured reconnaissance squadron and a host of minor units like an Intelligence Section and a helicopter flight for instance. It was, in effect, a mini-Brigade, and we liked to think that our standard of training was second to none.

During my time with the AMF(L) the infantry battalion was the 2nd Battalion the Royal Regiment of Fusiliers, or 2 RRF, under the command of Lieutenant Colonel Joe Gunnell. I was lucky enough to have this fine unit under my command in its second season with the AMF(L), and their expertise in that second winter in Norway developed into something quite exceptional. Our Norwegian liaison officers assured me after six weeks that they were the best ski-troops they had ever seen in Norway. I certainly put them to a severe test, by devising a very difficult battalion exercise as the finale to their training prior to coming under AMF(L) command for their major exercise in northern Norway. The exercise involved a long advance to contact across the highest part of the mountains in the Voss area. The terrain would not allow the BV 202 tracked oversnow vehicles to be used for most of the way, and much depended on the battalion's ability to ski at night and in deep snow carrying heavy loads of equipment and ammunition on each man.

The exercise started in bright sunny conditions, and all went according to plan for the first 24 hours, but then suddenly a raging blizzard descended on the mountain range. The Norwegians advised me to call off the exercise, but the battalion was already committed, and would have to sit tight on the mountains and wait for the storm to abate, coming down as best they could. Joe Gunnell decided to struggle on, and it was not long before he was reporting a number of cases of cold-exhaustion and exposure. One of these was very serious, and there was an urgent need for a rescue by helicopter. There was no way that a helicopter could get up to the battalion on the top of the mountain plateau in the blizzard, but by some brilliant flying, one pilot did get up to an agreed rendezvous point in a moderately well sheltered re-entrant. The casualty was taken there on a sled, and rushed off to hospital in the helicopter where, much to my relief, he survived. The way in which this incident was handled reflected very well on the determination of the young men involved, both on the ground and in the air. Indeed, the battalion pressed on in the most atrocious weather, and completed the advance to contact in a record time, some 24 hours sooner than our Norwegian advisers thought possible.

The Colonel-in-Chief of 2 RRF was the Duke of Kent, and he, an accomplished skier, flew over to join the battalion during their spell in Voss. I sat next to him at dinner one evening and we recalled our contemporaneous days at Sandhurst, although he was one term senior to me then. He held the record for a car journey back from the West End to the RMA before the motorway was built – 35 minutes I believe – a record that he maintained still stands. The following winter I invited Peter Carstens to come and join in this hard training, and he brought his son with him, a young Oberleutnant in the Gebirgsdivision, the German Mountain formation. The two of them rather fancied their expertise in winter-warfare, and initially showed their disdain for British winter-warfare equipment by bringing their own clothing and skis from the Bundeswehr. They camped out with our people in a snow hole and, to give Peter Carstens his due, he hid his age excellently. Peter and his son quickly learned to respect and admire the Fusiliers and Gunners with whom they exercised, and rightly so. I recommended Joe Gunnell for an OBE, not only for his exemplary leadership in these testing conditions but also for his initiatives in the field of international relations within the AMF(L). I am glad to report that my recommendation was supported and Joe duly received his award. He rang me and said, 'You naughty Brigadier, you!' – an unusual and friendly way of saying thank you.

I also had overall supervision of the training of our units in other situations, flying out to northern Italy for one exercise and to Sardinia for another. In all cases they performed superbly well, and I was very proud indeed of their fitness, professionalism and their spirit. I do not suppose there is another role, apart from the Airborne one, which brings the best out of our soldiers quite like that with the AMF(L). I relished it all and found it immensely fulfilling.

I managed to get Linda flown out by RAF Hercules transport aircraft in January 1989, as she had never been to Norway before. The weather was poor for winter warfare training up to that point, but that meant the waterfalls on the southern slopes of the mountains were in full flood, and really spectacular. We went to the obligatory Norwegian Ball in the old castle at Bergen, but did not enjoy the protocol much. We had doubtless had enough of it in America and Bonn. I was glad she came over, though. No sooner had she left for the UK again, than the snow came down in buckets, and the training took off in a big way.

Norway was also the scene of my own last skiing, a sport I had hitherto enjoyed enormously. One late afternoon at the top of a 'black' run, discretion seemed the better part of valour in the fast gathering dusk, so I decided to take the chair lift back down the mountain instead. I was the sole occupant when halfway down it stopped, leaving me stranded, swinging high above the darkening piste in rapidly decreasing tempera-tures. I hung there freezing, shouting for help into the emptiness for ages. Eventually a lift attendant skied past underneath and a few minutes later he restarted the lift and rescued me. I cannot imagine a more ignominious end to a skiing career!

Back in Marnhull in the summer of 1989 we had a wonderfully relaxed time. I enjoyed walking in the local lanes, and came across Fifehead Wood, a mile away across the Stour valley. It was an ancient wood, full of oak and other native trees, which abounded with bluebells in the spring. It was owned and managed by the Woodland Trust, which I immediately joined, and became a voluntary warden for this peaceful, beautiful wood. The summer also saw me elected to be President of the Royal Artillery Cricket Club, and I enjoyed many an afternoon at Woolwich or Sandhurst watching the team and doing my best to show an interest in them and encourage them. I also got my book *Ulster Snapshot* published at my own expense, and while I did receive some financial return on it, the marketing was woefully inadequate. I should have appointed an agent. I did take out Public Lending Rights and Linda went around Dorset libraries asking for a loan of it to boost my income! Libraries may not have been certain where to list it; was it military history or fiction? Those friends who read it, thought it good. They must have been good friends.

In August 1989 I heard that our long-standing friend, Mike Wilkes, now a Major General and GOC 3rd Armoured Division in Germany, was to be promoted again. When we were in Bonn, Linda and I had been to see Anne and him as they moved into the GOC's residence overlooking the Möhnesee. As ever Mike was a modest and warm-hearted host. Now I sent him a signal congratulating him yet again on another step in his meteoric career. Typically he sent me the following reply: 'Personal for Brig Pughe from GOC. My thanks for your kind signal. Any success which comes my way is based on my early tuition in the desert at your knee exclam Allah has indeed been merciful, much to my surprise. Salaams, MW.' It was the sort of response I would expect from Mike, but generous as it was, it was unduly self-deprecating. I was flattered by his remarks for his rise to fame was none of my doing. He was an exceptional officer in every way, charming and amusing too, possibly one of the least pompous men I have known, even when he reached the Army Board, was knighted and became Lieutenant-Governor of Jersey.

In the summer of 1989 I took Linda on a long-promised visit to Cyprus. Lieutenant Colonel Jim Evans, who had been with us in America, sponsored our visit so that we could fly out by RAF charter aircraft. He was now in charge of a Signals Intelligence regiment at Ayos Nikolius, and he loaned us his UN pass for both the Turkish north and the Greek south of the island. Starting with a short acclimatisation stay in the RAF Deputy Commander's lodge in the Troodos Mountains, we then spent a wonderful fortnight touring the whole island and visiting many of my old haunts. We swam in the sparklingly clear blue sea, visited the recently uncovered mosaics at Paphos, went to the beautiful port of Kyrenia and St Hilarion in the panhandle. Linda, though equipped with a walking stick, thrived on the heat of a Cypriot August and we were loath to come back to England so soon.

Once back, I started in earnest to look for a new job, not necessarily a second career, but a well-paid occupation, preferably within striking distance of Marnhull. One criterion I established from the start was a determination not to work in London, so that restricted my choice when casting my eye over the *Daily Telegraph* appointments page every week. I realised that it would be a long process, but in the end I had only made 35 applications before I was successful. One of the first jobs I felt certain was made for me was Bursarship of St Anthony's College, Oxford. Sir Ralph Darendorf was the Warden of this international post-graduate college, and I knew that Sir Christopher Mallaby and he were well acquainted. Sir Christopher kindly gave me a strong reference for the job, so I was convinced that it would be mine. When the College Warden's secretary then wrote to me saying that I had not been considered even for interview I was sufficiently nettled to write to Sir Ralph and ask him the reason. He wrote a charming reply, saying that it had long since been decided to appoint a strong internal candidate, a woman. I got the distinct impression that the advertisement for this post had only been made as a legal formality. I consoled myself with the thought that the salary was not very attractive anyway, and continued my search for a post which would entail a salary as good as a Brigadier's.

While thus engaged, I began to work hard at getting my pet idea of an Anglo-German Officers' Association off the ground. The germ for this ambition lay in those annual reunions of RCDS students in Bonn, and I was keen to build on that international rapport, extending the links to officers of all three Services who had served in any capacity with the other nation's forces. I foresaw that the respective nations' Defence Attachés in Bonn and London would be key players and I asked them to provide me with lists of former Attachés. I gathered names and addresses of students and instructors, Exchange Officers and Liaison Officers from far and wide, wrote to them and invited them to support the founding of an Association. I then asked the two current Chiefs of Army Staff to become the first Co-Presidents, Field Marshal Sir Nigel Bagnall and General Hans-Henning von Sandrart. To my delight, everyone to whom I wrote was supportive.

On 9 November 1989 I was on the point of calling the first meeting of the embryonic Association when that cataclysmic event occurred in Europe which had far-reaching consequences of historic proportions, namely, the collapse of communism in eastern Europe, the fall of the Iron Curtain and the Berlin Wall. We watched in fascination and considerable emotion at those unforgettable scenes of the Berlin Wall being ripped down and excited but dignified crowds surging over from the east. I was not unfamiliar with that grotesque monument to communist failure, of course, having seen its grisly form from the western part of Berlin. Only recently, when we were there on an Attaché tour from Bonn, Linda had been through to East Berlin by car with Fanny Van Orden, while I, being an Attaché with restricted access to the East, had to get Colonel Geoffrey van Orden, formerly our Liaison Officer at the Führungsakademie in Hamburg and now on the Intelligence staff in Berlin, to arrange a helicopter flight for me from which to peer over that dreadful wall.

Linda and I had also visited Adam von Trotz du Solz who had recently retired from his post with the protocol staff in the German MoD. We had much admired his family estate, Gut Bellers, right on the border between West and East Germany. The minefield and wire barricade cut right through his land, and we had stared at what had appeared to be a lasting spectacle in resignation and dismay. Little had we thought then how soon and how suddenly the situation would change. Not even our most optimistic friends among the Germans foresaw how soon the collapse of the Eastern regimes would occur.

Mixed with my emotional reaction to the event, which was derived directly from my deep understanding of just how the Germans felt themselves, was a slight feeling of satisfaction at the embarrassment it all caused the BND, the BundesNachrichtensDienst, in Munich. I had had my request to visit this civilian intelligence centre turned down while in Bonn, but now it was evident that military intelligence of what was going on in the East was far better than the BND's, who appeared to be completely taken by surprise and woefully ignorant of the true state of dilapidation and demoralisation in the former DDR.

The impact of the amazing events unfolding before our eyes every day on television could not yet be judged. What, for instance, would be the effect on NATO? Would there even be a need for NATO in future?

More importantly for me and my plans for an Anglo–German Officers' Association was the question over what would be the relation in future between the two former German states. Could we as British readily come to terms with making friends with our former East German enemies? How indeed would the Bundeswehr absorb the NVA? These and many more questions affecting our bilateral relationship could not be answered in 1989, nor, I suspected, for a year or more after that. So I suggested tactfully to General von Sandrart that we postpone the first meeting of the Association for a year and see how things settled down. He readily agreed, and my initiative was put to bed for a year.

By the end of the summer of 1989 I had received one invitation for a job interview. It was to be with Surrey Heath Borough Council who were looking for a new Chief Executive. Although I had hoped to find a job in the West Country, preferably near Marnhull, Surrey Heath BC's headquarters were in Camberley, and I knew this would appeal to Linda, being her town of origin, and where so many friends remained. Above all, however, the job looked as if it was well paid, about £58,000 starting salary, which was roughly what I was receiving as a Brigadier. I calculated that this, added to my Army pension, would enable us to buy a bigger and better house in Camberley and so at last catch up on the housing ladder which we had so badly fallen behind on over the years. A firm called PE Incubon, based in Egham, was doing the recruiting for this post, and I was invited to go there and see Bill Penny, the Executive dealing with this appointment.

I had long since prepared my *Curriculum Vitae*, on the basis of which Bill told me I had been selected for interview from a long list of sixteen, which had been whittled down to five. I thought the job was well within my capabilities, being largely administrative, but also entailing strategic management and leadership of a multi-disciplined professional work force. I was well aware that the view was held widely among civilians that senior Army officers were all 'Colonel Blimps' and couldn't add up, let alone deal with major financial matters. I was therefore careful to include in my CV the fact that, as Deputy Commander South West District, I was responsible for a devolved operating budget of £231 million! This was theoretically true, as the MoD had recently begun to devolve financial accountability to Districts, much to the dismay, I might add, to most officers having to deal with it. To many, endless committee meetings deciding how much to cut from the local training budget to pay for a recent rise in the total salary bill over which they had no control, was both frustrating and boring, and certainly not what they joined the army to do.

I went to see Bill Penny at Egham, and he was extremely helpful, giving me an invaluable insight into the financial problems which Surrey Heath Borough Council had run into. I had no doubt when I left his office, that in Bill, strangely a former priest, I was going to have a strong supporter. In early October I went to Camberley for the interview, which stretched over two days. On the first evening the five candidates were invited to a cocktail party in the Members' Room. I thought I was rather good at cocktail parties, but I was cornered by an attractive lady Councillor called Jill White who proceeded to talk to me almost exclusively the whole evening, much as I tried to circulate. Not surprisingly, but somewhat to my amusement, I learned later that I was by no means the front runner with the appointments panel after this stage of the process.

That evening we were all given a problem to solve overnight, our individual solutions to which we were to present to the appointment panel the next day. The exercise envisaged that a multi-story car-park had been built, but the entrance to it, owned by the County Council, had not been secured as the County were demanding a £2 million payment. The question was: 'How can we get into the car-park we have built?' It turned out that this was a real life problem facing the Borough Council, and the interview process for their new Chief Executive appeared to these poor councillors to be an opportunity too good to miss to get their problem solved! One of the candidates, already a Chief Executive of another local authority, readily divulged his solution to the others of us. He would build a ramp from the road beyond the railway line, with a fine bridge over that line. It would cost a lot, but it would be a poke in the eye for the County Council. I tackled the problem like a small military appreciation, and decided that the best thing to do would be to negotiate with the County Council for a reduction in the purchase price of the land, but in the meantime, to use a rather less ideal, but sufficiently satisfactory route into the car-park from the main road nearby. This was the solution the Council eventually adopted, I am thankful to relate.

I was told immediately after the five interviews were concluded that I was the winner. The Leader of the Council, a former RAF Wing Commander, walzed into the small conference room where we were all waiting listening to the 'flyover' candidate announcing how certain he was that he would get the job, and he had already visited local schools, and so on, and announced curtly and briefly, 'Brigadier Pughe, you have won. Please come through.'

I was duly congratulated, and I thanked Bill Penny profusely. I promised that I would be able to start on 2 January 1990, and I returned much pleased to Marnhull.

The thought of leaving the Army after 35 years, however, did not please me as much. True, the Army was changing, and things were not quite what they were, especially as there were fewer long postings overseas and more short exercises. But I was having a ball in my present appointment, not only with the AMF(L), but in the new pleasure I was getting from various conservation projects around Salisbury Plain Training Area. We planted our one millionth tree that autumn, and when we had entertained the Royal Society of Foresters, my name had been placed on a huge plaque in a broadleaf forest where I planted an oak tree. There I was putting down eternal roots in one moment, only to uproot myself and Linda to step into the unknown life as a civilian. I reflected, however, that my maternal grandfather would have been pleased to see me go into local government, he having served with distinction on the Devonport Council many years before, a fact my dear mother reminded me of when she heard the news.

When it came to leave Bulford just before Christmas the farewells were embarrassingly profuse from every unit. I was sorry to leave but I was looking forward too to something different. The boys came down to Marnhull for Christmas. I fixed myself up with a small rented house on the Heatherside estate, in Camberley, Linda staying in Marnhull for the few months it would take to sell up there and find something of our own in Camberley. I started at the Borough of Surrey Heath head-quarters (BOSH HQ!) on 2 January 1990 as planned, convinced that my Army experience would stand me in good stead, but with some foreboding!

CHAPTER 16

Council of War

IT WAS A MICKEY MOUSE world into which I tentatively felt my way. The so-called 'officers' of the council, that is the staff, seemed a bit wary of me, expecting, I suppose, that I would set about giving orders in some stentorian manner to all and sundry. But I took some military leadership skills with me, I believe, and spent several days going round all the offices and out-stations, meeting people, just as one would on taking over a regiment. Somebody said that it was the first time they had met a Chief Executive, and it was evidently rare for one to get down to the coal-face. (I even donned overalls and went out on a refuse collection round!)

The Leader of the Council asked to have a chat with me. He told me that he wanted to have my recommendations within six weeks on how to reorganise the Council and do more training! I asked him if he had any strategic plans, and he hadn't heard of the words. I started with a clean sheet of paper and analysed what we were trying to do, divided the jobs sensibly, and finished up much with what was there already, with the exception of focus groups for strategy and the environment.

In due course I put my ideas to the Council, tactfully consulting the senior management, and they were accepted by all but one councillor who appeared to have taken an immediate dislike to me. I set up a working party of officials to work out the details of my proposals, to make them feel as if they were their own ideas, and started to change the very culture of the organisation onto more businesslike lines, even introducing an 'internal market' between the various reorganised departments. It was a long struggle, though, to persuade councillors to take the strategic and long-term aspects of their responsibilities, rather than the 'price of canteen coffee' and 'garden shed' view.

It all worked like clockwork, though it took more time to put in place than I had anticipated. In fact it took nine months grinding through committees, but I was content to let it go at their accustomed pace, the democratic rights of every councillor to have a say seeming to me to be important. To be honest, I did not expect any opposition, as the council was in such a frightful financial mess that they were looking to me to sort it out, albeit the Councillors were good people.

They had bought a chunk of Camberley for £14 million, half of which they 'borrowed' from the housing account, to which they then had to pay interest at £1.4 million per annum. Then they had spent another £9 million on re-locating churches which had been on the site and building the multi-storey car-park. All this was done speculatively on the understanding that a nationally well-known developer would build a large shopping centre on the site. Unfortunately nothing had been signed, and when I arrived, I found myself trying desperately to force the pace with developers who were clearly not getting the financial backing they had hoped for. Worse still, the developer had been allowed to lend the Council £2 million to build the multi-story car-park – the one which had no entrance! This loan was like a pistol to the Council's head, and after trying for three months to make some progress, I eventually backed the developer's MD up against one of our conference room walls and told him it was now or never, and the loan would be repaid in a fortnight. It called their bluff but the shopping centre scheme fell flat on its face. We subsequently tried valiantly for two or three years to obtain a properly financed offer for the site to no avail, there being a prolonged national economic recession. The Council had egg on its face to the tune of £23 million and, apart from a multi-story car-park which one couldn't get into properly, and the luxurious High Cross Church (which I called High *Cost* Church) off-site, the public had nothing but a bomb site to show for all this expenditure. Eventually we had the whole area covered in tarmac and converted into a surface car-park. Although even the national Press proclaimed this 'the most expensive car-park in Europe', by the time it was completed the Council's debts were paid off, and its popularity with the public assured us of a regular income and profit.

The debts I inherited and the monthly interest payments on it demanded immediate and severe economies in every department of the Council. I closed down offices, and staff numbers were reduced by a third, largely through natural wastage. Each department was put on a business-like internal budgeting basis and I looked for opportunities to privatise as many of our services as possible. Although this was a gradual process, within a few years we had sold off all the council houses to a Housing Association which we ourselves set up and manned, thereby in a trice closing the Housing account and avoiding the need for interest payments, put the entire Works Department out to private contract, and contracted out public relations, highway consultancy and a host of other operations. In several of these 'out-sourcings' we found ourselves in the forefront of national developments, and the District Audit team was on as steep a learning curve as we were. We also embarked upon a parallel programme of management training for the staff, and introductory courses for new councillors. I took extra care, too, to improve relations with the local Press, whose reports on the Council's affairs before I arrived had been severely critical to say the least. I can only summarise it all by relating that within four years or so the Council's financial situation and reputation had dramatically altered for the better. Instead of being in the red by £15 million without much in the way of capital reserves, we were running at a £750,000 per annum profit, free of all debts, and setting one of the lowest Poll Tax/Council Tax rates in the land. It was quite an achievement, and one on which the councillors congratulated themselves roundly.

We had a lot of laughs over everyday life with the Council. I began to write it all down, with a view to writing book on the subject. Most of the entertaining incidents are therefore recorded elsewhere and space here does not permit a detailed account of those remarkable years. For this record I will only mention a few of the events which ensured that life was not all plain sailing, however, and it was on occasions stressful.

I was very glad when Linda joined me in July 1990 and we bought 'Woodstock's', a nicely proportioned large white bungalow in Paddock Close, just behind and in sight of the Frimley Hall Hotel, where I had first met Judy Shepherd when I was a Sandhurst cadet in 1954 and where David decided to have his wedding reception in September 1994! My dear mother never saw 'Woodstock's', for she was by now 83 years old and confined to bed in considerable abdominal pain. She sadly died of what turned out to be bowel cancer on 4 October 1992.

In August 1990 we took a long weekend's leave and drove north to take part in the happy event of Richard's wedding to Caroline Nayler. I arranged a dinner party for all the close relations the night before the wedding itself. Twenty-six of us sat down to a four-course meal at the Bowmans' famous Inn at Whitewell. The wedding service took place in Waddington parish church, with Richard and Caroline being driven across the hills afterwards to Dunsop Bridge in a gleaming white open-topped Rolls-Royce. The reception was a splendid affair, in a magnificently decorated marquee on the lawn of Staple Oak, the Naylers' country house. Lord Waddington, then Home Secretary and later Governor of Bermuda, was there. Leslie, and many of our old friends like the Dickins, Whiteheads and Westons also motored long distances to be present. All in all it was a superb start to what was to prove a gratifyingly good marriage.

On 24 September 1994 David followed suit, marrying Vanessa at St Paul's Church, Camberley, with an unforgettable reception at the Frimley Hall Hotel. After their honeymoon on the Gulf shores of Muscat and Oman, another old stamping ground of mine, David and Vanessa sold their two houses and, while searching for a new one, stayed with us in 'Woodstock's'. We wondered whether this arrangement would work, but it proved to be fine, and Linda got on famously with Vanessa. As the months and years went by thereafter, Vanessa grew to become very much one of the family, with a great many foibles and amusing ways in common with Linda. Not only did they, like Richard and Caroline, produce some gorgeous grandchildren for us, but they flourished in what was clearly a happy and successful married life.

Finally on the domestic front, Linda and I took some well-earned leave a year later, and went to South Africa. November and early December 1993 were spent first with my sister Maggie in their house in Robindale, a northern suburb of Johannesburg, and then touring the eastern half of the country. We stayed a night at Cathedral Peak Hotel in the Drakensberg Mountains, where, in one of those curious coincidences in life, we bumped into 'Jungly' Drake, with whom I had played rugger at Shrivenham years before. We then went to Fugitives' Drift and enjoyed an unforgettable and magic tour of the battlefields of Isandlwhana and Rorke's Drift led personally by David Rattray. Following that we motored to Colenso, the battle from which one of my batteries in 26th Regiment took its name and battle honour. For the last four days of this holiday we roamed the vast Kruger Park. Quite wonderful.

Back in Camberley the pace of life increased markedly after a while when a dispute broke out between two leading councillors over a planning matter. I was invited by the Ombudsman to investigate a complaint by a couple who were seeking planning permission for increased polo activities at their farm near Windlesham. Since I appreciated the delicacy of the situation between these councillors, I decided to conduct the inquiry personally under my newly acquired responsibilities as the Council's 'Monitoring Officer'.

The planning issues were simple, and not wholly relevant to the inquiry, which focused on whether the local councillor, the leading opponent, who lived near the polo field in question, had declared a personal interest in a timely manner. The wording of the Local Government Code of Conduct was not entirely clear on certain aspects of interest declarations, or at least was open to misinterpretation, and this councillor had mistakenly, but possibly quite unintentionally, not observed the spirit of the Code as well as he might have. The councillor who supported the applicant was he who had kept me on tenterhooks from the beginning of my tenure, and I was worried lest his support for the applicant could be deemed to be a way of getting at the local man and the planning staff. My investigation could not ignore any hostility between councillors for it might affect the issue; the farming couple had raised an appeal against a contentious planning decision and complained to the Local Government Ombudsman about the Council's handling of the case. The Ombudsman promptly referred the matter back to me!

I duly took statements from councillors, officials, the complainants and even members of the public, and wrote my report. I showed it to the Borough Solicitor, who said he thought that I had gone too far in bringing in both the councillors. I thought about that for a while, but concluded that without the full analysis, the report could be faulted for incompleteness. I chose my words with some care but the conclusions included a mild reproof for both councillors. The local councillor took it in good heart, indeed he thanked me profusely and paid tribute to my 'integrity' while his wife unofficially presented Linda with a splendid print of the old clubhouse at Camberley Heath Golf Club where we had had our wedding reception in 1963. The other man, however, was incensed by my report and threatened to sue me for libel! He even went as far as instructing a solicitor, and I was forced to call upon the Council's insurers to provide a defence for me. The matter dragged on for over six months, during which Linda and I were placed in a very difficult position, not without much anxiety. I always knew that my report was protected under the rules of qualified privilege, and libel could only be accepted if malice was involved. I bore no malice to the councillor whatever, and I had a file of letters between him and 'The Boss' as he called me, as evidence. I even presented him with a copy of my book! But nevertheless Linda and I suffered badly from tension over this period. Linda's brother Denis, an excellent solicitor, was a source of much comfort to us throughout, and in the end, the councillor withdrew his threatened action after, I presume, abortively spending quite a lot on legal fees. It was considered that he had been disloyal to the Council and to the Leader of the Council, and he was later asked to resign from the

Conservative Group on the Council, though he tried to contest that matter too. It was a shame that he then received some very unwelcome publicity, and his business and private affairs were splashed all over the national press. Eventually he stood down from the Council and some councillors breathed a sigh of relief, though his dynamism, for which I had much admiration, was sorely missed.

In January 1995 I had reached the five year mark, but I had an open-ended contract, and my salary was pretty good, rising to £62,000 by then. House prices had fallen fairly seriously too, so it would not have been a good time to retire and try to redeem our large mortgage on the house. So I soldiered on, but really, in retrospect, I should have left then. I had by now achieved all I had set out to do, the Council was running well, and I was popular with the staff and nearly all Members of the Council. For my last two years things did not work out quite so happily for me, of which more anon.

Despite the pressures of life with the Council and the long hours, I did find time for my principal hobby, Anglo-German relations. During 1990, my first year in Surrey Heath, the situation in Germany had stabilised and on 3 October 1990 the two formerly separated German states were finally reunited. I thereupon revived my idea of forming an Anglo-German Officers' Association, and we duly held our inaugural dinner at the Staff College in Camberley in November of that year. From then on it went from strength to strength, agreeably along the lines I envisaged, namely with a living, current purpose, involving studies and seminars and not purely reunion dinners. At the behest of Secretary of State for Defence, George Robertson, the name was later changed to The British-German Officers' Association. After I had struggled for some time with the Charity Commission, Alan Dickins, now retired from the army and a qualified solicitor, successfully achieved charitable status for the Association. Annual meetings soon gained quite a high international profile, attracting prominent speakers, including Ministers, Ambassadors and all the senior Servicemen from both nations. I worked very hard at it, and every day spent time on my computer enlarging the membership and arranging meetings in the UK and Germany. This task was made much easier when the family clubbed together and bought me the latest computer technology, complete with Windows 95 and Word 6 software. David, by then an enthusiastic expert on computers, installed up-grades every time he visited us. I believed I was past being up-graded myself, but the Association was a hobby and an all-consuming one.

As Chief Executive, with the German medal, 1994

In 1994 I was honoured by being awarded the German Presidential Order of Merit 1st Class and received a nice letter from Buckingham Palace permitting me to wear this decoration alongside my existing paltry two medals. The award ceremony was conducted in the German Embassy in London, and Linda, Leslie and the boys were able to be present. It was a proud moment. My linguist skills also helped the Council in their rather feeble Town-Twinning efforts with the delightful people of Bietigheim-Bissingen, near Stuttgart.

In terms of local leadership the Council was not terribly good. It had had a 100 per cent Conservative majority for many years and had become very complacent about its role in local governance, especially in relation to local businessmen, who were regarded rather as a threat in their quest for industrial sites, especially to the rural end of the Borough. I endeavoured to redress the balance a little by forming the Surrey Heath Business Association, and got Sir Michael Grylls, our local Member of Parliament, to be a patron and launch its first meeting. I regarded it as a useful forum for maintaining an interface and understanding with commerce and industry in the Borough, and it was certainly something which the Government of the day encouraged. Not all my councillors seemed to agree, however, and treated it with suspicion.

Tony Brown was the dynamic MD of Bisley Furniture Ltd, a company which had secured countless overseas export orders, but some hostility too from a few local residents in Bisley, most of whom had moved there long after the factory expanded. He was a former Gunner officer, we got on well, and I had much sympathy with his position *vis à vis* the noise and fumes inevitably generated by his factory, even though it annoyed a few neighbours. He told me that he had got a big export order for furniture which would need his factory to work a late shift for three months in the summer. This required an agreement from the Council to vary the restrictive terms of the planning permission, but it meant extra jobs and a boost for the local economy. As he felt it was unlikely that the Council officers would agree to this extension, he asked me if I could help in any way. I said I would see, but made no promises. Certainly, if the Council were to take action against a company when it was at that moment receiving a prestigious Queen's Award for Industry it risked another PR disaster. As it was I felt all sides would be satisfied in the end.

I popped my head round the corner into the Borough solicitor's section and enquired about the state of play regarding Tony Brown's request. It appeared that the complaints of the neighbours were already at such a pitch that an injunction was being prepared against the company to keep to its agreed hours, and there was nothing that could be done. I asked the solicitors how long such proceedings might take, and they said quietly that they thought it could be as long as three months.

A few weeks later, Tony Brown gave an inspiring address to the Surrey Heath Business Association, and I as secretary, wrote to him afterwards to thank him. In the same letter, rather in parenthesis, I said rather cryptically that I hoped that the Council solicitors were using their common sense over the injunction. Some weeks later I was suffering from a fit of frustration in the office and beginning to contemplate seriously looking for another job, when I thought of Tony Brown and his network of contacts, especially in continental Europe. On the spur of the moment I wrote to him asking him to bear me in mind if he heard of anyone looking for someone like me who could speak German. He did not reply.

A few days later the new Leader of the Council, a charming lady, dropped into my office for one of our weekly discussions, at the end of which she said, 'I want to speak to you about these two letters.' I did not know what she was talking about. She said, 'It has come to my notice that you have written two letters to Tony Brown, and they have been put together. The outcome is I have agreed that the Chairman of the Finance and Land Committee should conduct a formal investigation, and I shall be asking him, the Mayor, and one other councillor to interview you formally.'

To say I was thunderstruck would be an understatement. I protested my total innocence, and asked how the two letters in question had been seen and by whom, although they were in no way, in my mind, connected. The Leader was very evasive, and evidently embarrassed. It transpired that the Internal Auditors of the Council had been looking into the computer which my Secretary used, for what purpose I never discovered. They had seen these two letters, incorrectly put two and two together, and reported the matter to the Director of Finance.

The next step in this saga was my receipt of a formal letter from the Chairman of the Finance Committee, in which he asked me to attend a meeting with the Mayor, which would be recorded by another councillor who was legally qualified, and which listed a series of spurious charges against me. The charges included vague innuendos about, for example, my being 'too close' to the Business Association, and not securing a large enough compensation payment from our recently failed computer agents, ICL, and upsetting the Council's Directors by writing a 'spoof' letter to them one day, a piece of fun which evidently misfired. Although I had already joined the Association of Local Authority Chief Executives (ALACE), the Chief Executives' Union, the whole business was so laughable I did not bother to take legal advice, but went along to the meeting on the due date full of righteous indignation. Suffice to say I answered every charge put to me point by point, to the satisfaction of the Mayor and the other councillor, and some weeks later, secured from the Leader of the Council a letter confirming that all charges had been dropped and the matter was totally closed.

This brush with the Chairman of Finance did not please me, but showed me something of civilian life that I had never encountered in the Army and which filled me with dismay. At my next weekly Management Board meeting with my three Directors I demanded that they come to see me first if they ever had a problem with anything I did or said in future. Whereupon the Finance Director said that his first loyalty was to the Council! I suppose he was right, but it shook me to the core. The Mayor, a kindly former Army major, said to me afterwards that I should always remember that the people I was dealing with were not 'proper officers'. Yet most councillors and officials were really admirable folk.

There were, of course, many hilarious and lighter moments. The pomp and circumstance of attending mayoral events never ceased to tickle us, especially when all the District Council mayors of the county (the 'Chain Gang') met for dinner. Fortunately for our sanity we were able to maintain close links with the Army during our years at Camberley, attending international events and pantomimes at the Staff College. I also joined the RMA chapel choir, as I had as a cadet. Deepcut barracks too, on the edge of Camberley and Frimley, saw the formation of The Royal Logistic Corps while we were there. Anne, Princess Royal, was the Colonel-in-Chief, and her visits to the barracks caused me a small problem over protocol. The Mayor and I were invited to the inaugural parade, but to my astonishment and the Mayor's dismay, the mayoral Rolls-Royce was told to park some distance from the parade ground and we were bustled into third row seats. I wrote to the Lord Lieutenant afterwards, asking why the Mayor had not been treated appropriately for a Royal visit, and was told in no uncertain terms that it had been designated a 'private' visit. The Princess paid more visits, including one to our only prison, at Chobham, in which role she does wonderful work as patron of the association for drug rehabilitation among prisoners – one of her many unsung good works. I took extra care with these to establish the category of the visit in advance so the Mayor was not offended. We also had an opportunity to meet Her Majesty the Queen for a second time, when she presided over the formal return of Bagshot Park from the Army Chaplain's Department to the Royal Family. When we spoke to the Queen at Bagshot Park poor Linda was on crutches with her leg in an iron caliper, having dislocated her knee-cap in a nasty fall, of which she had increasing numbers as a result of her MS. The Queen didn't turn a hair, and nor did brave Linda, who looked as charming and elegant as ever for all that. Our final chance to meet Her Majesty was at a standard Garden Party at Buckingham Palace when, thanks to a friend of Linda's family, Alan Pemberton, an equerry to Prince Philip, we were placed in the front receiving line. I had been to the palace once before, in 1954, when stepfather Leslie received his MC for his Malayan exploits, before he left for the Far East on the cruiser HMS *Newcastle*.

The 50th anniversary of the end of World War Two (VE/VJ days combined) provided an especially amusing ceremonial occasion for me to organise. To cut a long story short, I managed to cobble together a parade of some thousand men, women and children, including three military bands and very reluctant police co-operation over the closure of the A30 London road along which to march. At the outset of the planning for this event, nobody at all thought it feasible. The ace up my sleeve was the RMA Academy Sergeant Major, and on the day he marshalled the diverse participants on the great surface car-park, and it all went like clockwork. Of course, the councillors congratulated themselves on their grand civic success. Such ceremonials and mayoral frolics were too numerous to relate here. Suffice it to say they were excellent for our sense of humour.

Eighteen months later my patience with the Council was definitely running out, and I was becoming increasingly short-tempered with the approach of a couple of Members to a much needed revision to staff pay and conditions of service. While pressing for change, I wanted to do it my way, and I knew that the staff and their representatives had confidence in me. A new councillor, who had been a personnel director in industry, I believe, had more draconian ideas, and his bullish attitude to the staff set serious vibrations of discontent running through the organisation. All the good work which I done in the times of major staff reductions without any Union trouble or disruptions seemed to me to be in danger of being undone.

At one of the Personnel Committee Meetings I was so incensed at remarks certain councillors were making about the staff that I felt I had no option but to protest by walking out. The lady Chairman later said that she tried to call me back, but if she did, I never heard her, and anyway I didn't think that I was actually obliged to attend any Committee meetings, but did so out of choice. The final straw, however, as far as she was concerned, came when a special meeting of the Policy and Resources (P & R) Committee was arranged to approve the selection of a new Public Relations agent for the Council. It was a relatively small contract, but one naturally not without significance for councillors. A special panel was therefore set up to make the final selection from two or three contenders, and both the Chairman of the Finance Committee and the Leader of the Council were on that panel. The officers on the Panel, which included myself and the Director of Finance, recommended a certain company on the grounds of experience and their imaginative presentation. Their material clearly indicated that the leading figure in this firm had worked with the BBC, and he explained that he had been a member of the supporting staff for a *Panorama* Programme which had looked into some alleged 'sleaze' by a couple of Conservative Members of Parliament. Neither the Director nor I thought anything of that, and the two councillors said nothing.

At 9 a.m. on the day on which the evening P & R Committee meeting was to take place, however, and at which we expected the Panel's recommendation to be approved without difficulty, the Chairman rushed into my office. She told me that the Conservative Group had held a meeting the night before and had decided that the P & R Committee meeting should be cancelled. I was therefore to cancel it and contact the Liberal Democrat and Labour members of the Committee to tell them. She told me that there was no need to contact the Conservative members as they had already been stood down. She said that they didn't like the recommended contractor as he had been connected with the BBC programme which criticised Conservative MPs.

I exploded. I said that this was no way to run a Council and it was almost certainly unconstitutional. More importantly, I said I thought that she could not refuse a contractor on political grounds, and we would have the book thrown at us. She left in a hurry, and I sought the experienced old Town Clerk's advice on whether it was in her power to cancel a committee meeting like that. He was non-committal, but it was a *fait accompli* to some extent, and I thought that the contract could be considered again anyway at the next regular meeting of the Committee in a few days' time. Unfortunately, when the Labour and Liberal councillors came to that regular meeting, which was in public, they gave the Conservatives an exceedingly hard time over their decision to cancel the earlier meeting, and asked me to stand up and give my version of events. I did so, but the Chairman's version was different. She said she had only sought my advice over cancellation of the meeting, and I had let her down. The writing was now on the wall. Hell hath no fury like a woman scorned, especially by the political opposition in public!

I suppose, therefore, I was half expecting a showdown when the new Mayor, previously that same Chairman of the Finance Committee, walked into my office ten days' later and handed me a brown envelope, saying that he was very sorry to be doing this, but he was only the messenger. I was nevertheless shocked when I read the letter. It was another 'charge sheet', listing all sorts of apparent misdemeanours, including giving the Chairman of the P & R Committee the wrong advice over the cancellation of the meeting, and walking out of one her

Personnel meetings. Some of the charges were so vague as to be meaningless, such as my having 'upset certain councillors', but this time I wasted no time in contacting ALACE for advice.

Bill Miles, the very helpful solicitor employed by ALACE, was well used to rescuing Chief Executives in trouble. The security of tenure of Local Authority Chief Executives was almost as weak as the average professional football club manager's, and Bill was a busy man. Over the telephone he asked whether I wanted to fight the charges or leave under the best terms he could secure. Although I felt the charges totally specious and unjust, I saw little point in prolonging the agony. The new Mayor, I was told, was determined to get rid of me. The Leader of the Council appeared unable to decide whether she wanted me to stay or go. I chose the second alternative, and Bill Miles came down to face a small panel of councillors, which the Mayor had set up in great secrecy. One of the members he appointed, in a rare show of democracy, was the Leader of the Opposition parties on the Council, and frankly one of our more sensible councillors. For several weeks he kept me informed of the farcical deliberations of this secret panel, for which I was very grateful. To my surprise, it soon transpired that only two or three councillors on the entire Council were aware of what was going on. But when the Mayor's fellow Conservatives at Divisional Headquarters like Barry Price OBE and Alan Cleverley OBE, and County figures like Joy Reid OBE JP, Bill Reid, and Anthony Tisdall, all of whose judgement was widely respected, heard what was happening, they hastened to offer me support.

When it came to the day to face the Panel and agree terms for my departure, the Mayor led the discussion aggressively from the start, and at one stage said that it 'was not the first time I had caused trouble'! (So much for my earlier 'total exoneration'!) Bill Miles said that the charges were totally unjustified and I could take the Council to an industrial tribunal, but I was prepared to accept a decent financial settlement with proper tributes being paid to me on departure and my reputation intact and untarnished. But it was possibly one of the Mayor's ideas during the final stages of the negotiations preceding the Panel meeting which caused me the most amusement and which was probably the most revealing aspect of this entire ludicrous business. He wanted a condition written into the agreement that I would not speak about the matter to anyone for ten years! Needless to say, Bill Miles quickly rejected that preposterous proposal.

So that was that. It was agreed that I was to retire on 2 January 1997, seven years to the day that I joined, and the Council would make up the years to my 65th birthday as far as pension was concerned. It was a decent settlement from which both sides considered they came out well enough. Several councillors came into my office to express regret at what had happened and said they were sorry to have been kept in the dark and I would be sorely missed. One or two good councillors had been told what was happening a few days before the Panel meeting but, thinking I wanted to leave with a good financial settlement, they ran for cover and did not get involved. The local newspaper was generous in its report on my departure, even though it did not publish quite all the friendly advice I had offered the Council in my valedictory speech. It took the Council six months to find a suitable successor.

Shortly before we left Woodstocks Linda suffered another bad fall, this time splitting her head open so badly that I and our German guest, Frau Sigrid Geisler just arrived from Bietigheim, had to mop up the blood with a bath towel. I could see that it would not be long before we had to surmount the psychological hurdle of Linda taking to a wheelchair.

During my time at Surrey Heath I had become a Fellow of the Institute of Personnel & Development, and a Fellow of the Institute of Management. I had learnt a great deal. The whole experience had also been stimulating for my sense of humour, though it was a pity that seven relatively successful years as Chief Executive came to an end in such strange circumstances. All things considered, those somewhat farcical events did not overshadow the amusing, interesting and valuable experience of a job which I, and I hope many others, regard as having been done well, if not gloriously.

CHAPTER 17

Beating Retreat

L INDA AND I had lived in 'Woodstock's' longer than in any other house
in our married life. The garden was small and bored me from time
to time, but it did look splendid in summer with my 103 roses and
Linda's magnificent array of pelargoniums in tubs and window boxes.
We were only on nodding acquaintance with our neighbours, although
the charming Sir Donald and Lady Spiers had been to drinks and dinner
with us on occasions. Nevertheless, I knew that we would not miss the
area nor the hectic pace of life, lack of places to walk and the
ever-present traffic noise.

We had bought 'Woodstock's' in 1990 and the Council had helped
me with the initial mortgage. When the prices started to drop in the
1992 recession, we bought out the Council's share and believed it was a
wise move. In November 1996, as my time at the Council drew to an
end, we put the house on the market through the agents Carsons, the
managing director of whom had been a friend of ours and of Linda's
brother, Tim Chetwood, an outstanding surveyor. We then received an
endless stream of potential purchasers, some from America, some from
Germany, but nobody made a firm offer. We dropped the asking price
but Linda was getting desperate by March 1997 and so we swopped
agents to Vickerys who, within two weekends, had found a purchaser
from just around the corner! This meant we could clear our mortgage
completely and buy something more to our liking back in Dorset.

Linda's parameters for our retirement home and the first house which
would be wholly our own were simple: she wanted a chalet bungalow
with a downstairs bedroom and bathroom for us, rooms upstairs for
visiting children and grandchildren, she wanted the house to be set well
within its own grounds all round the house, and she wanted an Aga
cooker. We asked Humberts of Shaftesbury to look for us, and Linda was
not all that fussed if we did not return to Marnhull, much as I thought
that would be nice. Linda would not begin the hunt until we had secured
the sale of 'Woodstock's' so we did not visit Humberts with a true
purpose until March 1997. One Victorian house was for sale in Marnhull
but we considered it in too poor a state to set right economically, and

229

so we looked at one other possibility in Hazelbury Bryan, but a look at the map suggested that that one might be subject to winter flooding. Finally we saw Glebe Cottage in Donhead St Mary, and, almost derelict as the house and garden were after being empty for two years, we were at once taken with it. Our friends John and Jane Hill had lived in the Donheads for some time and assured us they were very sociable villages, which was another prerequisite for my ever-gregarious Linda.

We arrived to take over the house on Thursday 24 July 1997. I had arranged for the water to be turned on that afternoon, the oil heater to be fired up, the electricity to be checked and a firm of cleaners to come in on the following day to start attacking the effects of two years of dampness and water leaks, and fly-blown, spider-webbed walls and cupboards. On the Thursday afternoon we were shown the water and heating systems and all seemed well. We were staying at the nearby Grove House Hotel for the weekend and the following morning at 9.00 a.m. I arrived a few minutes in advance of the cleaners, only to find that the water system was not operating, no water at all coming from the taps. I telephoned the firm we had seen the previous afternoon to no avail, so with the cleaners borrowing buckets of water from the neighbours, we waited until another local firm from Shaftesbury could arrive and sort out the plumbing system. It took an excellent plumber 4½ hours to sort the system out, and this was at emergency rates, producing a bill of £534! Not a very auspicious start, but the cleaners did a great job, and so did Richard the window cleaner, and by the end of a long Friday things were beginning to look more shipshape, the spiders and flies mostly gone, and the carpets dry-cleaned superbly. Malcolm Cullimore the carpenter started work too on dozens of minor jobs, and we found him to be the source of information on a typical network of village tradesmen.

The removal lorries arrived promptly on the Monday morning while a number of workmen were still getting to grips with various defects in the house. Although there was unlimited time to get settled in, we had moved 23 times in our married life, so Linda, almost out of habit, insisted on getting everything shipshape and like a home as quickly as possible – so we unpacked 115 boxes in 4½ days!

The previous owners had been the Tetley-Jones, thought to be related to the Tetley tea company, and Anne Tetley-Jones had been a knowledgeable and accomplished gardener. Under the nettles and brambles lurked originally a beautiful garden. In it also stood an ornate well-head in the middle of the back lawn. Linda and I said at once that it would have to go, as would some light oak cupboards in the drawing-room and hall, and also an ornately carved, ugly wooden fireplace surrounding the small drawing room fire. Malcolm Cullimore dismantled the cupboards and we got Semley Auctioneers to collect them and the fireplace surround. They subsequently sold them for £382 and, to our amazement, £1,635 respectively. This would help pay for local stonemason, Harry Jonas, to build us a new drawing room fireplace out of Chicksgrove stone, which was completed in late October. The well-head, however, created much more amusement. I was seriously considering getting the Royal Engineers to come in and blow it up, when a local builder said he knew a chum who had a tractor and they could drive in over the overgrown flower-beds, removing a couple of fences as they did so, and drag it away free of charge. We agreed and it was arranged that the tractor would come along the next Saturday morning about 9.30 a.m. Earlier in the week Linda had the bright idea of approaching Talisman, a shop specialising in garden statues the other side of Gillingham, and we showed them a photograph of the well-head. They were non-committal at first but on the Thursday morning the manager of Talisman rang and said he would like to have a quick look at it. Linda said, 'You'd better be quick, as it is going to be taken away on Saturday at 9.30.' The manager said he would be with us on Friday at 10.00 then.

When the manager came, I took him down the garden. I said nothing as he approached the monstrous object, hoping that he might give us a few pounds for it. When he reached it he peered closely at it and said: 'You know I thought it was concrete at first, but it is actually carved Istern marble, probably eighteenth century. I'll give you £2,000 for it right now. If I do it up a bit it will possibly fetch £3,500.' I asked him if he had said £2,500, but he declined to raise his offer. He signed the cheque there and then and had it removed very professionally a few days later.

And so we set about renovating the house and garden. The views were stunning. I lost 1 ½ stone in weight in the first three months' graft in the garden, clearing undergrowth and weeds and cutting back trees and shrubbery. It was a labour of love, and I revelled in the peace and interest of the garden and its bird-life. The house, ready equipped with a Stannah stair lift, was soon made thoroughly waterproof, carpeted, curtained and redecorated, all of which took from 24 July until the middle of

November. We used local tradesmen, one of whom said to me, 'Surr,' in his Dorset accent, 'I wuddent dew yew a shoddy job, Surr, 'cos I've gotta lewk yew in the oye when I sees yer in the 'igh Street o' Shaftesbury.' That seemed a truism and a very good reason for persisting with local craftsmen.

In between hordes of workmen arriving at the house, and Linda keeping them tended with cups of tea all day, we felt we were on perpetual holiday. Malcolm Cullimore became such a regular visitor that he took to calling in at tea-time, and we had a lot of fun teasing each other. People in the shops too were so nice, always having a polite chat and taking their time. One day I was taking my time choosing local cheeses in Farmer Bailey's in Shaftesbury and I turned to apologise to an old lady behind me for taking so long. 'Never yew mind, m'dear,' she replied. 'This be Dorset!' Village life too proved every bit as lively, even hectic, as the Hills had suggested. Glebe Cottage lies 50 yards from the lovely church of St Mary one way and 50 yards from the Village Hall in the other direction. Linda joined the local Women's Institute, and an embroidery class, and we threw ourselves into the local social life wholeheartedly.

And so we settled in to a blissful retirement. In between running Help the Aged and Age Concern in Dorset, struggling to maintain a large garden, taking an Open University diploma in German, actively involving myself in a host of Conservative Association, village and church activities, I somehow found time to write a novel based on my experiences in Local Government, and some short stories, including several about red dragons, about which my grandchildren thought I was quite obsessed. Also, before leaving Camberley, and simply out of interest, I had joined a London-based Venture Capital ('Business Angels') company. My job was to seek out embryonic business ventures, advise them on business planning, and make recommendations or otherwise as to their suitability as an investment opportunity. I looked at one case: a young couple living in Frimley, who had obtained degrees in commercial art at Bristol University and who had secured a contract with an international fashion house to design their window display in, I believe, Regent Street. They had now been asked to repeat the work in Paris and they wanted to expand their workshop. I was amazed when interviewing them that they did not know how to go about making a business plan, and more seriously, had not taken out Intellectual Property Rights on their London window display, something that anyone might have copied. I helped them with both, but left Camberley before knowing whether they received their much-needed investment. I stayed on the Venture Capital firm's books for a year after we left Camberley, but I was not comfortable with them when they adopted a more intrusive method of finding potential investment opportunities. So this was a case of nothing ventured and nothing gained.

So I then consigned other writings to the attic, and set about these memoirs, the main purpose of which is to record for posterity within our family what life was like in our generation. Unless somebody writes such an account, our lives and times will be lost for ever. It may not be of much interest to our three sons now, but it may be one day. At all events, it was now time to beat retreat and to reflect.

I have had a fortunate life and have much for which to be extremely thankful. I never cease to thank God for this lovely life and the beauty of nature around us. Most of all I thank Him for the gift of a wonderfully secure and happy marriage, for this has been the basis of such success as I have had, and, I firmly believe, the success which the boys have enjoyed. There is much evidence to show that a secure family background provides an important launch pad for children's achievements and can exert a crucial influence on their lifestyle. I hope that Linda and I have provided that environment for them at all times. Judging by the way they keep in touch with their mother, I feel perhaps they do appreciate what we have tried to do for them. Certainly in their success as businessmen, although they may not win medals or fame thereby, and in the decent way they lead their lives, we count ourselves lucky and we are also proud.

The background I refer to is not created by accident. People say you have to work at a marriage, and it is true that in our early days there were fleeting moments of irritation or tension, but they were always shortlived and we never went to sleep angry with each other. Good marriages are made in heaven, and that has also been the firm basis for our loving relationship. I have always been robustly religious, no time for mealy-mouthed-ness, nor excessive ritual, but we have attended church regularly, I have directed and sung in choirs, played the organ, and been inspired by cathedral music. I am convinced that, whatever degree of faith in the after-life one may possess, the Christian ethics are the proven best set of rules by which to regulate one's personal and communal life. British society is presently going through a spell of decline in Christian belief and following, and the deplorable results in drug-taking, broken marriages, housing shortages, crime and misery are plain to see. Linda and I have loved each other passionately and strongly, with a deep abiding Christian belief in complete fidelity. Indeed I have never accepted that sexual activity outside marriage is anything but sinful, and today's promiscuity is leading to nothing but disease, divorce and unhappiness for the individuals involved, their children and society as a whole. The consequences of continuing along these lines cannot be imagined.

Linda too, especially in recent years when she has been so troubled with her multiple sclerosis, now being wheelchair-bound, has developed a very strong Christian faith. She regularly attends bible studies, we go to church nearly every Sunday, and I know she prays fervently for God's continued help in her brave battle. I hope that my prayers help her too. It would be nice to think that the boys would come to take such a firm hold on Christianity as we have. Maybe when their children have grown up a bit, they will. I know that it could certainly be of help to them all.

We did our best for the boys in all ways, giving them as good an education as we could afford. Linda never contributed to the family finances in a big way, only having a secretarial job for a short period when we were in Camberley, when she worked for a blind solicitor. But I never wanted her to work professionally anyway. I needed her by me, and she considered it her duty to follow the flag. Gifted with an enormous amount of practical commonsense, she was always very self-deprecating about her childhood academic attainments, and she was often teased about her supposed shortage of brain-power by our three clever sons. However, Linda's domestic talents were boundless and the range of them truly impressive. She was an accomplished cook and read her large collection of cookery books avidly. She was a brilliant hostess, demanding nothing short of perfection down to the smallest detail in the arrangements for dinner and lunch parties. Her skills were not only demonstrably good in handicrafts like lampshade and curtain making, and needlework of all sorts, including dressmaking for many of her own clothes as well, but from time to time she also turned her hand to chair upholstery and French polishing. Artistic flower-arrangements too, everything from those massive displays in the Ambassador's Residence in Bonn to tiny twig-like creations exemplified her patience, creativity and eye for detail. Above all she was brilliant at home-making wherever we went, and often in the most atrocious places where younger Service wives these days would not condescend to go. Her greatest contribution to the comfort of me and the welfare and future of our sons was in creating a happy, caring, tasteful, and stable home.

It was satisfying that the boys responded so well to this matchless foundation and were deservedly successful in their school, university and professional careers. At some time or other during their childhood I tried to encourage each or some of them in varying degrees according to their talents and inclination to take an interest in piano-playing, singing, bird-watching, gardening, cricket, rugby and hockey, sailing, skiing, stamp collecting, walking and chess. Though they all did well in various sports, Richard excelling at hockey of course, David at running and Jonathan even tackling rowing at University, it will be up to them to what extent they take up any of these activities in later life, but there must be some relief from work. I was particularly pleased to see how Richard has taken to gardening and stuck to the piano, he having inherited Aunt Pin's soft-toned upright piano.

Above all, however, it is reassuring to see the boys taking to family life. All three appear to be happily married, and their lovely respective wives, Vanessa, Caroline and Clare, get on well with Linda, which is

Linda (left) with Vanessa and granddaughters at home

fine. They are bringing up their children, our delightful grandchildren, with care and imagination. I trust they have the good sense and devotion to maintain these stable relationships all their lives.

Professionally my life was rather more disappointing than distinguished. My Army career was far from illustrious; more lacklustre I must admit. True, nobody in the Pughe line had ever reached the rank of Brigadier before me. My dear mother was very proud of that, and I know my father would have been too. Leslie was a quite marvellous stepfather to me and grand-stepfather to the boys. His interest in and affection for us all was undiminished. I owe him a lot, and look back to those early days when I struggled with my physics prep, and how he helped me tackle it from basic principles, with pleasure and gratitude. How he managed to support and educate my two sisters and me on a Captain's pay was a small miracle that confounds me to this day. I know that it meant my mother and him making considerable personal and financial sacrifices to do it. I hope they would think that whatever professional luck I have enjoyed was worth their great efforts.

But I did only finish my military career with two British medal ribbons and one German one, to which, admittedly the honour of being designated an ADC to HM The Queen could be added for a couple of years. It was little enough to show for a lifetime's service, and I felt somewhat cheated that I was not in the right place at the right time for a proper war. Of course, I may have lost my life in it or been wounded, so I cannot but count my blessings, and hope that I served and contributed to the community and country wherever I was, however unpretentiously .

On the other hand Linda and I will always cherish the opportunities Service life gave us to travel. We relished the international postings and all the friends we made. We saw a lot of the world, and never took a package holiday! Looking in the back of one of our family photograph albums I see that I recorded that in a spell of 5 ½ years between May 1986 and October 1991 we lived in or visited nine countries together: Germany, Austria, Portugal, Norway, France, Scotland, Cyprus, England and Switzerland; while I visited a further four: Denmark, the Channel Islands, Sardinia and Italy. We certainly saw much of the world, and treasure our memories of Canada, Mexico, South Africa, Australia and New Zealand especially. Our sons, not being in the Services, which I am still a little sad about, may seldom get such opportunities as we had, but they will doubtless have more money to spend on holidays abroad, though I cannot believe those fleeting visits can be as fruitful as our experiences were, or the insights we gained.

My contribution has, I trust, been useful. My adult life has seen a kaleidoscopic 42 years of public service, both in the Army and in Local Government. Money was never plentiful, but we managed to squeeze a lot out of life and the wonderful situations in which we were placed – dirty Dortmund included! I feel satisfied that I have done my best, and have few regrets, except perhaps, that I am left with a sneaking feeling that, with a little more drive and speed in the uptake, I might actually have achieved that elusive glory.

> Remember me when I am gone away,
> Gone far away into the silent land;
> When you can no more hold me by the hand,
> Nor I half turn to go, yet turning stay.
>
> Remember me when no more day by day
> You tell me of our future that you planned:
> Only remember me: you understand
> It will be late to counsel then or pray.
>
> Yet if you should forget me for a while
> And afterwards remember, do not grieve:
> For if the darkness and corruption leave
> A vestige of the thoughts that once I had
> Better by far you should forget and smile
> Than that you should remember and be sad.

Christina Rossetti

Index